ERIC PUGH, ALA

THIRD DICTIONARY OF ACRONYMS & ABBREVIATIONS

more abbreviations in management, technology and

information science

ERIC PUGH, ALA

THIRD DICTIONARY OF ACRONYMS & ABBREVIATIONS

more abbreviations in management, technology and

information science

CLIVE BINGLEY
LONDON

ARCHON BOOKS
HAMDEN · CONN

FIRST PUBLISHED 1977 BY CLIVE BINGLEY LTD
16 PEMBRIDGE ROAD LONDON W11 UK
SIMULTANEOUSLY PUBLISHED IN THE USA BY ARCHON BOOKS
AN IMPRINT OF THE SHOE STRING PRESS INC
995 SHERMAN AVENUE HAMDEN CONNECTICUT 06514
SET IN 10 ON 12 POINT PRESS ROMAN BY ALLSET
AND PRINTED AND BOUND IN THE UK BY
REDWOOD BURN LTD OF TROWBRIDGE & ESHER
COPYRIGHT © ERIC PUGH 1977
BINGLEY ISBN: 0-85157-224-3
ARCHON ISBN: 0-208-01535-3

cc

INTRODUCTION

This third volume contains 5,000 entries. Most of them are new; the remainder up-date entries in the previous two volumes. Again it must be stressed that some of the acronyms and abbreviations listed are registered trade names and care should be taken in their use.

As in the previous volumes the word 'PROGRAM'—the accepted term relative to software in computer data processing—has not been used in that sense. 'PROGRAMME' has been used to cover data processing and 'PROGRAM' reserved to cover proceedings or projects undertaken by institutions, etc, in the USA.

I am pleased to acknowledge the support inherent in the interest shown by J C Andrews, S G Berriman and A J Walford in the continuation of this dictionary.

Although this volume is shorter than the previous two the work of compilation has been more difficult. The necessary checking against the already published works to avoid duplication and to up-date entries has only been possible by the constant assistance of my wife, who also typed the proof. It is a joint compilation in every respect and is dedicated to her alone.

ERIC PUGH

Teddington, Middlesex
July 1976

CONTENTS

A

A A	Ascorbic Acid
A A B	American Association of Bioanalysts (USA)
A A B S H I L	Aircraft Anti-collision Beacon System High Intensity Light
A A C	Association of American Colleges (USA)
A A C C	Airport Associations Co-ordinating Council
A A C O	Advanced and Applied Concepts Office (US Army)
A A C P	American Academy for Cerebral Palsy (USA)
	American Academy of Child Psychiatry (USA)
A A C R	Anglo-American Cataloguing Rules
A A D	American Academy of Dermatology (USA)
A A E E	American Association of Electromyography and Electrodiagnosis (USA)
A A E L S S	Active Arm External Load Stabilization System
A A E S	Advanced Aircraft Electrical System
A A F C E	Allied Air Forces Central Europe (of NATO)
A A F E	Advanced Applications Flight Experiment
R A D S C A T	Radiometer-Scatterometer sensor
A A F S	American Academy of Forensic Sciences (USA)
A A H	Anti-Armour Helicopter
A A I M S	An Analytical Information Management System
A A L S	Acoustic Artillery Location System
A A M A	Architectural Aluminum Manufacturers Association (USA)
A A M C A	Army Advanced Materiel Concepts Agency (US Army)
A A M D	American Association on Mental Deficiency (USA)
A A N	Aminoacetonitrile
A A O	Authorized Acquisition Objective
A A O S	American Academy of Orthopaedic Surgeons (USA)
A A P C	Afro-American Purchasing Center (USA)
A A P S	Alternative Automotive Power Systems (a program of EPA (USA))
A A P S C	American Association of Psychiatric Services for Children (USA)
A A P S D	Alternative Automotive Powersystem Division (of EPA (USA))
A A R B	Australian Road Research Board (Australia)

7

A A R F	Australian Accounting Research Foundation (Australia)
A A S C	Aerospace Applications Studies Committee (of AGARD (NATO))
	Australian Accounting Standards Committee (Australia) (of Institute of Chartered Accountants in Australia *and* Australian Society of Accountants)
A A S H T O	American Association of State Highway and Transportation Officials (USA)
A A S I R	Advanced Atmospheric Sounder and Imaging Radiometer
A A T	Alanine Amino-transferase
A A T B	Army Aviation Test Board (US Army)
A A U P	Association of American University Presses (USA)
A A V	Adeno Associated Virus
A B A A	Antiquarian Booksellers Association of America (USA)
A B B A	American Brahman Breeders Association (USA)
A B C	Automation of Bibliography through Computerization
A B C A	American, British, Canadian, Australian
A B C I L	Antibody Mediated Cell Dependent Immune Lympholysis
A B C M	Association of Building Component Manufacturers
A B C U	Association of *Burroughs* Computer Users
A B D P	Association of British Directory Publishers
A B E	Association of Business Executives
A B F L	Auke Bay Fisheries Laboratory (of NMFS (NOAA) (USA))
A B H P	American Board of Health Physics (USA)
A B I H	American Board of Industrial Hygiene (USA)
A B I I S E	Agrupación de Bibliotecas para la Integración de la Información Socio-Económica (Perú) (Association of Libraries to Pool Social and Economic Information)
A B I R	All-Band Intercept Receiver
A B I R D	Aircraft Based Infra-Red Detector
A B L E	A Better Language Experiment
A B L I S S	Association of British Library and Information Science Schools
A B L R	American Burkitt Lymphoma Registry

A B O	Aviator's Breathing Oxygen
A B P	American Business Press (USA) (association of specialized business publications publishers)
A B P	Androgen Binding Protein
A B P M	American Board of Preventive Medicine (USA)
A B S	Australian Bureau of Statistics (Australia)
A B T I C S	Abstract and Book Title Index Card Service (now of the Metals Society)
A C A	Acetylacetone
	American Chiropractors Association (USA)
	Arms Control Association (USA)
	Association of Canadian Archivists (Canada)
	Association of Chartered Accountants
A C A A I	Air Cargo Agents Association of India (India)
A C A B	Air Conditioning Advisory Bureau (of the Electricity Council)
A C A S	Advisory, Conciliation and Arbitration Service
A C C	Adaptive Control Constraint
	Amateur Computer Club
	Army Communications Command (US Army)
	Asian Coconut Community
A C C C I	American Coke and Coal Chemicals Institute (USA)
A C C E S S	Architects Central Constructional Engineering Surveying Service (Greater London Council)
A C C O M P	Academic Computer Group (USA)
A C C U	Automatic Combustion Control Unmanned
A C C V	Armoured Cavalry Cannon Vehicle
A C D L	Asynchronous Circuit Design Language
A C E	Association for Cooperation in Engineering (USA)
A C E A R T S	Airborne Countermeasures Environment And Radar Target Simulator
A C E C	Advisory Council on Energy Conservation
A C E I	Association of Consulting Engineers of Ireland
A C E N Z	Association of Consultant Engineers of New Zealand (New Zealand)
A C E Q	Association of Consulting Engineers of Quebec (Canada)
A C E S A	Arizona Council of Engineering and Scientific Associations (USA)
A C F	Air Combat Fighter
	Australian Conservation Foundation (Australia)

9

A C F H E	Association of Colleges for Further and Higher Education
A C F O D	Asian Cultural Forum on Development (Thailand)
A C H	Acetone Cyanohydrin
A C h R	Acetylcholine Receptor
A C I A	Asynchronous Communications Interface Adapter
A C L	Audit Command Language
A C L I C S	Airborne Communications Location, Identification and Collection System
A C L O	Association of Cooperative Library Organizations
A C M	Air Combat Manoeuvering
	Associative Communications Multiplexer
A C O	Adaptive Control Organization
A C O D A C	Acoustic Data Capsule
A C O D S	Army Container-Oriented Distribution Systems (US Army)
A C O M P L I S	A Computerized London Information Service (of the Greater London Council)
A C O M R	Advisory Committee on Oceanic Meteorological Research (of WMO (UN))
A C O R D	Advisory Council on Research and Development for Fuel and Power (of Dept of Energy)
A C O S	Advisory Committee on Safety (of IEC)
A C O S H	Appalachian Center for Occupational Safety and Health (of NIOSH (USA))
A C O U S I D	Acoustic Seismic Intrusion Detector
A C P	African, Caribbean and Pacific countries
	Association of Canadian Publishers (Canada)
A C P S	Arab Company for Petroleum Services (of OAPEC)
A C R A	Association of Company Registration Agents
A C R E	Automatic Call Recording Equipment
A C R i L I S	Australian Centre for Research in Library and Information Science (Riverina College of Advanced Education (Australia))
A C R S	Advisory Committee on Reactor Safeguards (USA) (absorbed into Nuclear Regulatory Commission 1974 (USA))
A C S	Air Coating System
A C S / D C I	American Chemical Society/Division of Chemical Information (USA)

A C S F	Artificial Cerebrospinal Fluid
A C T	Advanced Concept Tyre
	Autocoder to COBOL Translator
A C T I	Advisory Committee on Technology Innovation (of BOSTID (NAS) (USA))
A C T S U	Association of Computer Time-Sharing Users (USA)
A C T V	Armored Cavalry TOW Vehicle
A C U	Asian Clearing Union (Bangladesh, India, Iran, Nepal, Pakistan and Sri Lanka)
A C U G	Association of Computer User Groups
A C U P	Association of Canadian University Presses (Canada)
A C U R I L	Association of Caribbean University and Research Libraries
A D	prefix to dated-numbered series of Airworthiness Directives issued by FAA (USA)
A D A	Allgemeiner Deutscher Automobile Club (Germany) (German Automobile Association)
	American Diabetes Association (USA)
A D A B A S	Adaptable Data Base System
A D A L	Action Data Automation Language
A D A M H A	Alcohol, Drug Abuse and Mental Health Administration (USA)
A d B	Acceleration Decibel
A D C	Armament Development Center (US Army)
A D C A	Advanced Design Composite Aircraft
A D C I S	Association for the Development of Computer-based Instruction Systems (USA)
A D C O M	Aerospace Defense Command (USDOD)
A D C T	Assisted-Draught Crossflow Tower
	Association of District Council Treasurers
A D D M	Automated Drafting and Digitizing Machine
A D E	Automatic Data Entry
A D H	Alcohol Dehydrogenase
A D I C E P	Association des Directeurs des Centres des Matières Plastiques (Association of Directors of Plastics Materials Centres)
A D L I P S	Automatic Data Link Plotting System
A D M	Air-launched Decoy Missile
A D M A	Abu Dhabi Marine Areas (a company) (Abu Dhabi)
A D N O C	Abu Dhabi National Oil Company (Abu Dhabi)

11

A D O P T	Approach to Distributed Processing Transactions
A D P	Aggregate Demand Potential
A D P A	American Defense Preparedness Association (USA)
A D P C	Abu Dhabi Petroleum Company (Abu Dhabi)
A D P C M	Adaptive Differential Pulse Code Modulation
A D P E S O	Automatic Data Processing Equipment Selection Office (USN)
A D S	Atmospheric Diving Suit
A D S I D	Air Delivered Acoustic Implant Seismic Intrusion Detector
A D S S	Australian Defence Scientific Service (of DSTO (Dept of Defence) (Australia))
A D S Y M	Automobile De-fog/de-frost System Model
A D T	Automatic Detection and Tracking
A D V	Air-Defence Variant (of the MRCA *"Tornado"*)
	Aleutian Disease Virus
A D V U L	Air Defence Vulnerability
A E A	Association of European Airlines
A E B	Atomic Energy Bureau (of STA (Japan))
A E B I G	*Aslib* Economic and Business Information Group
A E C	Atomic Energy Commission (USA) (disbanded in 1974 and replaced by ERDA and Nuclear Regulatory Commission)
A E C B	Association for the Export of Canadian Books (Canada)
A E C E	Automotive Electronics Conference and Exposition
A E C M A	Association Européenne des Constructeurs de Matériel Aérospatiale (European Association of Manufacturers of Aerospace Material)
A E G	Association of Engineering Geologists (USA)
A E I	Americans for Energy Independence (USA) (a non-profit group)
A E I M S	Administrative Engineering Information Management System
A E M	Acoustic Emission Monitoring
A E M P	Association of European Management Publishers
A E O	Association of Exhibition Organisers
A E O S	Astronomical, Earth and Ocean Sciences (a directorate of NSF (USA))
A E Q A	Alabama Environmental Quality Association (USA)

12

A E R	Apical Ectodermal Ridge
A E R A L L	Association d'Études et de Recherches sur les Aéronefs Allégés (France)
A E R O S O L	Aero dynamic-solar
A E S	American Electroencephalographic Society (USA)
	Anti-eosinophil
	Auger Electron Spectroscopy
A E S D	Acoustic Environment Support Detachment (of the Office of Naval Research (USN))
A E S O	Aircraft Environmental Support Office (of NEPSS (USN))
A E W B	Army Electronic Warfare Board (US Army)
A E W I S	Army Electronic Warfare Information System (US Army)
A E W S P S	Aircraft Electronic Warfare Self-Protection System
A F A C O	Association Française des Amateurs Constructeurs l'Ordinateurs (France) (French Association of Amateur Computer Builders)
A F A M	Airfield Attack Munition
	Automatic Frequency Assignment Model
A F B M A	Anti-Friction Bearing Manufacturers Association (USA)
A F C F S	Advanced Fighter Control Flight Simulator
A F C M A	Aluminium Foil Container Manufacturers Association
A F C R	American Federation of Clinical Research (USA)
A F D S C	Air Force Data Services Center (USAF)
A F E C O G A Z	Association des Fabricants Européens d'Appareils de Contrôle pour le Gaz et l'Huile (European Association of Gas and Oil Control Manufacturers)
A F E I	Association Française pour l'Étiquetage d'Information (France) (French Association for Informative Labelling)
A F F	An Foras Forbartha (Eire) (Institute for Physical Planning and Construction Research)
A F F F	Aqueous Film-Forming Foam
A F H F	Air Force Historical Foundation (USA)
A F I S	Air Force Intelligence Service (USAF)
A F L I R	Advanced Forward Looking Infra-Red
A F L O S H	AUDDIT Fault Logic Simulation Hybrid
A F M E A	Air Force Management Engineering Agency (USAF)

A F M M F O	Air Force Medical Materials Field Office (USAF)
A F M P C	Air Force Military Personnel Center (USAF)
A F M S	Association of Fleet Maintenance Supervisors (USA)
A F N I L	Agence Francophone pour la Numérotation Internationale du Livre (France) (acts also for Belgium and Switzerland) (Agency for International Standard Book Numbering)
A F O G	Asian Federation of Obstetrics and Gynaecology
A F O S	Advanced Field Operating System
	Automation of Field Operations and Services (of National Weather Service (USA))
A F P	Alpha Foetoprotein
A F P A	Association pour la Formation Professionnelle des Adultes (France) (Association for the Professional Training of Adults)
A F P R O	Air Force Plant Representative Office (USAF)
A F R C C	Air Force Rescue Coordination Center (USAF)
A F S	Atomic Fluorescence Spectrometry
A F T E C	Air Force Test and Evaluation Center (USAF)
A F T I	Advanced Fighter Technology Integration (a project of USAF)
A F V O A	Aberdeen Fishing Vessel Owners Association
A G	Aktiengesellschaft (Public Stock Company)
A G E	Asian Geotechnical Engineering (an information centre of the Asian Institute of Technology (Thailand))
A G I L E	Analytic Geometry Interpretive Language
A G I P A	Adaptive Ground Implemented Phased Array
A G L	Above Ground Level
A G L I N E T	Agricultural Libraries Information Network (of IAALD & FAO (UN))
A G O	Atmospheric Gas Oil
A G R	Advanced Gas-cooled Graphite-moderated Reactor
A G R E	Atlantic Gas Research Exchange (of British Gas Corporation, American Gas Association and Gaz de France)
A G R E E	Advanced Ground Receiving Equipment Experiment (of NASA (USA) and Nippon Hoso Kyokai (Japan))

A G R E P	Permanent Inventory of Agricultural Research Projects (in the EEC)
A G R I / M E C H	prefix to numbered series issued by the Group of Experts on Mechanization of Agriculture (of ECE (UNO))
A G T E L I S	Automated Ground Transportable Emitter Location and Identification System
A G T V	Advanced Ground Transportation Vehicle
A H	Adenohypophysis
A H A B	Attacking Hardened Air Bases
A H A S	Acetohydroxy Acid Synthase
A H C	Acute Haemorrhagic Conjunctivitis
A H E A D	Army Help for Education and Development (a project of the US Army)
A H L	Alcohol Induced Hyperlipidemia
A H M S A	Altos Hornos de México SA (Mexico)
A I A	Association for Industrial Archaeology
A I B	Accident Investigation Branch (of Dept of Trade) Anti-Inflation Board (Canada)
A I B F	Advanced Internally-Blown jet Flap
A I C A	Associazione Italiana per il Calco Automatico (Italy) (Italian Association for Automatic Data Processing)
A I C C	Antibody-Induced Cell-mediated Cytoxicity
A I C H	Automatic Integrated Container Handling
A I C M A	Association Internationale des Constructeurs de Matériel Aérospatial (now AECMA)
A I C M R	Association Internationale des Constructeurs de Matériel Roulant (International Association of Rolling Stock Manufacturers (federated into UNIFE in 1976))
A I C R O	Association of Independent Contract Research Organisations
A I C S	Air Intake Control System
A I D	Automatic Interaction Detector
A I D A	Automatic Intruder Detector Alarm
A I D A T S	Army In-flight Data Transmission System (US Army)
A I D S	Aircraft Intrusion Detection System
A I D U S	Automated Information Directory Update System Automated Input and Document Update System
A I E I	Association of Indian Engineering Industry (India)

A I F T A A	Anglo-Irish Free Trade Area Agreement
A I F V	Armoured Infantry Fighting Vehicle
A I H A	American Industrial Hygiene Association (USA)
A I M	Accuracy In Media (an organization) (USA)
	Association des Ingénieurs Électriciens sortis de l'Institut Électrotechnique Montefiore (Belgium)
	Atlantic International Marketing Association (USA)
	Automated Inventory Management
A I M A V	Association Internationale pour la Recherche et la Diffusion des Méthodes Audio-Visuelles et Structuroglobales
A I M I C	Association of Insurance Managers in Industry and Commerce (now AIRMIC)
A I M S	Airport Income Management System
	Altitude Identification and Military System
A I N	Australian Institute of Navigation (Australia)
A I N A	American Institute of Nautical Archaeology (USA)
A I N D T	Australian Institute for Non-Destructive Testing (Australia)
A I O P I	Association of Information Officers in the Pharmaceutical Industry
A I O T T	Action Information Organisation and Tactical Trainer
A I P	Aldosterone-Induced Protein
	Automated Imagery Processing
A I P A	Associazione Italiana Planificazione Aziendale (Italy)
A I P S	Australian Institute of Political Science (Australia)
A I R C A T	Automated Integrated Radar Control for Air Traffic
A I R / M M H	Acoustic Intercept Receiver/Multimode Hydrophone system
A I R M A P	Air Monitoring, Analysis and Prediction
A I R M I C	Association of Insurance and Risk Managers in Industry and Commerce
A I R S	Advanced Inertial Reference Sphere
	Airborne Integrated Reconnaissance System
A I S	Answer in Sentence
A I S B	Artificial Intelligence and Simulation of Behaviour (a group of the British Computer Society)
A I S M	Association Internationale de Signalisation Maritime (International Association of Marine Signalling)

A I U F F A S	Association Internationale des Utilisateurs de Files de Fibres Artificielles et Synthétiques (France) (International Association of Users of Artificial and Synthetic Yarn)
A I U M	American Institute of Ultrasound in Medicine (USA)
A L A D	Aminolevulinic Acid Dehydratase
A L A I R S	Advance Low Altitude Infra-Red Reconnaissance Sensor
A L B	Arbeitsgemeinschaft Landwirtschaftliches Bauwesen (Germany) (Working Committee on Farm Buildings)
	Assembly Line Balancing
A L B A N Y	Adjustment of Large Blocks with *any* number of photos, points and images, using *any* photogrammetric measuring instrument and on *any* computer
A L C	Amoeba-less Life Cycle
	Armament Logistics Command (US Army)
A L C M	Air-Launched Cruise Missile
A L C O R	*ARPA* (USA) *Lincoln* (Laboratory of MIT (USA)) C-band Observable Radar
A L E C S	Automated Law Enforcement Communications System (USA)
A L E C S O	Arab League Educational, Cultural and Scientific Organization (Egypt)
A L E G E O	Latin American Association of Editors in the Earth Sciences
A L I R T	Adaptive Long Range Infra-Red Tracker
A L I T	Advanced Technology Light Twin (a project of NASA (USA))
A L L	Airborne Laser Laboratory
A L M I D S	Army Logistics Management Integrated Data System (US Army)
A L O F T	Airborne Light/Optical Fiber Technology (a program of the USN)
A L Q A S	Aircraft Landing Quality Assessment Scheme
A L S S	Advanced Location Strike System
	Airborne Location and Strike System
A L T	Airborne Laser Tracker system
A L V A O	Association des Langues Vivantes pour l'Afrique Occidentale (Nigeria) (West African Modern Languages Association)
A L W I N	Algorithmic Wiswesser Notation

A M A	Air Materiel Area (USAF) (now known as Air Logistics Center)
	Association of Metropolitan Authorities
A M A C O N	a division of American Management Association
A M A D	Aircraft Mounted Accessory Drive
	Airframe Mounted Accessory Drive
A M A R C	Army Materiel Acquisition Review Committee (US Army)
A M C	Army Materiel Command (US Army) (became DARCOM in 1976)
A M C A W S	Advanced Medium-Calibre Aircraft Weapon System
A M C M	Airborne Mine Counter Measures
A M C O	International Conference on Atomic Masses and Fundamental Constants
A M C O S	*Aldermaston* Mechanized Cataloguing and Ordering System (of AWRE (MOD))
A M D A	Airline Medical Directors Association
A M E	Automatic Microfiche Editor
A M E D A	Automatic Microscope Electronic Data Accumulator
A M I	Association of Medical Illustrators
A M I C	Aerospace Materials Information Center (operated by University of Dayton Research in conjunction with AFML (USAF))
	Asian Mass Communications Research and Information Centre (Singapore)
A M I E V	Association Médicale Internationale pour l'Étude des Conditions de Vie et de Santé (International Medical Association for the Study of Living Conditions and Health)
A M I N A	Association Mondiale des Inventeurs (Belgium) (World Federation of Inventors)
A M I O	Arab Military Industrialisation Organisation
A M I S	Automated Mask Inspection System
A M M I N E T	Automated Mortgage Management Information Network
A M M R P V	Advanced Multi-Mission Remotely Piloted Vehicle
A M O P	Association of Mail Order Publishers
A M O S	Anti-reflection coated Metal Oxide Semiconductor
A M P A	American Medical Publishers Association (USA)
A M P L	A Macro Programming Language
A M P P	Advanced Microprogrammable Processor

A M P S	Atmospheric, Magnetospheric and Plasmas-in-Space
A M P T C	Arab Maritime Petroleum Transport Company (jointly owned by a number of Arab oil exporting companies)
A M Q U A	American Quaternary Association (USA)
A M R A D –	ARPA (USDoD) Measurements Radar
A M S	Acoustic Measuring System
	Advanced Metallic Structures (a project of USAF)
	Anti-reflection Metal Semiconductor
	Automatic Meteorological System
A M S A	American Metal Stamping Association (USA)
A M S A C	Advanced Multi-Stage Axial-flow Compressor (a program of NASA (USA))
A M S S E E	Area Museums Service for South-Eastern England
A M T	Audio-frequency Magneto-tellurics
A M T E X	Air Mass Transportation Experiment
A M T R A K	formal title is National Railroad Passenger Corporation (USA) (a quasi-governmental agency)
A M V E R	Automated Merchant Vessel Report system (of the United States Coast Guard)
A N A	Anti-nuclear Antibodies
	Automated Naval Architecture
A N B F M	Adaptive Narrow-Band Frequency Modulation Modem
A N C E	Associazione Nazionale Costruttori Elili (Italy) (National Association of Building Constructors)
A N C H O R	Alpha-Numeric Character Generator
A N C I R S	Automated News Clipping, Indexing, and Retrieval System
A N C O V A	Analysis of Covariance
A N F I	Automatic Noise Figure Indicator
A N G	Air National Guard (USA)
A N M C	American National Metric Council (of ANSI (USA))
A N M I	Air Navigation Multiple Indicator
A N M R C	Australian Numerical Meteorology Research Centre (Australia)
A N N A F	Joint Army/Navy/NASA/Air Force (USA)
A N O M	Analysis of Means
A N P R M	prefix to dated-numbered series of Advanced Notices of Proposed Rule Making issued by FAA (USA)
A N Q U E	Associación Nacional de Químicos de España (Spain) (National Chemical Association)

A N S T E L	Australian National Scientific and Technological Library (Australia)
A N Z	Air New Zealand (New Zealand)
A N Z W O N A	Australian and New Zealand Web Offset Newspaper Association (now PANPA)
A O A C	Association of Official Agricultural Chemists (title changed in 1965 to Association of Official Analytical Chemists (USA))
A O C	Association of Old Crows (USA)
A O C M	Advanced Optical Counter-Measures
A O H C	American Occupational Health Conference
A O M A	American Occupational Medical Association (USA)
A O R S	Army Operations Research Symposium (US Army)
A O S T R A	Alberta Oil Sands Technology and Research Authority (Canada)
A P	Associative Processor
A P A	American Polygraph Association (USA)
	Anthracite Producers Association (South Africa)
A P C	Accounting Principles Committee (South Africa)
	Agricultural Productivity Commission (Philippines)
A P C	Armour Piercing, Capped
A P C A	Air Pollution Control Association (Canada)
A P C B C	Armour Piercing, Capped, Ballistic Cap
A P C M	Authorized Protective Connecting Module
A P C O M	International Symposium on the Applications of Computers in the Mining Industry
A P C R	Armour Piercing, Composite Rigid
A P C S	Associative Processor Computer System
A P D L	Algorithmic Processor Description Language
A P E T	Application Programme Evaluator Tool
A P F	Association of Paper Finishers (of BPBIF)
A P F S D S	Armour Piercing, Fin Stabilised, Discarding Sabot
A P H A	American Printing History Association (USA)
A P I D C	Andhra Pradesh Industrial Development Corporation (India) (government owned)
A P L	Aluminium-Polythene Laminate
A P L L	Analog Phased-Locked Loop
A P M	Air Power Museum (USA)
A P M C	Andhra Pradesh Mining Corporation (India) (government owned)

A P O	Australian Post Office (Australia) (split into Australian Postal Commission *and* Australian Telecommunications Commission in 1975)
A P P	Ammonium Polyphosphate
A P P A	Association des Pilotes et Propriétaires d'Aéronefs (France) (Association of Private Aircraft Owners)
A P P L E	*Ariane* (artificial satellite) Passenger Payload Experiment
	Associative Processor Programming Language
A P R	Association of Petroleum Re-Refiners (USA)
A P R A G A Z	Association des Propriétaires de Récipients à Gaz Comprimés (Belgium)
A P R G	Air Pollution Research Group (NPL (CSIR)) (South Africa)
A P R O C	Adaptive Statistical Processor
A P R S	Association of Professional Recording Studies
A P S	American Proctologic Society (USA)
	Appearance Potential Spectroscopy
A P S A	American Political Science Association (USA)
A P S T C	Andhra Pradesh State Road Transport Corporation (India) (Govt owned)
A P T	Association of Photographic Technicians (now Technicians Section of Institute of Incorporated Photographers)
A P T A	American Public Transit Association (USA)
A P V	Automatic Patching Verification
A Q C R	Air Quality Control Regions (USA)
A R B	Air Registration Board (replaced by the Airworthiness Requirements Board of the CAA in 1972)
A R B S	Angular Rate Bombing System
A R C	Accounting Research Committee (Canada)
	Ames Research Center (of NASA (USA))
A R C A D E	Automatic Radar Control and Data Equipment
A R C A S	Automatic Radar Chain Acquisition System
A R D C	Agricultural Refinance and Development Corporation (India)
A R D I	Analysis, Requirements Determination, Design and Development, and Implementation and Evaluation

A R D U	Analytical Research and Development Unit (of AERE (UKAEA))
A R E A	American Recreational Equipment Association (USA)
A R E N B D	Armor and Engineer Board (US Army)
A R E T O	Arab Republic of Egypt Telecommunications Organization (Egypt)
A R H	Advanced Reconnaissance Helicopter
A R H / I R	Anti-Radiation Homing/Infra-Red
A R I E S	Astronomical Radio Interferometric Earth Surveying
A R I M A	Autoregressive Integrated Moving Average
A R I S	Activity Reporting Information System
A R L I S / N A	Art Libraries Society of North America
A R M C O M	Armament Command (US Army)
A R M C O M S A T	Arab Communications Satellite System
A R M E	Automatic Reseau Measuring Equipment
A R M I S	Agricultural Research Management Information System
A R M O P	Army Mortar Program (US Army)
A R M S	preface to numbered series on Aerial Radiological Measuring System issued by Atomic Energy Commission (USA)
	Atmospheric Roving Manipulator System
A R P A C	Agricultural Research Policy Advisory Committee (of ARS (USDA))
A R P E G E	Air Pollution Episode Game
A R P L	A Retrieval Process Language
A R P S	Advanced Radar Processing System
	Arab Physical Society (Lebanon)
	Australian Radiation Protection Society (Australia)
A R R A	Amateur Radio Retailers Association
A R R E S	Automatic Radar Reconnaissance Exploitation System
A R R S	Aircraft Refueling and Rearming System
A R S	Acoustic Rate Sensor
	Active Radar Seeker
A R S	Atmosphere Revitalization System
A R S P A	Aerial Reconnaissance and Surveillance Penetration Analysis
A R T E M I S	Administrative Real Time Express Mortgage and Investment System

A R T I N S	Army Terrain Information System (US Army)
A R T T	Automatic Rubber Tensile Tester
A S	Amorphous Semiconductor
A S A	American Soybean Association (USA)
	American Surgical Association (USA)
	Australian Society of Authors (Australia)
A S A L M	Advanced Strategic Air-Launched Multi-mission Missile
A S A P	Aircraft Synthesis Analysis Programme
	Antennas-Scatterers Analysis Programme
A S A R	Advanced Surface-to-Air Ramjet
A S A S	*Atkins (Computing Services Ltd)* Stress Analysis System
A S A T T	Advanced Small Axial Turbine Technology
A S B	Asymtomatic Bacteriuria
A S C	Accounting Standards Committee (of ICAEW, ICAS, ICAI, ACA, ICMA and CIPFA)
	Advanced Science Computer
A S C C	Aeronautical Services Communications Centre
	Air Standardization Coordinating Committee (of NATO)
A S C D	Association for Supervision and Curriculum Development (USA)
A S C N	American Society for Clinical Nutrition (USA)
A S C O	American Society on Contemporary Opthamology (USA)
A S D F	Air Self-Defence Force (Japan)
A S E	Aircraft Stabilization Equipment
	Amplified Spontaneous Emission
A S E B	Assam State Electricity Board (India)
A S E D	Aviation and Surface Effects Department (of NSRDC (USN))
A S E R / C o E D	American Society for Engineering Education, Computers in Education Division (USA)
A S E T	Aeronautical Satellite Earth Terminal
	Author System for Education and Training
A S E T A	Association Suisse pour l'Équipement de l'Agriculture (Switzerland) (Swiss Association for Agricultural Technology)
A S E W	Airborne and Surface Early Warning
A S H	Aerial Scout Helicopter
A S I	Advanced Study Institute (conferences held by NATO)

A S I A C	Aerospace Structures Information and Analysis Center (USAF)
A S I C	Avionics Subsystems Interface Contractor
A S I D I C	Association of Scientific Information Dissemination Centers (USA) (changed title in 1975 to Association of Information and Dissemination Centers)
A S I L	Asymptotic Stability In the Large
A S I S	*Aoki* (*Construction Company* (Japan)) Shadow Investigation System
A S L A B	Atomic Safety and Licensing Appeal Board (USA)
A S L B	Atomic Safety and Licensing Board (USA) (absorbed into the Nuclear Regulatory Commission in 1974)
A S M	American Society of Mammalogists (USA)
A S M D / E W	Anti-Ship Missile Defence/Electronic Warfare
A S M T	American Society of Medical Technologists (USA)
A S N A P	Automatic Steerable Null Antenna Processor
A S O	Antistreptolysin 0
	Aviation Supply Office (USN)
A S P	Accelerated Surface Post
	All Altitude Spin Projectile
	American Society for Photobiology (USA)
	Astronomical Society of the Pacific (USA)
A S P A	Alloy Steel Producers Association (India)
A S P E C	Association pour la Prévention et l'Étude de la Contamination (France) (Association for the Prevention and Study of Contamination)
A S P E C T	Acoustic Short-Pulse Echo-Classification Techniques
A S R	Air-Sea Rescue
A S R A D I	Adaptive Surface Signal Recognition And Direction Indicator
A S R C	Atmospheric Sciences Research Center (of SUNY (USA))
A S R O	Astronomical Roentgen Observatory Satellite
A S R Y	Arab Shipbuilding and Repair Yard (at Bahrain; financed by OAPEC)
A S S C	Accounting Standard Steering Committee (became ASC in 1975 with membership of ICAEW, ICAS, ICAI, ACA, ICMA and CIPFA)
	Automatic Support Systems Symposium

A S S E S S	Airborne Science/Spacelab Experiments Simulation System
A S S E T	Advanced Systems Synthesis and Evaluation Technique
A S S H	American Society for Surgery of the Hand (USA)
A S S I F O N T E	Association de l'Industrie de la Fonte de Fromage (of EEC) (Association of the Processed Cheese Industry)
A S S O C H A M	Associated Chambers of Commerce and Industry (India)
A S S W	Anti-Strategic Submarine Warfare
A S T	Air Service Training (an aviation school at Perth Aerodrome, Scotland)
A S T A	American Seed Trade Association (USA)
	American Society of Travel Agents (USA)
A S T A P	Advanced Statistical Analysis Programme
A S T C	Airport Surface Traffic Control
A S T E C	Australian Science and Technology Council (Australia)
A S T I	Anti-Submarine Training Indicator
A S T R A	Advanced Structural Analyzer
	Advanced System for Radiological Assessment
	Automatic Scheduling and Time-dependent Resource Allocation
A S T T	Action-Speed Tactical Trainer
A S U	Arizona State University (USA)
A S U T S	American Society of Ultrasound Technical Specialists (USA)
A S V	Anodic Stripping Voltammetry
A S W	Artificial Seawater
A S W F	Arithmetic Series Weight Function
A T / G W	Anti-Tank Guided Weapon
A T A	American Transit Association (USA) (merged into APTA, 1974)
A T A	American Translators Association (USA)
	Automatic Threat Alert
A T A C	Air Transport Association of Canada (Canada)
A T A C C	Advanced Technology Axial Centrifugal Compressor
A T A F C S	Airborne Target Acquisition and Fire Control System
A T A R	Airborne Tracking, Acquisition and Recognition

A T A R S	Anti-Terrain Avoidance Radar System
A T C	Advanced Technology Components
A T C A	Advanced Tanker/Cargo Aircraft
A T C A S	Air Traffic Control Automated System
A T Case	Aspartate Transcarbamylase
A T C S	Air Traffice Control Board (of MoD and Dept of Industry)
A T D A	Army Training Device Agency (US Army)
A T E C	Aviation Technician Education Council (USA)
A T E G	Asociatión Técnica Española de Galvanización (Spain) (Spanish Technical Association of Galvanising)
A T E M I S	Automatic Traffic Engineering and Management Information System
A T E N	Association Technique pour l'Énergie Nucléaire (France) (Nuclear Energy Technology Association) (disbanded in 1975)
A T E W S	Advanced Tactical Electronic Warfare System
A T F A S	Association of Teachers of Foundry and Allied Subjects
A T I	Association of Technical Institutions (changed to ACFHE in 1970)
	Automotive Tyre Industry (India) (a manufacturers association)
A T I C	Australian Tin Information Centre (Australia) (of the Tin Research Institute)
A T I S	Airborne Tactical Jamming System
A T L A	American Theological Library Association (USA)
A T L A S	Advanced Tactical Lightweight Air Superiority radar
A T L I S	Automatic-Tracking Laser Illumination System
A T M	Advanced Technology Mining
	Association of Teachers of Management
A T N A V	Acoustic Transponder Navigation
A T S	Acoustic Target Sensor
	American Tentative Society (USA)
	Automated Telemetry System
A T S / J E A	Automated Test System/Jet Engine Accessories
A T S U	Association of Time-Sharing Users (USA)
A T T R	Advanced Threat Reactive Receiver
A T U	Arab Telecommunication Union

26

A T W S	Anticipated Transients Without Scram
A U C A N U K U S	Australia, Canada, United Kingdom, United States
A U C A S	Association of University Clinical Academic Staff
A U D D I T	Automatic Dynamic Digital Test System
Aus I M M	Australian Institute of Mining and Metallurgy (Australia)
A U S T R I A T O M	Österreichische Interessengemeinschaft für Nukleartechnik (Austria) (Austrian Nuclear Industry Group)
A U T A	Association of University Teachers of Accounting
A U T E	Association of University Teachers of Economics
A U T O C O M	Automated Combustor design code
A U T O P R O S	Automated Process Planning System
A U T R A N	Automatic Translation
A U T R A N A V	Automated Transponder Navigation system
A U V M I S	Administrative Use Vehicle Management Information System (US Army)
A V - M F	Aviatsiya Voennomorskovo Flota (USSR) (Naval Air Force)
A V A	Automatic Voice Alarm
A V A D S	Autotrack Vulcan Air Defence System
A V A S I	Abbreviated Visual Approach Slope Indicator
A v c a t	Aviation High-flash Turbine Fuel
A V I D	Audio Visual Instructional Division (of ISRO (India))
A V L O C	Airborne Visible Laser Optical Communications
A V L S	Automatic Vehicle Location System
A V M F	Aviatsiya Voenno-Morskava Flota (USSR) (Naval Air Force)
A V P	Arginine Vasopressin
A V R S	Audio/Visual Recording System
A V S T	Automated Visual Sensitivity Tester
A v t a g	Aviation Wide-cut Turbine Fuel
A v t u r	Aviation Turbine Fuel
A W	Augmentor Wing
A W A D S	Adverse Weather Aerial Delivery System
A W A N S	Aviation Weather and Notice to Airmen System
A W A R E	Advance Warning Equipment
A W A R S	All-Weather Airborne Reconnaissance System
A W A S	Airborne Wind-shear Alert Sensor
A W E S	Association of Western Europe Shipbuilders

A W I S	Association for Women in Science (USA)
A W J S R A	Augmentor Wing Jet STOL Research Aircraft
A W S G	Army Work Study Group (MOD) (now Army Management Services Group (Work Study))
A W W F	All-Weather Wood Foundations
A Z T R A N	Azimuth from Transit

B

B A - S I S	Bibliographic Author of Subject Interactive Research
B A - S I S - H	BA-SIS-History
B A - S I S - P	BA-SIS-Political Science, Public Administration, Urban Studies, and International Relations
B A - S I S - S	BA-SIS-Sociology
B A A	British Anodising Association
B A B O	Boolean Approach for Bivalent Optimization
B A C	British Atlantic Committee (of the Atlantic Treaty Association)
B A D A D U Q	Banque de Données à Accès Direct de l'Université du Québec (Canada) (On-line Bank of Quebec University)
B A E D	British Airways European Division
B A F M	British Association of Friends of Museums
B A G D A	British Advertising Gift Distributors Association
B A H	British Airways Helicopters (a part of British Airways)
B A H P A	British Agricultural and Horticultural Plastics Association
B A L U N	Balance to Unbalanced
B A M P	Basic Analysis and Mapping Programme
B A N S	Bright Alphanumeric Sub-system
B A O D	British Airways Overseas Division
B A R	Browning Automatic Rifle
B A R B I	Baseband Radar Bag Initiator
B A R C	Bay Area Reference Center (administered by California State Library (USA))
B A R C S	Battlefield Area Reconnaissance System
B A R O N	Business/Accounts Reporting Operating Network
B A R V	Beach Armoured Recovery Vehicle
B A S	British Acoustical Society (in 1974 merged into the Institute of Acoustics)

B A S A M	British Association of Grain, Seed Feed and Agricultural Merchants
B A S E	Bank-Americard Service Exchange (USA)
	Business Assessment Study and Evaluation
B A S E C	British Approvals Service for Electric Cables
B A S I L	*Barclays (Bank)* Advanced Staff Information Language
B A S S	Basic Analogue Simulation System
B A S Y C	Benefit Assessment for System Change
B A T H Y	Bathythermograph
B A U	Bangladesh Agricultural University (Bangladesh)
B B A C	Bus-to-Bus Access Circuit
B C A B	British Computer Association for the Blind
B C C	Bharat Coking Coal Ltd (India) (Government owned)
B C C A	Beer Can Collectors of America (USA)
B C C D	Buried-Channel Charge-Coupled Device
B C C S	British Carpet Classification Scheme (now operated by BCMA)
B C F	Bulked-Continuous-Filament
B C G	Bacillus Calmette-Guerin
B C I S C	British Chemical Industry Safety Council (of CIA) (replaced in 1975 by CISHEC (of CIA))
B C I T A	British Carpet Industry Technical Association (disbanded 1976)
B C M	Budget Correcting Mechanism (of EEC)
B C M A	British Carpet Manufacturers Association
B C M E A	Bureau Commun du Machinisme et de l'Équipment Agricole (France)
B C O A	Bituminous Coal Operators Association (USA)
B C S A A	British Computer Society ALGOL Association
B C S L A	British Columbia School Librarians Association (Canada)
B C T	Building Centre Trust
B C U A	Business Computers Users Association
B D A	British Diabetic Association
	Bomb Damage Assessment
B D A M	Basic Direct Access Method
B D D T	Bench Detergency-Dispersancy Test
B D P A	British Disposable Products Association

B D W T T	*Batelle* Drop Weight Tear Test
B E A	British European Airways (now BEAD of British Airways)
B E A M O S	Beam-Addressable Metal Oxide Semiconductor
B E C	Board for Engineering Cooperation (USA) (governing body of the Association for Cooperation in engineering)
	Business Education Council
B E C A M P	Ballistic Environmental Characterization and Measurements Program (US Army)
B E R U	Building Economics Research Unit (of University College, London)
B F I	Beam-Forming Interfact
B F I C C	British Facsimilie Industry Compatibility Committee
B F M P	British Federation of Master Printers (now British Printing Industries Federation)
B G C	British Gas Corporation
B G T A	Birmingham Group Training Association
B G W	Battlefield Guided Weapon
B H A	Butylated Hydroxyanisole
B H G M F	British Hang Glider Manufacturers Federation
B H M A	British Hard Metal Association
B H P	Biological Hazard Potential
B H T	Butylated Hydroxytoluene
B I A	Binding Industries of America (of PIA (USA))
B I A L L	British and Irish Association of Law Librarians
B I F N	Banque Internationale pour le Financement de l'Énergie Nucléaire
B I M	An Bord Iascaigh Mhara (Eire) (Sea Fisheries Board)
B I N D T	British Institute of Non-Destructive Testing
B I N S	*Barclays (Bank)* Integrated Network System
B I P S	British Integrated Programme Suite
B I R S	British Institute of Recorded Sound
B I S	Biological Information Service (of the Institute of Biology *and* the British Library)
B I S I T S	British Industrial and Scientific International Translations Service (now of the Metals Society)
B J C G	British Joint Corrosion Group (disbanded 1974)
B L E A P	Bought Ledger and Expenditure Analysis Package

B L E U	Blind Landing Experimental Unit (of RAE) (now RAE Flight Systems Division 2)
B L H S	Ballistic Laser Holographic System
B L I P	Background-Limited Infra-red Photography
B L M	Bilayer Lipid Membrane
B L O C S	*Bucknell (University)* (USA) On-Line Circulation System
B M A T	Beginning of Morning Astronomical Twilight
B M D A T C	Ballistic Missile Defense Advanced Technology Center (US Army)
B M D C A	Ballistic Missile Defense Communications Agency (USACC)
B M D S C O M	Ballistic Missile Defense System Command (US Army)
B M E	Bundesverband Materialwirtschaft und Einkauf (Germany) (National Association of Materials Management and Purchasing)
B M L	Bundesministerium für Ernahrung, Landwirtschaft und Forsten (Germany) (Federal Ministry of Food, Agriculture and Forestry)
B M L A	British Maritime Law Association
B M M F F	British Man-Made Fibres Federation
B M P	National Council of Building Material Producers
B M P A	British Medical Pilots Association
B M R	Basal Metabolic Rate
B M S	Balanced Magnetic Switch
B N A	Beta-naphthylamine
B N B	British National Bibliography (now part of the Bibliographic Services Division of the British Library)
B N D C	British Nuclear Design and Construction Ltd (absorbed into NNC in 1975)
B N F M R A	British Non-Ferrous Metals Research Association (became British Non-Ferrous Metals Technology Centre in 1973)
B N O C	British National Oil Corporation
B O A C	British Overseas Airways Corporation (now British Airways Overseas Division)
B O D S	British Oceanographic Data Service (now of the Institute of Oceanographic Services)
B O L D S	*Burroughs* Optical Lens Docking System

31

B O S S	*BRE (Building Research Establishment)* On-line Search System
	International Conference on the Behaviour of Off-Shore Structures
B O T A C	British Overseas Trade Advisory Council (a channel of communication between BOTB and industry and commerce)
B O T E X	British Office for Training Exchange (of BACIE)
B P & B M A	British Paper and Board Makers Association (now BPBIF)
B P A	Byggproduktion AB (Sweden)
B P A S	British Pregnancy Advisory Service (a non-profit registered charitable trust)
B P B F	British Paper Bag Federation
B P B I F	British Paper and Board Industry Federation
B P D C	Book and Periodical Development Council (Canada)
B P D M S	Basic Point-Defence Missile System
B P I F	British Printing Industries Federation
B P M	Beam Path Multiplier
B P P M A	British Power Press Manufacturers Association (now MMMA)
B P S	Balanced Pressure System
B P S	Benchmark Portability System
	Bureau of Product Safety (of FDA (USA)) (now Consumer Product Safety Commission)
B P T	Bound Plasma Tryptophan
B P T I	Bovine Pancreatic Trypsin Inhibitor
B Q S F	British Quarrying and Slag Federation
B R A Z O	Spanish word for Arm—used as a name for an Air-to-Air Anti-radiation missile guidance concept by the USN and USAF
B R I N D E X	British Independent Oil Exploration Companies Association
B R I S C	Buffered Remote Interactive Search Console
B R I T S H I P S	British Shipbuilding Integrated Production System
B R M C	Business Research Management Center (USAF)
B R U F M A	British Rigid Urethane Foam Manufacturers Association
B S	Back-scattering Spectrometry

32

BSA	Bearing Specialists Association (USA)
B S A	Boundary-Spanning Activity
B S A C	British Sub-Aqua Club
B S C	Biological Stain Commission (USA)
B S F	British Shipping Federation (merged into GCBS in 1975)
B S F C	Bihar State Finance Corporation (India)
B S M V	Barley Stripe Mosaic Virus
B S O	Benzene-Soluble Organics
	Business Statistics Office (a branch of the Government Statistical Service)
B S P	Binomial Sampling Plan
B S R C	British Sporting Rifle Club
B S R D	Behavioural Sciences Research Division (of the Civil Service Department)
B S R I A	Building Services Research and Information Association
B S S	Biological and Social Sciences (a directorate of NSF (USA))
B S T M	Biaxial Shock Test Machine
B T	Body Temperature
B T A	Benzotriazole
	British Tourist Authority
B T C	British Textile Confederation
B T E A	British Textile Employers Association
B T F	Binary Transversal Filter
B T H	Beyond The Horizon
B T L V	Biological Threshold Limit Value
B T S A	British Tensional Strapping Association
B T V	Basic Transportation Vehicle
B Tx	Batrachotoxin
B T X	Benzene, Toluene, and Xylenes
B U C C S	Bath University Comparative Catalogue Study
B U D W S R	*Brown University* (USA) Display for Working Set Reference
B U E T	Bangladesh University of Engineering and Technology (Bangladesh)
B U R D	Biplane Ultra-light Research Device
B U S S	Balloon-born Ultraviolet Stellar Spectrometer

B V A	British Radio Valve Manufacturers Association (ceased to operate in 1973) (member companies became direct members of the Electronic Components Board)
B W B	Bundestamt für Wehrtechnik und Beschaffung (Germany) (Federal Office for Military Technology and Procurement)
B W P A	British Wood Pulp Association
B W R	Boiling Light-water Cooled and Moderated Reactor

C

C A	Common Antigen
	Corpus Allatum
Ca - A T Pase	Calcium-dependent Adenosine Triphophatase
C A A	Cement Admixtures Association
	Conformal-Array Antenna
C A B	Corrosion Advice Bureau (of BISRA) (now part of the British Steel Corporation)
C A B L E	Collaborative Atmospheric Boundary Layer Experiment
Ca B P	Calcium Binding Protein
C A B S	Computer Aided Batch Scheduling
	Computer Augmented Block System
	Computerised Annotated Bibliography System
C A B S II	Computer Automated Block System — Two Station Separation
C A B W A	Copper and Brass Warehouse Association (USA)
C A C	Central Arbitration Committee (of ACAS)
	Codex Alimentarius Commission (of FAO (UN))
C A C C I	Confederation of Asian Chambers of Commerce and Industry
C A C L	Canadian Association of Childrens Librarians (Canada)
C A D	Computer Aided Detection
	International Conference and Exhibition on Computers in Engineering and Building Design
C A D C	Computer Aided Design Centre (now of Dept of Industry)
C A D C / C C	Central Air Data Computer/Central Computer
C A D D	Computer Aided Design-Drafting
C A D E	Computer Aided Design Engineering

34

C A D E	Computer Aided Design Evaluation
C A D E T	City Air Defense Evaluation Tool (a computer model used by the US Army)
C A D S	Containerized Ammunition Distribution System (US Army)
C A D S Y S	Computer-Aided Design System
C A E	Computer-Assisted Electrocardiography
C A F S	Cartridge-Actuated Flame System
C A G	Centre for Applied Geology (Saudi Arabia)
C A H O F	Canadian Aviation Hall of Fame (Canada)
C A I R S	Computer Assisted Information Retrieval System
C A I S	Central Abstracting and Indexing Service (of the American Petroleum Institute)
C A J E	Consolidated Anti-Jam Equipment
C A L	Computer Assisted Learning
C A L A S	Computer-Assested Language Analysis System
C A L B	Computer Aided Line Balancing
C A L L	Canadian Association of Law Libraries (Canada)
C A L M	Crane Attachment Lorry Mounted
C A L P	Computer Analysis of Library Postcards (of library buildings)
C A L P H A D	Calculation of Phase Diagrams (an international working group on thermo-chemistry)
C A L S	Committee for Ammunition Logistics Support (US Army)
C A M	Communications Access Manager
	Crassulacean Acid Metabolism
C A M A L	*Cambridge (University)* Algebra System
C A M E L	Computer Aided Machine Loading
C A M E T	Centre for Advancement of Mathematical Education in Technology (Loughborough University)
C A M O L	Computer Assisted Management Of Learning
C A M O S	Computer-aided Abrasive Machining Oscillation Studies
C A M P	Craft Attitude Monitoring Package
C A M R A	Campaign for Real Ale (an organisation)
C A N / O L E	Canadian On-Line Enquiry (of CISTI (Canada))
C A N / S D I	Canadian Selective Dissemination of Information (of CISTI (Canada))

C A N / T A P	Canadian Technical Awareness Programme (of CISTI (Canada))
C A N C E E	Canadian National Committee for Earthquake Engineering (of NRC (Canada))
C A N F A R M	Canadian Farm Management Data System
C A N P	Civil Air Notification Procedure
C A N T A P	Canadian Technical Awareness Programme (a service of CISTI (Canada))
C A P	College of American Pathologists (USA)
	Configuration Analysis Programme
C A P A	Corrosion and Protection Association (became the Corrosion Science Division of the Institution of Corrosion and Technology in 1975)
C A P A B L E	Controls And Panel Arrangement By Logical Evaluation
C A P C I S	Corrosion and Protection Centre, Industrial Services unit (of Dept of Industry and UMIST)
C A P E	Conduction Analysis Programme using Eigenvalues
C A P E R	Combined Active/Passive Emitter Rangings
	Computer Aided Perspective
C A P E X I L	Chemicals and Allied Products Export Promotion Council (India)
C A P F C E	Comité Administrador del Programa Federal de Construcción de Escuelas (Mexico) (Administrative Committee of the Federal Programme for the Building of Educational Institutes)
C A P L	Canadian Association of Public Librarians (Canada)
C A P M S	Central Agency for Public Mobilisation and Statistics (Egypt)
C A P O S S	Capacity Planning and Operation Sequencing System
C A P P S	Computer Aided Project Planning System
C A P S	Cassette Programming System
	Coastal Aerial Photo-laser Survey
	Collins (Radio) Adaptive Processing System
	Combat Air Patrol Support Aircraft
	Computer-Aided Planning System
	Computer Aided Project Study
	Computer-based Aid to Aircraft Project Studies
C A P T	Clearinghouse for Applied Performance Testing (Northwest Regional Educational Laboratory, Portland (USA)

C A R	Change Agent Research
C A R A	Circular Active Reflector Antenna
C A R B S	Computer-Aided Rationalised Building System
C A R D	Continuous Automatic Remote Display
C A R D S	Computer Aided Recording of Distribution Systems
C A R I C O M	The Caribbean Community
C A R I S	Current Agricultural Research Information System (a project of FAO (UN))
C A R I S E D	Caribbean Surveying Education
C A R M L	County and Regional Municipality Librarians (an association of librarians in Ontario (Canada))
C A R S	Central America Research Station (of Center for Disease Control) (of PHS (USA))
	Computer-Assisted Reliability Statistics
C A R T	Cargo Automation Research Team (of IATA)
C A R T S	Computer Automated Reserved Track System
C A S	Computer Accounting System
	Conciliation and Arbitration Service (name changed in 1975 to ACAS)
C A S A O	Chartered Accountants Students Association of Ontario (Canada)
C A S C	Computer-Assisted Cartography
C A S C A D E	Computer Aided Scantling Determination
C A S C O M P	Comprehensive Airship Sizing and Computer Programme
C A S E	Coordinated Aerospace Supplier Evaluation (name now changed to Coordinated Agency for Supplier Evaluation) (an organization of aerospace industrial concerns in USA)
	Counselling Assistance to Small Enterprises (of the Dept of Industry, Trade and Commerce (Canada))
C A S H	Charge Amplified Sample and Hold
	Commercial Applications Systems from *Hoskyns*
	Computer Aided Stock Holdings
C A S L E	Commonwealth Association of Surveying and Land Engineering
C A S L I S	Canadian Association of Special Libraries and Information Services (Canada)
C A S O E	Computer Accounting System for Office Expenditure

C A S P A R	Cushion Aerodynamic System Parametric Assessment Research (a programme of NRC (Canada))
C A S P E R S	Computer-Automated Speech Perception System
C A S T	Computer Assisted Scanning Techniques
C A S T A R A B	Conference of Ministers in Arab States responsible for the Application of Science and Technology to Development
C A T	Consolidated Atomic Time
C A T C C - D A I R	Carrier (warship) Air Traffic Control Centre—Direct Altitude Identity Readout
C A T S S	Cataloguing Support System (of Library Automation Systems Division, University of Toronto (Canada))
C A T T	Controlled Avalanche Transit-Time
C A T T S	Combat Arms Tactical Training Simulator
C A U S E	College and University Systems Exchange (USA)
C A T V A	Computer Assisted Total Value Assessment
C A V E A	Connecticut Audio-Visual Education Association (USA)
C A V E A T	Code and Visual Entry Authorisation Technique
C A W S	Central Aural Warning System
C A W S P S	Computer-Aided Weapons Stowage Planning System (a project of NAEC (USN))
C B A	Canadian Booksellers Association (Canada)
	Christian Booksellers Association (USA)
C B C T	Customer Bank Communication Terminal
C B E M A	Computer and Business Equipment Manufacturers Association (USA)
C B F M	Constant Bandwidth Frequency Modulation
C B M P E	Council of British Manufacturers and Contractors serving the Petroleum and Process Industries
C b O	Compensation by Objectives
C B O	Congressional Budget Office (USA)
C B P D C	Canadian Book and Periodical Development Council (Canada)
C C	Corpus Cardiacum
C C A	Chick Cell Agglutination
	Current Cost Accounting
C C A B	Consultative Committee of Accountancy Bodies
C C C	Classified Catalogue Code (of *Ranganathan*)

C C C	Customs Co-operation Council (68 countries are members)
C C E T S W	Central Council for Education and Training in Social Work
C C F	Carbonaceous Chondrite Fission
	Conglutinating Complement Fixation
C C I R I D	Charge-Coupled Infra-Red Information Device
C C L	Commodity Control List (USA)
C C L C	City Company Law Committee (of the Bank of England)
C C L N	Council for Computerized Library Networks (USA)
C C M	Counter-Countermeasures
C C M V	Cowpea Chlorotic Mottle Virus
C C N A	Canadian Community Newspapers Association (Canada)
C C O P / S O P A C	Committee for Co-ordination of Joint Prospecting for Mineral Resources in South Pacific Offshore Areas (of ECAFE)
C C O U	Construction Central Operations Unit (of Health and Safety Executive)
C C P I T	China Council for the Promotion of International Trade (China)
C C R	Coastal Confluence Region
C C R E S P A C	Current Cancer Research Project Analysis Center (USA)
C C R S	Canada Centre for Remote Sensing (Canada)
C C R T	Cathodochromic Cathode Ray Tube
C C S E M	Computer-Controlled Scanning Electron Microscope
C C S S	Commodity Command Standard System (US Army)
C C U R R	Canadian Council on Urban and Regional Research (Canada)
C D	Common Digitizer
C D C	Canada Development Corporation (Canada) (government sponsored)
	Chenodeoxycholic acid
	Cathodic Dichromate
C D F	Contiguous-Disk File
C D H S	Comprehensive Data Handling System
C D I	Centre de Diffusion de l'Innovation (of ANVAR (France)) (Information Centre on Innovation)

C D P	Continuous Distending Pressure
C D R A	Canadian Drilling Research Association (Canada)
C D R S	Control and Data Retrieval System for remotely piloted vehicle concepts
C D S	Compatible Discrete
C D W	Charge Density Wave
C E A	Comité Européen des Assurances (European Committee for Security)
C E B L S	Council of EEC Builders of Large Ships
C E C C	California Educational Computer Consortium (USA)
C E C I M O	Comité Européen de Coopération des Industries de la Machine-Outil (European Committee for Coóperation of Machine Tool Industries)
C E D	Committee for Economic Development (USA) (non-profit and educational organisation)
C E D A	Canadian Electrical Distributors Association (Canada)
C E D D A	Center for Experimental Design and Data Analysis (of NOAA (USA))
C E D P A	California Educational Data Processing Association (USA)
C E E F A X	See-the-Facts
C E E M A	Centro de Enseñanza y Experimentación de Maquinaria Agrícola (Argentina) (Training and Research Centre of Agricultural Machinery)
C E E M A T	Centre d'Études et d'Expérimentation du Machinisme Agricole Tropicale (France) (Study and Experimentation centre of Tropical Agricultural Machinery)
C E F	Chick Embryo Fibroblasts
C E H	Conférence Européenne des Horaires et des Services directs (European Conference of Timetables and Direct Services)
C E I	Centre d'Études Industrielles (Switzerland) (Centre for Education in International Management)
C E L	Central Electronics Limited (India) (government owned)
C E L A D E	Centro Latinoamericano de Demografía (Chile) (Latin-America Centre of Demography)
C E L O S	Centrum voor Landbouwkundig Onderzoek in Suriname (Surinam) (Centre for Agricultural Research in Surinam)

C E L S	Continuing Education for Library Staffs in the Southwest (a project of the Southwestern Library Association (USA))
C E L T E	Constructeurs Européens de Locomotives Thermiques et Électriques (European Association of Manufacturers of Thermal and Electric Locomotives (Federated into UNIFE in 1976)
C E M	Conventional Electron Microscope
C E M A	Council for Economic Mutual Assistance *see under* COMECON
C E M A C	Committee of European Associations of Manufacturers of Active Electronic Components (now merged into CEMEC)
C E M A G	Centre d'Étude de la Mécanisation en Agriculture (Belgium) (Centre for the Study of Mechanisation in Agriculture)
C E M E C	Committee of European Associations of Manufacturers of Electronic Components
C E N C E R	Certification Body of CEN (Comité Européen de Normalisation)
C E N C O M S	Center for Communications Sciences (of Comm/ADP (US Army))
C E N D H R R A	Centre for the Development of ﬁuman Resources in Rural Asia (Philippines)
C E N I M	Centro Nacional de Investigaciones Metalúrgicas (Spain) (National Centre for Metallurgical Research)
C E N S A	Council of European and Japanese National Shipowners Associations
C E N T A	Committee for Establishing a National Testing Authority
C E N T A C S	Center for Tactical Computer Sciences (of Comm/ADP (US Army))
C E N T R O M I N	Empresa Minera del Centro del Perú (Peru) (government controlled)
C E P	Co-operative Engineering Program (a branch of SAE (USA))
	Counter Electrophoresis
C E P A C	Conféderation Européenne de l'Industrie des Pâtes, Papiers et Cartons (European Confederation of the Paper and Card-board Industries)

41

C E P A C S	Customs Entry Processing And Cargo System
C E P E C	Committee of European Associations of Manufacturers of Passive Electronic Components (now merged into CEMEC)
C E P R I G	Centre de Perfectionnement pour la Recherche Industrielle et sa Gestion (France) (Centre for Improving Industrial Research and its Management)
C E R	Cross-linking Electron Resist
C E R I	Centre d'Études sur la Recherche et l'Innovation (France) (a non-profit association)
	Clean Energy Research Institute (University of Miami (USA))
C E R L	Central Electricity Research Laboratories (of CEGB)
C E S	Committee of European Shipowners (merged with CENSA in 1974)
C E S M M	Civil Engineering Standard Method of Measurement (of ICE and FCEC)
C E T	Council for Educational Technology for the United Kingdom
C E T F	Clothing and Equipment Test Facility (of US Army Infantry Board)
C E T I E	Centre Technique Internationale de l'Embouteillage (France) (International Technical Centre of Bottling)
C E W T	Central England Winter Temperature
C F	Cystic Fibrosis
C F A D C	Canadian Forces Air Defence Command (Canada)
C F E	*Caterpillar (Company of America)* Fundamental English
C F F	Critical Flicker Frequency
C F I A	Cavity Foam Insulation Association
C F I T	Committee for Industrial Technology (of DTI) (now of Dept of Industry)
C F R	Civil Fast Reactor
C F R G	Carbon Fibre Reinforced Glass
C F R G C	Carbon Fibre Reinforced Glass-Ceramic
C F T	Complement-Fixation Test
C F T C	Commodity Futures Trading Commission (USA)
C F V	Conventional Friend Virus
C G A	Clean *Gulf (of Mexico)* Associates

C G E R	Centre de Gestion et d'Économie Rurale (France) (Centre of Rural Management and Economy)
C G H	Computer-Generated Hologram
C G I	Computer-Generated Imagery
C G I A R	Consultative Group on International Agricultural Research (of the World Bank, UN Development Programme and FAO (UN))
C G I T	Compressed-Gas-Insulated Tube
C G L	Chronic Granulocytic Leukaemia
C G U	Canadian Geophysical Union (Canada)
C H A M	Combusion, Heat and Mass transfer
C H A M P V A	Civilian Health and Medical Program of the Veterans Administration (USA)
C H A P S	Chance-constrained Programming System
C H A U D	Chemical Audit and Distribution
C H D L	Computer Hardware Description Language
C H E M S A F E	Chemical Industry System for Assistance in Freight Emergencies
C H G	Chlorhexidine Glucomate
C H I P S	Calculator Help In Processing Signals
	Clearing House Interbank Payment System
C H S L	Cleveland (Ohio) Health Sciences Library (USA)
C H S S	Co-operative Health Statistics System
C H T	Collection, Holding, and Transfer
C I A C	Construction Industry Advisory Council
C I A G	CAMAC Industry Applications Group (USA)
C I B C	Confédération Internationale de la Boucherie et de la Charcuterie (Switzerland) (International Federation of Meat Traders Association)
C I B S	Chartered Institution of Building Services
C I C A	Centro de Investigaciones Ciencias Agronómicas (Argentina) (Scientific Agriculture Research Centre)
	Confederation of International Contractors Associations (France)
C I C A S	Computer Integrated Command and Attack Systems
C I C H	Comité International de la Culture du Houblon (Hop Growers International Committee)
C I D B E Q	Centre d'Informatique Documentaire pour les Bibliothéques d'Enseignement du Québec (Canada)

C I D E C T	Comité Internationale pour le Développement et l'Étude de la Construction Tubulaire (International Committee for the Development and Study of Tubular Construction)
C I D E P	Chemically Induced Dynamic Electron Polarization
C I D N P	Chemically Induced Dynamic Nuclear Polarization
C I D S T	Committee for Information and Documentation on Science and Technology (of the European Communities)
C I E	Counter-immuno electrophoresis
C I E C	Conference on International Economic Co-operation
C I E P	Counter Immunoelectrophoresis
C I E T A	Calcutta Import and Export Trade Association (India)
C I F	Construction Industry Federation
C I F A	Committee for Inland Fisheries of Africa (of FAO (UN))
C I G R	Commission Internationale du Génie Rural (France) (International Commission of Agricultural Engineering)
C I I T	Chemical Industry Institute of Toxicology (USA)
C I L A	Casualty Insurance Logistics Automated
C I M	Co-operative Investigations in the Mediterranean (of IOC (UNESCO))
C I M C	Colombian Internal Medical Congress
C I M M Y T	Centro Internacional de Mejoramiento de Maíz y Trigo (International Maize and Wheat Improvement Centre)
Ci M O S	*Cincinnati Milacron (Ltd)* Operating System
C I M S	Computer Integrated Manufacturing System
C I N C C H A N	Commander-in-Chief Allied Command Channel (of NATO)
C I N C N O R T H	Commander-in-Chief Allied Forces Northern Europe (of NATO)
C I N C S O U T H	Commander-in-Chief Allied Forces Southern Europe (of NATO)
C I N C U K A I R	Commander-in-Chief United Kingdom Air Force (of NATO)
C I N P	Collegium Internationale Neuro-Psychopharmacologicum
C I O A	Centro Italiano Assidatori Anodici (Italy) (Italian Centre of Aluminium Anodizers)

44

C I O M R	Confédération Interalliée des Officiers Médicaux de Réserve (of NATO) (Inter-Allied Confederation of Reserve Medical Officers)
C I O S	Conseil International pour l'Organisation Scientifique (International Council for Scientific Management) (now known as the World Council of Management)
C I P A	Comité Internationale de Photogrammétrie Archtectural (International Committee for Architectural Photo-grammetry)
C I P F A	Chartered Institute of Public Finance and Accountancy
C I P I	Comité Interministériel de Politique Industrielle (France) (Inter-Ministerial Committee on Industrial Policy)
C I P R A	Commission Internationale pour la Protection des Régions Alpines (International Commission for the Protection of Alpine Regions)
C I R A	Centro Italiano Radiatori Alluminio (Italy) (Italian Aluminium Radiators Manufacturers Association)
C I R I T	Comité Interprofessionel de Renovation de l'Industrie Textile (France) (Inter-professional Committee for the Restructuring of the Textile Industry)
C I R N A	Compagnie pour l'Ingenierie des Reacteurs au sodium (France)
C I S C O	The Civil Service Catering Organization
C I S H E C	Chemical Industry Safety and Health Council (of CIA)
C I S I	Command Inspection System Inspection (of AFISC (USAF))
	Compagnie Internationale de Service et Informatique (France)
C I S O	Comité International des Sciences Onomastiques (International Committee of Onomastic Sciences)
C I S T I	Canada Institute for Scientific and Technical Infor-mation (of National Research Council (Canada))
C I S T I P	Committee on International Scientific and Technical Information Programs (of Commission on Inter-national Relations (NAS/NRC (USA))
C I T	Carnegie Institute of Technology (USA) (now Carnegie-Mellon University)
	Charcoal Inhalation Tester
C L	Cathodoluminescence

C L A	Computer Law Association (USA)
C L A I M S	Class Codes, Assignee, Index, Method, Search (of the Patent Office (USA))
C L A M	*Control Data Corporation* LISP Algebraic Manipulator
C L A M P	Closed Loop Aeronautical Management Program (of USN Aviation Supply Office)
C L A S P	Coded Label Additional Security and Protection system
C L A S S	*Canberra (Industries)* (USA) Laboratories Automation Software System
C L A S S I C	Class-room Interactive Computer
C L C C S	*Cammell Laird* Cable Control System
C L D	Crystal Lattice Dislocation
	Current-Limiting Device
C L E A N	Comprehensive Lake Ecosystem Analyzer
C L E O P A T R A	Comprehensive Language for Elegant Operating system And Translator design
C L E O S	Conference on Laser and Electro-optical Systems
C L I C S	Computer-Linked Information for Container Shipping
C L I M A P	Climate Long-range Investigation, Mapping and Prediction study
C L I P	Cellular Logic Image Processor
	Computer Layout Installation Planner
C L I S P	Conversational LISP
C L M	Crane-Load Moment-indicator
C L M S	Company Lightweight Mortar (artillery) System
C L O D S	Computerized Logic-Oriented Design System
C L O G	Computer Logic Graphics
C L S D	*Culham (Laboratory)* Language for System Development
C L T A	Canadian Library Trustees Association (Canada)
C L U M I S	Cadastral and Land-Use Mapping Information System
C L W	Council for a Livable World (USA)
C M A	Canadian Manufacturers Association (Canada)
	Cement Manufacturers Association (India)
	Coal Mines Authority Ltd (India) (government owned)
	Colonic Mucoprotein Antigen
	Computerized Management Account
C M A A	Crane Manufacturers Association of America (USA)

46

C M A L	Coal Mines Authority Ltd (India) (government owned)
C M A S	Circular Map Accuracy Standard
	Confédération Mondiale des Activités Subaquatiques (France) (World Confederation of Underwater Activities)
C M B	Composite Minimum Brightness
C M C	Cell-Mediated Cytotoxicity
C M D	Central Marine Depot (of the British Post Office)
	Count Median Diameter
C M M	Computerized Modular Monitoring
C M N	Cerous Magnesium Nitrate
C M P	COBOL Macro Processor
C M P C	Compañía Manufacturera de Papeles y Cartones (Chile)
C M R B	Chemicals and Minerals Requirements Board (of DoI)
C M S	Christian Medical Society (USA)
C N	Cetane Number
C N C / I A P S	Canadian National Committee for the International Association on the Properties of Steam (Canada)
C N D	Comité National de Documentation (France) (National Committee for Co-ordinating Government Information)
C N D O	Complete Neglect of Differential Overlap
C N E L	Community Noise Equivalent Level
C N I	Consolidated National Intervenors (USA) (an environmental conservation group)
C N I F	Conseil National des Ingénieurs Français (France) (National Council of French Engineers)
C N L	Corrected Noise Level
C O - A S I S	Central Ohio Chapter of ASIS (USA)
C O A T	Coherent Optical Adaptive Technique
C O B	Commission des Opérations en Bourse (France) (Stock Exchange Commission)
C O B R A	Computadores Brasileiros (Brazil)
C O C E R A L	Federation of Trade Associations for Grain and Feeding-Stuffs (of EEC)
C O C H A S E	Code for Coupled Channel Schrödinger Equations
C O C O M	Consultative Group-Coordinating Committee (comprising Japan and the NATO countries except Iceland)

C O C O R	Commission de Coordination pour la Nomenclature des Produits Sidérurgiques (of ECSC) (Commission for Co-ordinating the Naming of Metallurgical Products)
C O C S	Container Operating Control System
C O D A P	Client-Oriented Data Acquisition Programme
	Comprehensive Occupational Data Analysis Programme
C O D A S	Council of Departments of Accounting Studies
C O D P	prefix to numbered series of reports issued by Cranfield Institute of Technology, Department of Aircraft Design
C O E	Cross-Over Electrophoresis
	Crude Oil Equivalent
C O E A	Cost and Operational Effectiveness Analysis
C O F A D	Computerized Facilities Design
C O F I P S	Central Ohio Federation of Information Processing Societies (USA)
C O F R E N D	Comité Français pour l'Étude des Essais Non Destructifs (France) (French Committee for the Study of Non-Destructive Testing)
C O G S	Combat Oriented General Support
C O I	Crack Opening Interferometry
C O I E	Committee on Invisible Exports
C O I P M	Comité International Permanent pour la Recherche sur la Préservation des Matériaux en Milieu Marin (of OECD) (Permanent International Committee for Research on Corrosion in a Marine Environment)
C O L A	Co-operation in Library Automation (a project of LASER)
COLCIENCIAS	Fondo Colombiano de Investigaciones Científicas y Proyectos Especiales "Francisco José de Caldas" (Colombia)
C O L I N G	International Conference on Computational Linguistics
C O L I P A	Comité de liaison des Syndicats Européens de l'Industrie de la Parfumerie et des Cosmétiques (of the EEC) (Liaison Committee of European Groups of the Perfumery and Cosmetics Industry)
C O L M I S	Collection Management Information System (solid waste collection)

48

C O L R A D	College on Research and Development (of TIMS (USA))
C O M A R	Committee on Man and Radiation (of IEEE (USA))
C O M B I M A N	Computerized Biomechanical Man-model
C O M E C O N	Council for Economic Mutual Assistance (comprising Poland, Czechoslovakia, Hungary, Romania, East Germany, Mongolia, Cuba, and USSR) (administrative headquarters in USSR)
C O M E D S	Continental (USA) Meteorological Data system (USAF)
C O M E T	Controllability, Observability and Maintenance Engineering Technique
C O M F O R T	Compulogic FORTRAN Tidy
C O M I C O R D	Association des Industries de Corderie-Ficellerie de la CEE (merged into EUROCORD in 1975)
C O M I C S	Computer-Oriented Managed Inventory Control System
C O M I N T	Communications Intelligence
C O M I T E X T I L	Co-ordinating Committee of the European Textile Industries (of EEC)
Comm/ A D P	Communications/Automatic Data Processing Laboratory (of ECOM (US Army))
C O M P A C	Computer Output Microfilm Package
C O M P A C S	Computer Output Microforms Program And Concept Study (of US Army)
C O M P A S S	Computerized Movement Planning And Status System
C O M P C O N	IEEE (USA) Computer Society International Conference
C O M P E C	Computer Peripheral, Small Computer and Systems Exhibition and Conference
C O M P R Os	colllective name for the European Community's national bodies for the Simplification of International Trade Procedures
C O M P S T A T	Conference on Computational Statistics
C O M P U M A G	Conference on Computations of Magnetic Fields
C O M R A T E	Committee on Mineral Resources and the Environment (of NRC (USA))
C O M S A T	Communications Satellite Corporation (USA) (management services contractor for INTELSAT)
Com S E C	Communications Security
C O N A C S	Contractors Accounting System

C O N A D	Continental Air Defense Command (US DOD) (inactivated 1975)
C O N C A P	Conversational Circuit Analysis Programme
C O N C E P T	Computation Online of Networks of Chemical Engineering Processes
C O N C E R T	Consultative Group on Certification (of CEN (France))
C O N D E E P	Concrete Deepwater Structure
C O N D R I L L	Concrete Drilling Semi-submersible
C O N I D A	Comisión Nacional de Investigación y Desarrollo Aeroespacial (Peru) (National Commission for Aerospace Research and Development)
C O N R A D	Contour Radar Data
C O N S E R	Consolidation of Serial data bases (a project of Council on Library Resources (USA)) Conversion of Serials
C O N S I D E R	Conselho Nacional da Industria Siderurgica (Brazil) (National Council of the Steel Industry)
C O N S T R O N I C	Conference on Mechanical Aspects of Electronic Design
C O N S U B	Continental Shelf Submersible
C O N T R A C	Conversational Transient Radiation Analysis Programme
C O N T U	National Commission on New Technological Uses of Copyrighted Works (USA)
C O P	Compact Periscope
C O P E	CAMA (Centralised Automatic Message Accounting) Operator Position Exercise Compagnie Orientale des Pétroles d'Egypte (Egypt) (partly government owned)
C O P I C S	Copyright Office Publication and Interactive Cataloging System (of the Library of Congress (USA))
C O P Q	Committee on Overseas Qualifications (Australia)
C O P R	Centre for Overseas Pest Research (of ODM)
C O P T E C	Controller Overload Prediction Technique
C O Q	Cost-of-Quality
C O R A L	Coherent Optical Radar Laboratory (USAF)
C O R E P E R	Comité des Représentants Permanents (Committee of Permanent Representatives) (of the EEC)
C O R M	Council for Optical Radiation Measurements (USA)

50

C O R M A R	Coral Reef Management and Research (a group at the University of Hawaii)
C O R R I M	Committee on Renewable Resources for Industrial Materials (of NAS/NRC (USA))
C O R S P E R S	Committee on Remote Sensing Programs for Earth Surveys (of NAS/NRC (USA))
C O R T E Z	COBOL Oriented Real Time Environment
C O S	Canadian Otolaryngological Society (Canada)
	Contaminated Oil Settlings
C O S A M C	Commission for Special Applications of Meteorology and Climatology (of WMO (UN))
C O S A R	Compression Scanning Array Radar
C O S B A	Computer Services and Bureau Association (merged into Computer Services Association, 1975)
C O S E B I	Corporación de Servicios Bibliotecarios (Puerto Rico)
C O S F A D	Computerized Safety and Facility Design
C O S M O S	Comprehensive Option Stiffness Method of Structural Analysis
	a European Industrial Consortium (consisting of ETCA (Belgium), GEC-Marconi (UK), MBB (Germany) and SNIAS (France))
C O S S A C K	Computer Systems Suppliers Advisory Committee (of BETA)
C O S T E D	Committee on Science and Technology in the Developing Countries (India) (of ICSU)
C O T	Cyclooctatetraenyl
C O T A M	Commandement du Transport Aerien Militaire (France) (Air Transport Command of the French Air Force)
C O T C	Canadian Overseas Telecommunications Corporation (Canada)
C O T R A N S	Coordinated Transfer Application System (of the Association of American Medical Colleges (USA))
C O T T U	Committee on Technology Transfer and Utilization (of National Academy of Engineering (USA))
C O V I N C A	Corporación Venezolana de la Industria Naval CA (Venezuela) (government owned corporation)
C O W	Chlorinated Organics in Wastewater analyzer
C P	Companhia dos Caminhos de Ferro Portugueses (Portugal)

C P A	Chicago Publishers Association (USA)
	Combat Pilots Association (USA)
	Commonwealth Preference Area
C P A C	Centre for Protection Against Corrosion (of the Fulmer Research Institute)
	Corrosion Prevention Advisory Centre
C P A R	Co-operative Pollution Abatement Research (a programme of the Environment Dept (Canada))
C P A R S	Compact Programmed Airline Reservation System
C P C	Ceylon Petroleum Company (Sri Lanka) (government owned)
	Computerized Production Control
	Controlled-Pore Ceramic
C P C H	Controllable Pitch propellor
C P D A	Council for Periodical Distributors Association (USA)
C P D M	Centre for Physical Distribution Management
C P D S	Computerized Preliminary Design System
C P E A	Confederation of Professional and Executive Associations
C P E U G	Computer Performance Evaluation Users Group (USA)
C P F A	Cyclopropenoid Fatty Acid
C P H A	Commission on Professional and Hospital Activities (USA) (non-profit, non-governmental research and education center)
C P I	Council of the Printing Industries of Canada (Canada)
C P I C	Canadian Police Information Centre (Canada) (nationwide automated police information service)
C P L	Chemistry and Physics Laboratory (of EPA (USA))
C P L E E	Charged Particle Lunar Environment Experiment (part of ALSEP)
C P M	College of Petroleum and Minerals (Saudi Arabia)
C P P A	Canadian Periodical Publishers Association (Canada)
C P P G	Construction Programme Policy Group
C P R	Center for Population Research (of NICHD (NIH) (USA))
C P R M	Companhia de Pesquisas de Recursos Minerais (Brazil) (Mineral Resources Research Group of the Ministry of Mines and Energy)

C P S	Capacitance Proximity Sensor
	Creative Problem-Solving
C P S A	Clay Pigeon Shooting Association
	Commonwealth Preference Standstill Area
C P Sase	Carbamyl Phosphate Synthetase
C P S C	Consumer Product Safety Commission (USA)
C P S U	California Polytechnic State University (USA)
C P T	Continuous Performance Test
C P T S	Council of Professional Technological Societies
C P V	Cytoplasmic Polyhedrosis Virus
C Q M S	Circuit Quality Monitoring System
C R A	Chemical Recovery Association
C R A B	Cement River Assault Boat
C R A B S	Close Range Analytical Bundle System
C R B R P	Clinch River Breeder Reactor Plant (USA)
C R C	Centre d'Études et de Recherches des Chefs d'Entre-prises (France)
C R D M	Control-Rod Device Mechanism
C R E	Commercial Relations and Exporters (a division of the Dept of Trade)
C R E D D	Customer Requested Earlier Due Date
C R E D O C	Centre de Recherche et de Documentation sur la Consommation (France) (Research and Documentation Centre on Consumer Affairs)
C R E S	Corrosion Resistant
C R F S	Copper Reverbatory Furnace Slag
C R I	Cure Rate Integrator
C R I L A	Credit Insurance Logistics Automated
C R I Q	Centre de Recherche Industrielle du Québec (Canada) (Quebec Industrial Research Centre)
C R I S P	Comprehensive RNSTS Inventory System Project
C R L S	Coastguard Radio Liaison Station
C R M	Centre de Recherches Mathématiques (Université de Montréal (Canada)) (Centre of Mathematical Research)
	Centre de Recherches Métallurgiques (Belgium) (Metallurgy Research Centre)
C R N	Cardiac-Recurrent Nerve
C R O	Companies Registration Office

53

C R O S S A	Centre Régional Opérationnel de Surveillance et de Sauvétage pour l'Atlantique (France) (Regional Operational Centre for Atlantic Search and Rescue)
C R O S S M A	Centre Régional Opérationnel de Surveillance et de Sauvétage pour la Manche (France) (Regional Operational Centre for the English Channel Search and Rescue)
C R P	Collaborative Reference Program (of NBS (USA) and TAPPI (USA))
C R S	Coast Radio Stations (of the British Post Office)
	Congressional Research Service (of the Library of Congress (USA))
C R U E S I	Research Centre for the Utilization of Saline Water Irrigation (Tunisia)
C S	Computer Simulation
	Cyrstallographic Shear
C S A	Central Surgical Association (USA)
	Colony-Stimulating Activity
	Computer Services Association
C S C	Centrifugal Shot Casting
	Computer Search Center (of IITRI (USA))
C S Ch E	Canadian Society for Chemical Engineering (Canada)
C S E E	Canadian Society for Electrical Engineering (Canada)
C S E I	Concentrated Solar Energy Imitator
C S E R B	Computers, Systems and Electronics Research Board (of the Dept of Industry)
C S H	Centralised Hydraulic System
C S I E	Center for the Study of Information and Education (Syracuse University (USA))
C S L	Coincidence Site Lattice
C S L A	Canadian School Library Association (Canada)
C S L C	Coherent Side Lobe Cancellation
C S M	Cerebrospinal Meningitis
C S N	Companhia Siderurgica Nacional (Brazil)
C S N T A	Committee on Societal Needs and Technology Assessment (of Federation of Materials Societies (USA))
C S O	Central Statistical Organization (India)
C S O C R	Code Sort Optical Character Recognition
C S P	Controlled Surface Porosity

C S P	Circum-Sporozoite
C S R A	Committee of Secretaries of Research Associations
C S R E	Committee for Social Responsibility in Engineering (USA)
C S S C G	Container Systems Standardization/Coordination Group (USDOD)
C S S I	Coriolis (Cross-coupled angular acceleration) Sickness Susceptibility Index
C S S L	Cyclical Stress Sensitivity Limit
C S S P	Committee of Scientific Society Presidents (USA)
C S T	Concentration Stress Test
C S T P	Committee for Scientific and Technological Policy (of OECD)
C S U	Central Services Unit for University and Polytechnic Careers and Appointments Services
C S U K	Chamber of Shipping of the United Kingdom (merged into GCBS in 1975)
C T /Cosba	Cape Town Computer Services and Bureaux Association (South Africa)
C T A	Committee on Thrombolytic Agents (of the National Heart Institute (USA))
	Cystine Trypticase Agar
C T C A	Canadian Telecommunications Carriers Association (Canada)
C T C S S	Continuous Tone Coded Squelch System
C T D	Conductivity-Temperature-Depth
C T F T	Centre Technique Forestier Tropical (France) (Tropical Forest Technical Centre)
C T H	Cure To Handling
C T I A C	Concrete Technology Information Analysis Center (US Army)
C T L	Compass Test Language
	Cytotoxic T Lymphocyte
C T M	Capacity Ton-Mile
C T M A	Commercial Truck Maintenance Association (USA)
C T O	Commonwealth Telecommunications Organisation
C T R	Controlled Thermonuclear Research (formerly of USAEC, now a division of ERDA (USA))
C T S	Centre for Transport Studies (Cranfield Institute of Technology)

C T S	Communications Technology Satellite
C T T	Capital Transfer Tax
C U A G	Computer Users Associations Group
C U E	Coastal Upwelling Experiment
	Configuration Utilization Evaluation
	Correction-Update-Extension
C U E A	Coastal Upwelling Ecosystem Analysis (a project of IDOE)
C U M A	Canadian Urethane Manufacturers Association (Canada)
C U M M	Council of Underground Mining Machinery Manufacturers
C U M R E C	College and University Machine Records Conference (USA)
C U P I D	Commercial Users Programme to Index Data
	Conversational Utility Programme for Information Display
C U R B	Campaign on the Use and Restriction of Barbiturates (an organisation)
C U R E	Computer Users Replacement Equipment (a non-profit organisation based at Charles Keene College of Further Education, Leicester)
C U V	Current Use Value
C V C C	Compound Vortex Controlled Combustion
C V C M	Collected Volatile Condensable Material
C V R	Cockpit Voice Recorder
C V R D	Companhia Vale do Rio Doce (Brazil) (Government controlled)
C V S	Combat Vehicle Simulator
C V S D	Continuously Variable Slope Delta Modulation
C W P U	Central Water Planning Unit (of DOE)
C Z T	Chirp-Z-Transform

D

D A	Dalniya Aviatsiya (USSR) (the Long Range Aviation— a group of the Soviet Air Force)
D A A C A	Department of the Army Allocation Committee, Ammunition (US Army) (became CALS in 1975)
D A B S - I P C	Discrete Address Beacon System with Intermittent Positive Control

D A C A	Diphenylaminochloroarsine
D A C O W I T S	Defense Advisory Committee on Women in the Services (USA)
D A C T	Dissimilar Air Combat Training
D A E C	Danish Atomic Energy Commission (Denmark) (replaced by Danish Energy Agency in 1976)
D A F	Dansk Arbejdsgiverforening (Denmark) (Danish Employers Confederation)
	Dissolved Air Flotation
D A G	Dysprosium Aluminium Garnet
D A I G C	Direct Aqueous Injection Gas Chromatography
D A I S Y	Decision Aiding Information System
	Displacement Automated Integrated Systems
D A L E	Digital Anemograph Logging Equipment
D A M E	Digital Automatic Measuring Equipment
D A M O S	Data Moving System
D A N T E S	Defense Activity for Non-Traditional Education Support (an off-duty general education plan of USDOD)
D A P	Deformation Alignment Phase
	Derived Attainable Performance
	Diaminopimelic Acid
D A P I	Diamidino-phenylindole
D A P P	Data Acquisition and Processing Program (of USAF) (name changed to DMSP, Dec 1973)
D A R C O M	Army Materiel Development and Readiness Command (US Army)
D A R I A S	Digico Automated Radio-Immunoassay Analytical System
D A R M S	Digital Alternate Representation of Music Scores
D A R T	Deployable Automatic Relay Terminal
	Detection, Action and Response Technique
D A S	Data Analysis System
	Directorate of Aerodrome Standards (of CAA)
D A S E	Differential Absorption and Scattering technique
D A S I	Diffusion of Arsenic in Silicon
D A S S	Defined Antigen Substrate Sphere
D A W N	Drug Abuse Warning Network (of Drug Enforcement Administration (USA))
D B A M	Data Base Access Method

D B A W G	Database Administration Working Group (of British Computer Society and CODASYL Data Description Language Committee)
D B B D	Dibromopolybutadiene
D B D A	Database Design Aid
D B M S	Data Base Management System
D B N	*De Beers* Boron Nitride
D B O M P	Data Base Organization and Management Processor
D B S	Division of Biological Standards (of MRC)
D B T T	Ductile to Brittle Transition Temperature
D B T U	Dibutyl Thiourea
D B V	Deutscher Bibliotheksverband (Germany) (German Library Association)
D C A	Deoxycholate-Citrate Agar
D C D	Digital Correlation Detector
D C D S	Digital Control Design System
D C E	Differential Compound Engine
D C G M	Decorticated Groundnut Meal
D C I	Dispersive Corrosion Inhibitor
D C L	Defence Contractors List (of MOD)
D C M A	Dry Color Manufacturers Association (USA)
D C P	Dicalcium Phosphate
D C P A	Dicyclopentenyl Acrylate
D C S	Data Control System
D C S R D A	Deputy Chief of Staff Research, Development and Acquisition (US Army)
D C T	Discrete Cosine Transform
D D A	Delhi Development Authority (India)
D D C M P	Digital Data Communications Message Protocol
D D S	Doped Deposited Silica
D E	Diatomaceous Earth
D E - H	Destroyer Escort Hydrofoil
D E A	Diethanolamine
	Diethylamine
	Drug Enforcement Administration (of Dept of Justice (USA))
D E E	Diethoxyethylene
D E E S	Dynamic Electromagnetic Environment Simulator
D E G	Diethylene Glycol
D E H	Deepwater Escort Hydrofoil

D E H	Direct Electrical Heating
D E H A	Diethylhydroxylamine
D E I S	*DOD* (USDOD) Worldwide Energy Information System
D E L S	Direct Electrical Linkage System
D E L T A	Daily Electronic Lane Tole Audit
D E M K O	Dansk Elektrische Materialkontrol (Denmark) (Danish Board for the Approval of Electrical Equipment)
D E M O S	Directorate of Estate Management Overseas (of PSA (DOE))
D En	Department of Energy
D E N A C A L	Departamento Nacional de Acueductos y Alacanta-rillados (Nicaragua)
D E P C T	Diethyl Phosphorochloridothionate
D E P M I S	Depot Management Information System (US Army)
D E R E	Dounreay Experimental Reactor Establishment (of UKAEA)
D E R T	Division Électronique, Radioélectricité et Télécommu-nications (of SEE (France))
D E S	Draft Environmental Statement
D E S C N E T	Data Network on Environmentally Significant Chemicals
D E T G	Defense Energy Task Group (USDOD)
D E T U	Diethyl Thiourea
D E U L A	Deutsche Lehranstaeten für Agrartechnik (Germany) (German Farm Machinery Schools)
D E V S I S	Development of Sciences Information System (a project of IDRC, ILO, OECD, UNDP, and UNESCO)
D F B	Distributed Feedback
D F D P	Distribution-Free Doppler Processor
D F G A	Distributed Floating Gate Amplifier
D F I	Direct Flame Impingement
D G A	Diglycolamine
D G A S	Double Glazing Advisory Service (of IGA)
D G M W	Double Gimballed Momentum Wheel
D H A A	Dehydro-Ascorbic Acid
D H A P	Dihydroxyacetone Phosphate
D H F D H	Dihydrofolate Dehydrogenase
D H L L P	Direct-High-Level Language Processor

D H N	Diretoria de Hidrografia e Navegacão (Brazilian Navy) (Directorate of Hydrography and Navigation)
D H Oase	Dihydroorotase
D H T	Dihydro-Testosterone
D I A M	Data Independent Architecture Model
D I A S	Dublin Institute for Advanced Studies (Eire)
D I C	Disseminated Intravascular Coagulopathy
D I C B	Demolition Industry Conciliation Board
D I C E	Digital Intercontinental Conversion Equipment
	Digital Interface Countermeasures Equipment
D I C E F	Digital Communications Experimental Facility (USAF)
D I D	Drainage and Irrigation Department (Malaysia)
D I D A	Differential In-Depth Analysis
D I D E N T	Distortion Identity
D I F A R	Directional-Frequency Analysis and Recording
D I M S	Data Information and Manufacturing System
D I M U S	Digital Multi-beam Steering System Sonar
D I N	Deutsches Institut für Normung (Germany) (German Standards Institute)
D I O D E	Digital Input/Output Display Equipment
D I O S	Distributed Input/Output System
D I R	Digital Instrumentation Radar
D I S	Dialectic Information System
	Distributed Intelligence System
D I S C	Distribution Stock Control System
	Domestic International Sales Corporation (of Domestic and International Business Administration (Dept of Commerce (USA))
D I S E	Digital Systems Education (a project of University of Pittsburgh Department of Electrical Engineering (USA))
D I S I D	Disposable Seismic Intrusion Detector
D I S S	Directorate of Information Systems and Settlement (of the Stock Exchange)
D I S T R I P R E S S	Association for the Promotion of the International Circulation of the Press
D I T E	Divertor Injection Tokamak Experiment (of Culham Laboratory)
D I W	Deutsches Institut für Wirtschaftforschung (Germany) (German Institute for Economic Research)

60

D K G A	Diketogulonic Acid
D L	prefix to numbered-lettered series of Defence Lists issued by the Ministry of Defence and published by HMSO
D L A	Documentation, Libraries and Archives Directorate (of UNESCO)
D L D	Dark Line Defect
D L G	Deutsche Landwirtschafts Gesellschaft (Germany) (German Agricultural Society)
D L I M P	Descriptive Language for Implementing Macro-Processors
D L P C	Dilauroylphosphatidylcholine
D L S	DME-based Landing System
D L T	Development Land Tax
D M A	Division of Military Application (of ERDA (USA)) (formerly of USAEC)
D M B C	Direct Material Balance Control
D M D	Duchenne Muscular Dystrophy
D M E T U	Dimethyethyl Thiourea
D M I	Department of Manufacturing Industry (Australia)
D M L	Dimyristoyl Lecithin
D M M P	Dimethyl Methylphosphonate
D M O	Demetallized Oil
D M O D	Displacement Measuring Optical Device
D M P C T	Dimethyl Phosphorochloridothionate
D M R	Data Management Routines
D M S P	Defense Meteorological Satellite Program (of USAF)
D M S P C	Defence Materiel Standardization Policy Committee (MOD)
D N A	Deutscher Normenasschuss (Germany) (German Standards Institute) (named changed in 1975 to Deutsches Institut für Normung)
D N C P	Dirección Nacional de Construcciones Portuarias y Vías Navegables (Argentina) (National Directorate of Harbour Construction and Shipping Routes)
D N I C	Data Network Identification Code
D N J	Drone Noise Jammer
D N P	Dinitrophenol
D N P T	Dinitrosopentamethylene Tetramine
D O C	Developmental Optical Correlator
D O C A	Deoxycorticosterone Acetate

D O E S	Direct Order Entry System
D O I	Department of Industry
D O L	Dioleoyl Lecithin
D O L A R S	Disk On-line Accounts Receivable System
D O M E S	Deep Ocean Mining Experimental Study (of NOAA (USA))
D O M I N A	Distribution-Oriented Management Information Analyser
D O Q	Dynamic Order Quantity
D O S S	Deep Ocean Search System
D O T	Deep Ocean Transponder
	Department of Trade
D P	Dynamic Programming
D P C	Data Protection Committee
	Defence Planning Committee (of NATO)
D P C C	Double Potential Step Chronocoulometry
D P C P	Department of Prices and Consumer Protection
D P D	Diethyl Paraphenylene Diamine
D P E W S	Design-to-Price Electronic Warfare System
D P G	Dugway Proving Ground (of TECOM (US Army))
D P L	Dipalmitoyl Lecithin
D P M	Disruptive Pattern Material
D P P C	Dipalmitoylphosphatidylcholine
D P R S	Dynamic Preferential Runway System
D P S	Distributed Processing Support
D Q A B E	Defence Quality Assurance Board Executive (MOD)
D Q E	Detective Quantum Efficiency
D R G	Detroit Rubber Group (USA)
D R G	Dorsal Root Ganglia
D R L	Direct Ranging LORAN
D R P G	Detroit Rubber and Plastics Group (USA) (became Detroit Rubber Group in 1975)
D R V I D	Difference Range Versus Integrated Doppler
D S A	Double-Submerged Arc
D S A I	Digital Solar-Aspect Indicator
D S C G	Disodium Cromoglycate
D S M	Dense-Staining Material
	Dried Skim Milk
	Dynamic Stiffness Modulus
D S R	Depolymerized Scrap Rubber

d s R N A	Double-stranded Ribonucleic Acid
D S S M	Dynamic Sequencing and Segmentation Model
D S T	Discrete Sine Transform
D S T O	Defence Sciences and Technology Organization (Dept of Defence (Australia))
D S T R	Dynamic Systems Test Rig
D T E	Data Ten to Eleven
D T I	Department of Trade and Industry (split into Department of Trade (DoT) and Department of Industry (DoI) in 1974)
D T N S R D C	*David W Taylor* Naval Ship Research and Development Center (USN)
D T O L	Digital Test Oriented Language
D T O T	Development Test, Operational Test
D T P	Diptheria Tetanus Pertussis
D T P E W S	Design-to-Price Electronic Warfare System
D T S	Dense Tar Surfacing
D T U O C	Digital Tire Uniformity Optimizer Computer
D T U P C	Design To Unit Production Cost
D T V	Diver Transport Vehicle
D U B S	Durham University Business School
D U C E	Denied-Usage Channel Evaluator
D U M A N D	Deep Underseas Muon and Detector (the name adopted by a group of physicists, oceanographers and oceanographic engineers in the USA)
D U S T S O N D E	Balloon-borne Particle Counter
D U V D	Direct Ultrasonic Visualization of Defects
D V A R S	Doppler Velocity Altimeter Radar Set
D V L C	The Driver and Vehicle Licensing Centre (of DoE)
D V T	Deep Vein Thrombosis
D W I	Driving While Impaired (by alcohol and/or drugs)
D W I M	Do-What-I-Mean
D W L	Derived Working Level
D W P	Dyna Whirlpool Process
D W T	Deutsche Gesellschaft für Wehrtechnik (Germany) (German Society for Defence Technology)
D Y N A M I T	Dynamic Allocation of Manufacturing Inventory and Time

E

E	Prefix to numbered-dated series of standards on Electronic Components issued by BSI

E A	Energy Analysis
E A C A	Epsilon Aminocaproic Acid
E A G G F	European Agricultural Guidance and Guarantee Fund (of EEC)
E A C S O	East African Common Services Organization (Kenya)
E A N R R C	East African Natural Resources Research Council (Kenya)
E A N S	European Article Numbering System
E A P	Environmental Analysis and Planning
E A R	Electronically-Agile Radar
	Electronic Array Radar
	European Association of Radiology
E A R B	European Airlines Research Bureau (now Association of European Airlines)
E A R D H E	European Association for Research and Development in Higher Education
E A R O P H	Eastern Regional Organization for Planning and Housing (India)
E A R P	Equipment Anti-Riot Projector
E A R S	Electronic Airborne Reaction System
	Electronically Agile Radar System
E A S	European Accident Statement
E A S A	Engineers Association of South Africa (South Africa)
E A S E	Electronic Airborne Systems Evaluator
E A S S	Engine Automatic Stop and Start System
E A S S G	European Accountancy Students Study Group
E A S T E C	Eastern Testing Exposition/Conference (of ASNDT (USA))
E A T	Employment Appeal Tribunal
E A T C	Ehrlich Ascites Tumor Cell
E A T C S	European Association for Theoretical Computer Science
E A T S	Extended Area Tracking System
E A U	Extended Arithmetic Unit
E B	Environmental Buoy
E B A M	Electron-Beam-Addressed Memory
E B E S	Electron Beam Exposure System
E B I V	Electron Beam Induce Voltage
E S V	Epstein-Barr Virus
E C & D	Electronic Cover and Deception

E C A F E	Economic Commission for Asia and the Far East (of UN) (became ESCAP in 1974)
E C A S	Energy Conversion Alternatives Study (by ERDA, NSF and NASA (USA))
E C C	Electro-chemichromic
	Electrodeposited Composite Coating
E C C S	European Convention for Construction Steelwork
E C D I N	European Chemical Data and Information Network
E C F	Electro-Chemical Forming
	Electro-Conductive Film
E C F A	European Committee for Future Activities
E C I	European Co-operation in Informatics (a partnership of European computer societies)
	Export Consignment Identifying number
E C M T	European Conference of Ministers of Transport (of OECD)
E C O P C	Experimental Changes of Practice Committees (of the British Post Office)
E C O R S	Eastern Counties Operational Research Society
E C P N L	Equivalent Continuous Perceived Noise Level
E C Q A C	Electronics Component Quality Assessment Committee (of CENEL)
E C R I M	Engineering, Construction, and Related Industries Manpower National Committee (of TSA)
E C R O	European Chemoreception Research Organization
E C S	Embedded Computer System
	European Components Service (of Dept of Industry)
E C S A	European Computing Services Association
E C T A	Everyman's Contingency Table Analyser
E C U B E	Energy Conservation Using Better Engineering
E C V	Extracellular Virus
E C W A	Economic Commission for Western Asia (of UN)
E D	Estate Duty (replaced by Capital Transfer Tax)
E d A	Ejercito del Aire (Spain) (Military Air Force)
E D A	European Disposables Association (Belgium) now EDANA (Belgium)
E D A C	Engineering Design Advisory Committee (of the Design Council)
E D A N A	European Disposables and Non-Wovens Association (Belgium)
E D C	European Documentation Centres (of the European Communities)
	Export Development Corporation (Canada) (a Federal Crown Corporation)

E D C C	Environmental Dispute Coordination Commission (Japan)
E D F	European Development Fund (of EEC)
E D G N	Ethylene Glycol Dinitrate
E D I T	Engineering Design Intelligent Terminal
E D I T E R R A	European Association of Earth-Science Editors
E D L	Electric Discharge Laser
E D M	Electromagnetic Distance Measuring
E D O S / R J E	Extended Disc Operating System with Remote Job Entry facilities
E D R A	Environmental Design Research Association (USA)
E E	Exoelectron Emission
E E A T	End of Evening Astronomical Twilight
E E C A	European Electronic Component Manufacturers Association
E E D	Elastic Energy Density
E E I A	Electrical and Electronic Insulation Association (part of BEAMA)
E E L	Environmental Effects Laboratory (of WES (US Army))
E E R A	Electrical and Electronic Retailers Association (merged with RTRA in 1974)
E E S	Electro-magnetic Environment Simulator
E E Z	Exclusive Economic Zone
E F	Electroflotation
	Engineering Foundation (USA)
E F A	Essential Fatty Acids
E F E	Early Fuel Evaporation
E F P B	Employers Federation of Papermakers and Board-makers (now part of British Paper and Board Industry Federation)
E F S	Equivalent Standard Fillet
E F T S	Electronic Funds Transfer System
E F V	Equilibrium Flash Vaporization
E G A M	Ente di Gestione Aziende Minerarie (Italy) (Govt controlled)
E G C L	Electro-generated Chemiluminescence
E G G A	European General Galvanizers Association
E G O T	Erythrocyte Glutamic-Oxaloacetic Transaminase

66

E G O T I	Egyptian General Organization for Trade and Industry (Egypt)
E G P A	Egyptian General Petroleum Authority (Egypt)
E G P C	Egyptian General Petroleum Corporation (Egypt) (replaced in 1976 by EGPA)
E H D	Electrohydrodimerization
E I	Embrittlement Index
E I A	Environmental Impact Assessment
E I A C	Ergonomics Information Analysis Centre (University of Birmingham)
E I B	European Investment Bank (of EEC)
E I C	Energy Information Center (University of New Mexico (USA))
E I C F	European Investment Casters Federation (Netherlands)
E I N	European Informatics Network
E I S	Environmental Impact Statement
E I S C A T	European Incoherent Scatter Organisation
E I T	Environmental Interaction Theory of Personality
E J C S C	European Joint Committee of Scientific Cooperation (of the Council of Europe)
E L D O	European Launcher Development Organisation (merged into ESA in 1975)
E L E P	European Federation of Anti-Leprosy Associations (name changed to ILEP in 1975)
E L I N T	Electro-magnetic Intelligence
E L I S A	Enzyme-Linked Immunosorbent Assay
E L M O	Engineering and Logistics Management Office (US Army)
E L M S	Earth Limb Measurement Satellite
E L M S I M	Engine Life Management Simulation Model
E L R A C	Electronic Reconnaissance Accessory system
E L R A T	Electrical Ram Air Turbine
E L S E	(European Life Science Editors) is the acronym adopted by the European Association of Editors of Biological Periodicals
E M A	Employment Management Association (USA) European Marketing Association
E M A S	Emergency Medical Advisory Service (now of the Health and Safety Commission)

E M B L	European Molecular Biology Laboratory (Germany)
E M C	Encephalomyocarditis
E M C - F O M	Electro-Magnetic Compatibility Figure of Merit
E M C F	European Monetary Co-operation Fund (of EEC)
E M C S R	European Meeting on Cybernetics and Systems Research
E M I S	Engineering Maintenance Information System International Electromagnetic Isotope Separators Conference
E M M S E	Educational Modules for Materials Science and Engineering (a project of NSF (USA) administered by Pennsylvania State University)
E M O R G	East Midland Operational Research Group
E M P C	Educational Media Producers Council (of the National Audio-Visual Association (USA))
E M S	Early MARC Search (Library of Congress (USA)) Energy Management System Expected Mean Squares
E M T N	European Meteorological Telecommunications Network
E M U	Economic and Monetary Union (being formed in stages by the European Communities)
E M V	Electro-Magnetic Vulnerability
E N A F	Empresa Nacional de Fundiciones (Bolivia) (State Smelting Enterprise)
E N A S A	Empresa Nacional de Autocamiones SA (Spain)
E N C C	Ente Nazionale Cellulosa e Carta (Italy)
E N C I	Empresa Nacional de Comercialización de Insumos (Peru)
E N C O T E L	Empresa Nacional de Correos y Telegrafos (Argentina)
E N D E X	Environmental Data Index (of EDS (NOAA) (USA))
E N E R G A S	Empresa Nacional de Gas (Spain) (National Gas Enterprise)
E N E W S	Effectiveness of Navy Electronic Warfare System
E N R I	Electronic Navigation Research Institute (Japan)

E N S	European Nuclear Society
E N S E C	European Nuclear Steelmaking Club
E N S I P	Turbine Engine Structural Integrity Program (of USAF)
E O D A P	Earth and Ocean Dynamic Applications Program (of NASA (USA))
E O G B	Electro-Optical Glide Bomb
	Electro-Optical Guided Bomb
E O R	Explosive Ordnance Reconnaissance
E O W	Engine-Over-the-Wing
E P C	Educational Publishers Council (of the Publishers Association)
E P D C	Electric Power Development Corporation (Japan) (a semi-governmental organisation)
E P I	Engineering Projects (India) Limited (India) (government owned)
E P I C	Electron-Positron Intersecting Complex
E P I C S	Energetic Pion Channel and Spectrometer
E P I T	Equipment Procurement and Installation Team
E P M A	Electron Probe Micro-Analysis
E P O	Energy Policy Office (USA) (abolished 1974)
E P O C S	Effectual Planning for Operation of Container System
E P O S S	Environmental Protection Oil Sands System
E P R O I	Expected Project Return On Investment
E P S	Econometric Programme System
	Electron Proton Spectrometer
E Q I	Environmental Quality Index
E Q U A T E	Electronic Quality Assurance Test Equipment
E R A	Electrical Research Association (now a commercial service company and not a research body)
	Electric Response Audiometry
E R D A	Energy Research and Development Administration (USA)
E R D I P	Experimental Research and Development Incentives Program (of NSF (USA))
E R G	Energy Research Group (of the Open University)
	Enrichment Reprocessing Group (Japan)
E R I C / C I R	ERIC Clearinghouse on Information Resources (Stanford University (USA))

ERIC/CLIS	ERIC Clearinghouse on Library and Information Science (of American Society for Information Science (USA)) (merged with ERIC Clearinghouse on Educational Media and Technology in 1974 to form ERIC/IR (USA))
ERIC/EM	ERIC Clearinghouse on Educational Media and Technology (merged with ERIC/CLIS in 1974 to form ERIC/IR (USA))
ERIC/IR	ERIC Clearinghouse on Information Resources (Stanford University (USA))
ERIM	Environmental Research Institute of Michigan (USA)
ERIW	European Research Institute for Welding
ERL	Environmental Research Laboratory (Arizona University (USA))
ERLS	Economic Release Lot-Sizes
ERNIC	Earnings Related National Insurance Contribution
ERRDF	Earth Resources Research Data Facility (of NASA (USA))
ERS	Engineering Research Station (of the Gas Council which became the British Gas Corporation in 1973)
ERSOS	Earth Resources Survey Operational Satellite
ERSTC	Ergonomics Research Society Training Committee
ERT	Electrical Resistance Thermometer
ERTS	Earth Resources Technology Satellite (now known as Landsat)
ES	prefix to numbered-dated series of Emergency Standards issued by ASTM (USA)
ESA	Department of Economic and Social Affairs (of UN)
	Employment Services Agency (of the Manpower Services Commission)
	European Space Agency
ESAEI	Electric Supply Authority Engineers Institute (New Zealand)
ESAN	Escuela de Administración de Negocios para Graduados (Peru) (Graduate School of Business Administration)
ESB	Electricity Supply Board (Eire)
ESC	Enrichment Survey Committee (Japan) (disbanded 1975)

70

E S C	European Space Conference (absorbed into ESA in 1975)
E S C A P	Economic and Social Commission for Asia and the Pacific (of UN)
E S C P	École Supérieure de Commerce de Paris (France) (Paris College of Commerce)
E S C S P	European Society of Corporate and Strategic Planners (Belgium)
E S D R	European Society for Dermatological Research
E S F	European Science Foundation
	European Social Fund (of the EEC)
E S F P	Environment-Sensitive Fracture Processes
E S G M	Electrostatically Supported Gyro Monitor
E S G M / S I N S	Electrostatically Supported Gyro Monitor/Ships Inertial Navigation System
E S I	Equivalent Spherical Illumination
E S M	Electronic Support Measures
E S M A	Essential Manning
E S M O C	European Solar Meeting Organizing Committee
E S O C	European Space Operations Centre (of ESA)
E S O P	Employee Stock Ownership Plan
E S O R	Electronically Scanned Optical Receiver
E S P	Economy Systems Plates
	Electro-Sensitive Paper
	Eosinophil Stimulation Promoter
E S P A	Electronically Steered Phased Array
E S P I	Electronic Speckle-Pattern Interferometer
E S P R I	Education Service of the Plastics and Rubber Institute (operated from Loughborough College of Education)
E S R	Electroslag Remelting
E S R C	European Science Research Council
E S R I N	European Space Research Institute (now of ESA)
E S R O	European Space Research Organisation (incorporated within ESA in 1975)
E S R U	Environmental Sciences Research Unit (Cranfield Institute of Technology)
E S S	Expendable Sound Source
E S S C I R C	European Solid-State-Circuits Conference

E S S E C	École Supérieure des Sciences Économiques et Commerciales (France) (College of Economic and Commercial Sciences)
E S S E X	Effects of Sub-Surface Explosions (a project of the US Army)
E S S W A C S	Electronic Solid-State Wide-Angle Camera System
E S T A	Electronically Synchronised Transmission Assembly
E S T E C	European Space Research and Technology Centre (formerly of ESRO, now part of ESA since 1975)
E S V	Earth-Satellite Vehicle
E T A A D S	Engine Technical And Administrative Data System
E T A S	Escort Towed Array System
E T A S S	Escort Towed Array Sonar System
E T C	Effluent Treatment Cell
E T E M A	Engineering Teaching Equipment Manufacturers Association
E T I A	European Tape Industry Association
E T L	Emergency Locator Transmitter
E T O C	Expected Total Operating Cost
E T R	Effective Thyroxine Ratio
E T S C	Engineering Terotechnology Steering Committee (of IEE, IMechE, IProdE, ICMA and BCMA)
E T S U	Energy Technology Support Unit (of Dept of Energy)
E T T	Evasive Target Tank (armoured fighting vehicle)
E T T D C	Electronics Trade and Technology Development Corporation (India) (government owned)
E T U C	European Trade Union Confederation
E U	prefix to Euronorms which are Standards issued by the European Coal and Steel Community
E U A	European Unit of Account
E U C O N	Energy Utilization and Conservation Exhibition and Conference
E U D I S E D	European Documentation and Information System for Education
E U M O T I V	European Association for the Study of Economic, Commercial and Industrial Motivation (Belgium)
E U R A S	European Anodisers Association
E U R E L	Convention of National Societies of Electrical Engineers of Western Europe

72

E U R I M A	European Insulation Manufacturers Association
E U R O C E A N	European Oceanographic Association (Monaco)
E U R O C O M P	European Computing Congress
E U R O C O O P	European Community of Co-operative Societies
E U R O C O R D	Fédération des Industries de Corderie-Ficellerie de l'Europe Occidentale (France) (Federation of Western Europe Rope and Twine Industries)
E U R O D I D A C	European Association of Manufacturers and Distributors of Education Materials
E U R O F I N A S	European Federation of Finance Houses Association (Belgium)
E U R O G R O P A	Union des Distributeurs de Papiers et Cartons (European Union of Paper, Board and Packaging Wholesalers)
E U R O M I C R O	European Association of Microprocessor Users
E U R O S T R U C T-P R E S S	European Association of Publishers in the Field of Building and Design
E U R O T E S T	European Association of Testing Institutions (association of European companies involved in the non-destructive testing of steel) (administered from Belgium)
E U S A F E C	Eastern United States Agricultural and Food Export Council (USA)
E V	Efficient Vulcanising
E V A	Electrical Vehicle Association of Great Britain
E V I C T	Evaluation of Intelligence Collection Tasks
E W A C	Electronic Warfare Anechoic Chamber
E W A C S	Electronic Wide Angle Camera System
E W B	Elektrizitätswerk der Stadt Bern (Switzerland)
E W E C	Electromagnet Wave Energy Conversion
E W G A E	European Working Group on Acoustic Emission
E W I	English Winter Index
E W M A	Exponentially Weighted Moving Average
E W S L	Equivalent Single Wheel Load
E W S M	Electronic Warfare Support Measures
E W Z	Elektrizitätswerk der Stadt Zurich (Switzerland)
E X A F S	Extended X-ray Absorption Fine-structure Spectroscopy
E X I A C	Explosives Information and Analysis Center (US Army)

E X O	European X-ray Observatory (later known as ASRO)
E X O S A T	European X-ray Observatory Satellite (previously known as HELOS)
E X R A Y	Expendable Relay
E Z P E R T	Easy PERT (Programme Evaluation and Review Technique)

F

F A	Frontoviya Aviatsiya (USSR) (the Frontal Aviation— a group of the Soviet Air Force)
F A B	Flour Advisory Board
F A C C	Food Additives and Contaminants Committee
F A C C M	Fast Access Charge-Coupled Memory
FA C E	Field Alterable Control Element
F A C E S	FORTRAN-Automatic Code Evaluation System
F A C E T	*Faber (Oscar Faber and Partners)* Cost Estimating Technique
F A C S	Federation of American Controlled Shipping (USA)
	Financial Accounting and Control System
	Fluorescence-Activated Cell Sorter
F A C T	Facility for Automation, Control and Test
F A E	Federation of Arab Engineers (Egypt)
	Fuerza Aérea Ecuatoriana (Ecuador) (Military Air Force)
F A E P	Federation of Associations of Periodical Publishers (of the EEC)
F A E S H E D	Fuel Air Explosive System, Helicopter Delivered
F A I R	Fly-Along Infra-Red
F A I R S	Failure Report Sorting and Analysis
	Fairchild (Camera and Instrument Corporation) Automatic Intercept and Response System
F A M O U S	French-American Mid-Ocean Undersea Study (of the Mid-Atlantic Ridge)
F A N	Free Amino Nitrogen
F A P	Failure Analysis Programme
F A R	The Foundation for Australian Resources (New South Wales Institute of Technology (Australia))
F A R R P	Forward Area Refueling and Rearming Point
F A S	European Federation of Associations of Industrial Safety and Medical Officers

F A S	Faculty of Architects and Surveyors (now incorporating the Institute of Registered Architects)
	Feel Augmentation System
	Fuerza Aérea Salvadorena (Salvador) (Military Air Force)
F A S C A M	Family of Scatterable Mines
F A S F I D	Fédération des Associations et Sociétés Françaises d'Ingénieurs Diplômés (France) (Federation of French Associations and Societies of Chartered Engineers)
F A S I I	Federation of Associations of Small Industries in India (India)
F A S O R	Forward Area Sonar Research
F A S T	File Analysis and Selection Technique
	Fleet-sizing Analysis and Sensitivity Technique
	Frequency Agile Search and Track Seeker
F A T A R	Fast Analysis of Tape and Recovery
F A T S	Fast Analysis of Tape Surfaces
F A T T	Fracture Appearance Transition Temperature
F B A	Fluorescent Brightening Agent
F B C M	Federation of British Carpet Manufacturers (merged into BCMA in 1976)
F B C S	Foreground/Background Operating System
F B S	Foetal Bovine Serum
F C C	Fluid Catalytic Cracking
F C C U	Fluid Catalytic Cracking Unit
F C C R	Fatigue Crack Growth Rate
F C I	Fuel-Coolant Interaction
F C L	Freon Coolant Loop
F D A A	Federal Disaster Assistance Administration (USA)
F D E S	Fonds de Développement Économique et Social (France) (Economic and Social Development Funds)
F D N B	Fluorodinitrobenzene
F D N R	Frequency-Dependent Negative Resistance
F D P	Falling Dilute-Phase
F D T E	Force Development Testing and Experimentation
F E A	Federal Energy Administration (USA)
	Federation of European Aerosol Associations (Switzerland)

F E A M I S	Foreign Exchange Accounting and Management Information System
F EC O N S	Field Engineer Control System
F E D E S	European Flexible Packagings Industry Association
F E D S I M	Federal Computer Performance Evaluation and Simulation Center (of General Services Administration (USA))
F E F	Fast Extrusion Furnace
F E F C	Far Eastern Freight Conference
F E I	Fluidic Explosive Initiator
F E I C R O	Federation of European Industrial Co-operative Research Organizations (of EEC)
F E L	Food Engineering Laboratory (US Army)
Fe L V	Feline Leukaemia Virus
F E O	Federal Energy Office (USA) (replaced by Federal Energy Administration in 1974)
F E P	Free Erythrocyte Protoporphyrin
F E P A S A	Ferrovia Paulista SA (Brazil)
F E S	Final Environmental Statement
	Fuze/Munitions Environment Characterization Symposium
F E S S	Flywheel Energy-Storage System
Fe S V	Feline Sarcoma Virus
F E U G R E S	Fédération Européenne des Fabricants de Tuyaux en Grès (European Federation of Manufacturers of Salt Glazed Pipes)
F F A R	Forward Firing Aerial Rocket
F F G	Forcing Function Generator
F F I	Finance for Industry (of Bank of England and major clearing banks)
F F V	Forenade Fabricksverken (Sweden) (government owned)
F F V M A	Fire Fighting Vehicle Manufacturers Association
F F W	Failure-Free Warranty
F G C B	Fast Gas Cooled Reactor
F G M C	Federal Government Micrographics Council (USA)
F H F	Fulminant Hepatic Failure
F I	Field Ionization
F I A	Forging Industry Association (USA)
F I A F	Fédération Internationale des Archives du Film (Belgium) (International Federation of Film Archives)

76

F I C S	Factory Information Control System
F I D / C A O	Fédération Internationale de la Documentation Commission for Asia and Oceania
F I D / C C C	FID Central Classification Committee (for the development of the UDC)
F I D / C L A	FID Regional Commission for Latin America
F I D / C R	FID Committee on Classification Research
F I D / D C	FID Committee on Developing Countries
F I D / D T	FID Committee on the Terminology of Information and Documentation
F I D / E T	FID Committee on Education and Training
F I D / I I	FID Committee on Information for Industry
F I D / L D	FID Committee on Linguistics in Documentation
F I D / R I	FID Committee on Research on the Theoretical Basis of Information
F I D / T M O	FID Committee on Theory, Methods and Operations of Information Systems and Networks
F I D A	Federal Industrial Development Authority (Malaysia)
F I D U R O P	Fédération des Fabricants de Ficelles et Cordages de l'Europe Occidentale (merged into EUROCORD in 1975)
F I L T A N	Passive Filter Analysis
F I M	Fédération Internationale Motocycliste
F I N A T	International Federation of Manufacturers and Converters of Pressure-Sensitive and Heatseal Materials on Paper and other Base Materials (Netherlands)
F I P A G O	Fédération Internationale des Fabricants de Papiers Gommes (Netherlands) (International Federation of Manufacturers of Gummed Paper)
F I R A	Federal Investment Review Agency (Canada)
F I R E S - T	Fire Response of Structures-Thermal (a computer programme)
F I R P	Foreign Inward Remittance Payment Scheme (of the Reserve Bank of India)
F I R T A	Far Infra-Red Technical Area
F I R T O	Fire Insurers Research and Testing Organisation
F I S A R	Fleet Information Storage and Retrieval (USN)
F I S C	Fédération Internationale des Chasseurs du Son
F I U	Federation of Information Users (USA)

F L A I R	Fleet Location And Information Reporting (for police patrol cars)
F L A N G	Flowchart Language
F L A P S	Flexibility Analysis of Piping Systems
F L E E	Fast Linkage Editor
F L I M B A L	Floated Inertial Measurement Ball
F L I P	Free-form Language for Image Processing
F L O A T	Floating Offshore Attended Terminal
F L O P A C	Flight Operations Advisory Committee (of IATA)
F L S	Forward Look Sonar
F L V	Friend Leukaemia Virus
F M C	Fleet Maintenance Council (USA)
F M C S	Federal Mediation and Concilliation Service (USA)
F M I	Functional Management Inspection system (of AFISC (USAF))
F M R	Fasting Metabolic Rate
F N A F	Federal Nigerian Air Force (Nigeria)
F N A L	Fermi National Accelerator Laboratory
F N P	Floating Nuclear Power Plant
F o B	Faculty of Building
F O C I S	Financial On-line Central Information System
F O C M A	Feline Oncornavirus-associated Cell Membrane Antigen
F O C S	Freight Operation Control System
F O M	Figure Of Merit
F O N A S B A	Federation of National Associations of Shipbrokers and Agents
F O R M S	Federation of Rocky Mountain States (USA)
F O R T S I M	FORTRAN Simulation
F O S P L A N	Formal Space Planning Language
F P A	Federal Preparedness Agency (of GSA (USA))
F P C C	Flight/Propulsion Control Coupling
F P E C	Four-Pile Extended Cantilever platform
F P L A	Fair Packaging and Labelling Act (USA)
	Field Programmable Logic Array
F P S	Financial Planning System
F P T	Free Plasma Trytophan
F R A C A	Failure Reporting, Analysis and Corrective Action
F R A M A T E G	Framatone Entreprise Générale (France)
F R T C	Fast Reactor Training Centre (UKAEA)

F R W I	Framingham Relative Weight Index
F S B	Floating Supply Base
F S C	Food Standards Committee (of MAFF)
F S G	First Stage Graphitization
F S G T R - N C	prefix to numbered series of Forest Service General Technical Reports of the North Central Forest Experiment Center (USA)
F S L	Food Science Laboratory (US Army)
F S S	Federal Supply Service (of GSA (USA))
F S S T	Flying Spot Scanner Tube
F S T	Functional Simulator and Translator
F S T T	Floating Shuttle Tape Transport
F T A	Fluorescent Treponemal Antibody
F T A - A B S	Fluorescent Treponemal Antibody Absorption
F T C S	International Symposium on Fault-Tolerant Computing .
F T I	Free Thyroxine Index
F T M A	Federation of Textile Manufacturers Associations
F U B A R	*Fangmeyer's* Utility, a Basic Algorithm for Revision
F U E	Federated Union of Employers (Eire)
F U F O	Fly Under, Fly Out
F W D	Front Wheel Drive
F W H	Flexible Working Hours
F W I D	Federation of Wholesale and Industrial Distributors
F W O	Federation of Wholesale Organisations (now FWID)

G

Ga As (Cs)	Gallium-Arsenide (Cesium)
G A C	Government Advisory Committee on International Book and Library Programs (USA)
G A D P E T	Graphic Data Presentation and Edit
G A L S	Generalized Assembly Line Simulator
	Geographic Adjustment by Least Squares
G A M T A	General Aviation Manufacturers and Traders Association
G A R B	Garment and Allied Industries Requirements Board (of DoI)
G A S P	Global Air Sampling Program (of NASA (USA))
G A S S S	Gas Steady State
G A S U S	Gas Unsteady State

G A T T	General Agreement on Tariffs and Trade (of UN) (administrative office in Switzerland)
G A W R	Gross Axle Weight Rating
G B D	Grain Boundary Dislocation
G B I L	Gosudarstvennaya Biblioteka SSR Imeni V I Lenina (USSR) (Lenin State Library)
G C	Gas Council (became British Gas Corporation in 1973)
G C - M S	Gas Chromatograph linked with a Mass Spectrometer
G C A	Glycosphingolipid Sorbent Assay
G C B S	General Council of British Shipping
G C L	General Control Language
G C M R U	Genetic Control of Mosquitoes Research Unit (of ICMR (India))
G C M S	Gas Chromatograph Mass Spectrometer
G C R	Gas-cooled Graphite-moderated Reactor
G D B M S	Generalized Data Base Management Systems
G E A	Garage Equipment Association (absorbed into SMMT in 1976)
G E L I S - H	Ground Emitter Location Identification System - High
G E E C	General Egyptian Electricity Corporation (Egypt)
G E M	Ground Elevation Meter
G E M S	*Goodyear (Aerospace Corporation)* Electronic Mapping System
G E O D S S	Ground Electro-Optical Deep Space Surveillance
G E O M E D	Geometric Editor
G E P O C	Gesellschaft für Polymerchemie (Germany)
G E S	Government Economic Service (of H M Treasury)
Ge Se	Germanium Selenide
G E S M A	Groupe d'Études Sous-Marines de l'Atlantique (of the French Navy)
Ge Te	Germanium Telluride
G F E C	Graphite-Fibre Epoxy-Composite
G G E	General Graphical Editing
G I	Gesellschaft für Informatik (Germany) (Society for Data Processing)
G I D E P	Government-Industry Data Exchange Program (USA)
G I F A S	Groupement des Industries Françaises Aéronautiques et Spatiales (France) (French Aerospace Industry Association)
G I M I C	Guard Ring Implanted Monolithic Integrated Circuit

GINO-F	GINO FORTRAN IV
GIPSSY	Generalised Interactive Programme for the Simulation of Systems
GIRL	Generalized Information Retrieval Language
GISP	Greenland Ice Sheet Program (of USA, Denmark, and Switzerland)
GLAD	GALS LESA-A-A AGILE Dialogue
GLBSA	Greater London Building Surveyors Association
GLERL	Great Lakes Environmental Research Laboratory (of ERL (NOAA) (USA))
GLLD	Ground Laser Locator Designator
GLR	Generalized Likelihood Ratio
GLS	Graduate Library School (Illinois University (USA))
	Graduate Library School (Indiana University (USA))
	Graduate Library School (Rutgers University (USA))
GMBF	Gesellschaft für Molekularbiologische Forschung (Germany) (Society for Molecular Biology Research)
GMCC	Geophysical Monitoring for Climatic Change (a program of the Air Resources Laboratories (ERL) (NOAA) (USA))
GMPA	Gas-Metal-Plasma-Arc
GMT	Geometric Mean Titre
GNC	Graphical Numerical Control
GNT	Gesellschaft für Nuklear-transporte (Germany)
GOCO	Government-owned Contractor-operated production plant
GODAS	Graphically Oriented Design and Analysis System
GOLD	Geometric On-Line Definition
GOX	Gas Oxygen
GPA	Gas Processors Association (USA)
GPL/1	Graph Programming Language One
GPRSS	General Purpose Remote Sensor System
GPS	Global Positioning System
GPT	Guild of Professional Translators (USA)
GRAMS	Ground Recording And Monitoring System
GRASER	Gamma Ray Laser
GRASP	General Risk Analysis Simulation Programme
	Generation of Random Access Site Plans
GRC	Glass-Reinforced Cement
GRG	Gravimetric Rain-Gauge

81

G R P	Glass-fibre Reinforced Polyester
G S C	Group Switching Centre
G S C C M F	Gujarat State Co-operative Cotton Marketing Federation (India)
G S F C	*Goddard (Robert Hutchings Goddard)* Space Flight Center (of NASA (USA))
	Gujarat State Fertiliser Company (India)
G S H Px	Gluthathione Peroxidase
G S I	Geological Survey of India (India)
G S L	Geographic Sciences Laboratory (of USAETL)
G S P	Generalised System of Tariff Preferences
G S R	Galvanic Skin Resistance
G S T	General Systems Theory
G S T P	Generalised System of Tariff Preferences
G T - H T G R	Gas Turbine High Temperature Gas-cooled Reactor
G T E	Gunner Tracking Evaluator
G T M S	Graphic Text Management System
G T S C	Ground Testing and Simulation Committee (of AIAA (USA))
G T T	Glucose Tolerance Test
G U A T E L	Empresa Guatemalateca de Telecomunicaciones (Guatemala) (Telecommunications Agency of Guatemala)
G U G K	Glavnoje Upravlenije Geodesii i Kartografii (USSR) (Administrative Agency for Geodesy and Cartography)
G U G M S	Glavnoje Upravlenije Gidrometeorologicheskoi Sluzhby (USSR) (Administrative Agency for the Hydrometeorological Service)
G U P C O	Gulf of Suez Petroleum Company
G U R C	Gulf Universities Research Consortium (USA)
G V	Granulosis Virus
G V B	Gelatine Veronal Buffer
G V M D S	Ground Vehicle Mine Dispensing System
G V O	Gross Value of Output
G W K	Gesellschaft zur Wiederaufarbeitung von Kernbrennstoffen (Germany)
G W S	Grid Wire Sensor
G W U	George Washington University (USA)

G Z G	Gutegemeinschaft Zinngerat (Germany) (Pewter Quality Association)

H

H A B I T A T	United Nations World Conference on Human Settlements
H A C	High Alumina Cement
H A C C	High Alumina Cement Concrete
H A C L S	*Harpoon* (missile) Aircraft Command and Launch Sub-system
H A D I S	Hadamard Imaging Spectrometer
H A E S	High Altitude Effects Simulation (a program sponsored by Defense Nuclear Agency (USDOD))
H A F	Hellenic Air Force (Greece)
H A I S S	High Altitude Infra-red Sensor System
H A L	Health Affairs Library (East Carolina University (USA))
H A N E	High-Altitude Nuclear Explosion
H A N E S	Health and Nutrition Examination Survey (of National Center for Health Statistics (USA))
H A R E S	High Altitude Radiation Environment Study (by FAA, USAF, USN and NASA (USA))
H A R I S	High Altitude Radiation Instrument System
H A R M	High-speed Anti-Radiation Missile
	Hyper-velocity Anti-Radiation Missile
H A R V	High Altitude Research Vehicle
H A S A W A	Health and Safety at Work Act, 1974
H A S P A	High-Altitude Superpressure Powered Aerostat
H Bs Ag	Hepatitis B Surface Antigen
H B V	Hepatitis B Virus
H C F	Haemolytic Complement Fixation
H C G	Human Chorionic Gonadotrophin
H C H P	Harvard Community Health Plan (USA)
H C M	Health Care Management
H C O	Hydrogenated Coconut Oil
H C P	Hexachlorophane
H C S A	Hospitals Consultants and Specialists Association
H C U A	*Honeywell* Computer Users Association
H D D	Housing Development Directorate (of DoE)
H D H C	High-Density Hydrocarbon

H D L	Hardware Description Language
H D L	Hydrologic Data Laboratory (of Agricultural Research Service (USDA))
H E	Hydrogen Embrittlement
H E A D S - U P	Health Care Delivery Simulator for Urban Population
H E A F S	High-Explosive Anti-tank Fin-Stabilised
H E B A	Home Extension Building Association
H E I	High-energy Electronic Ignition
H E I A C	Hydraulic Engineering Information Analysis Center (US Army)
Hel C I S	Helicopter Command Instrumentation System
H E L L F I R E	Heliborne Laser Fire and Forget missile sytem
	Helicopter Launched, Fire and Forget missile
H E L P	Health Evaluation through Logical Processing
	High Energy Level Pneumatic automobile bumpers
H E L P I S	Higher Education Learning Programmes Information Service (of Council for Educational Technology)
H E L T A	High-Energy Laser Technology Assessment
H E M E L	Hexamethylmelamine
H E M L A W	Helicopter Mounted Laser Weapon
H E M L O C	Heliborne Emitter Location-Countermeasures
H E N I L A S	Helicopter Night Landing System
H E P	High Energy Physics
	High Explosive, Plastic
H E R M E S	Helicopter Energy and Rotor Management System
H E S C	International Congress of Scientists on the Human Environment
He S C A	Health Sciences Communication Association (USA)
H F F	Horizontal Falling Film
H F I	Hydraulic Fluid Index
H F M D	Hand-Foot-and-Mouth Disease
H F P A C	High Frequency Powder Air Conveyor
H F R O	Hill Farming Research Organisation
H F R T	High-Frequency Resonance Technique
H G R T	Hypoxanthine Guanine Phosphoribosy Transferase
H G S	Hydrologic Growing Season
H H C C	Higher Harmonic Circulation Control rotor
H H T	High-temperature Helium Turbine
H H T V	Hand-Held Thermal Viewer
H I - P I	High Performance Intercept

84

H I L A	Health (and accident) Insurance Logistics Automated
Hi M A T	Highly Manoeuvrable Aircraft Technology (a project of NASA (USA))
Hi N i L	High Noise Immunity Logic
H I P	Hierarchical Information Processor
H I P O	Hierarchical Input-Process-Output
H I S S G	Hospital Information Systems Sharing Group (USA)
H I T	Homing Intercept Technology
H L L	High-Level Language
H L S U A (Europe)	*Honeywell* Large Systems Users Association in Europe
H M B P	Heavy Machine Building Plant (India)
H M D	Hyaline Membrane Disease
H M D E	Hanging Mercury Drop Electrode
H M F I	Her Majesty's Factory Inspectorate (formerly of the Department of Employment, now of the Health and Safety Executive)
H M G	Human Menopausal Gonadtrophin
H M O	Health Maintenance Organization (organization here means the state of being organized and not the name of a body)
H M S S	Hospital Management Systems Society (USA)
Hn R N A	Heterogeneous nuclear Ribonucleic Acid
H O B	Horizontal Oscillating Barrel
H O E	Holographic Optical Element
H O P E S	High Oxygen Pulping Enclosed System
H O S T	Hardened Optical Sensor Testbed
H P C L	Hindustan Petroleum Corporation Limited (India)
H P D O	High Performance Diesel Oil
H P H F	Hereditary Persistence of Foetal Haemoglobin
H P I	Hydrocarbon Processing Industry
H P L C	High Pressure Liquid Chromatography
H P L L	Hybrid Phase-Locked Loop
H P M V	High Pressure Mercury Vapour
H P S E B	Himachal Pradesh State Electricity Board (India)
H P S N	Hot Pressed Silicon Nitride
H P T A	Hire Purchase Trade Association
H R A	Hypersonic Research Airplane
H R C C	Humanities Research Council of Canada (Canada)

H R D	High Roughage Diet
H R D	Human Resources Development
H R I R S	High Resolution Infra-red Radiation Sounder
H R I S	Human Resource Information System
H R P	Horizontal Radiation Pattern
H R R M	High Range-Resolution Monopulse
H R S	High Resolution Spectrometer
	Human Resource System
H S A	Human Serum Albumin
H S C	Health and Safety Commission
	Health Service Command (US Army)
H S C R	High-Strength Cold-Rolled
H S D	High Speed Diesel oil
H S D T	Hypersonic Small Disturbance Theory
H S E	Health and Safety Executive (of the Health and Safety Commission)
H S I	Heat Stress Index
H S R C	Health Sciences Resource Centre (of CISTI (Canada))
H S S	High-strength Stainless Steel
H S T R U	Hydraulic System Test and Repair Unit
H S V	Herpes Simplex Virus
	Highly Selective Vagotomy
H T A	Horticultural Trades Association
H T C	Heat Transfer Coefficient
H T G R	High-temperature Gas-cooled Graphite-moderated Reactor
H T O L	Horizontal-Take-Off and Landing
H T O T	High-Temperature Operating-Test
H T R B	High-Temperature Reverse-Bias
H T S	Hadamard Transform Spectrometer
	High-Temperature Storage
H U D W A C	Head-Up Display Weapon Aiming Computer
H U S A T	Human Sciences and Advanced Technology (a research group at Loughborough University)
H U T C H	Humidity-Temperature Charts
H V A P	Hyper-Velocity, Armour Piercing
H V B	Heptyl Viologen Bromide
H V D B	Heptyl Viologen Dibromide
H V E M	High Voltage Electron Microscope
H V G O	Heavy Vacuum Gas Oil

86

H V H M D	Holographic Visor Helmet Mounted Display
H V J	Haemagglutinating Virus of Japan
H V R A	Heating and Ventilating Research Association (became Building Services Research and Information Association in 1975)
H V R A P	Hyper-Velocity Rocket-Assisted Projectile
H W G C R	Heavy-Water-moderated, Gas-Cooled Reactor
H W L W R	Heavy-Water-moderated, Boiling Light-Water-cooled Reactor
H W M	Hot-Water-cure Mortar
H W M D	Hazardous Waste Management Division (of EPA (USA))
Hy S A S	Hydrofluic Stability Augmentation System
H Y S T U	Hydrofoil Special Trials Unit (USN)

I

I & O	Individual and Organization performance
I A	Institute of Actuaries
I A A	International Association of Allergology (USA)
I A A I	International Airports Authority of India (India)
I A A P	International Association of Applied Psychology
I A A P E A	International Association Against Painful Experiments on Animals
I A B	Industry Advisory Board (of IEA (OECD))
I A C	Industries Assistance Commission (Australia)
	Institute of Company Accountants (merged into the Society of Company and Commercial Accountants in 1974)
I A C A	International Association of Consulting Actuaries
I A C I A	Incorporated Association of Cost and Industrial Accountants (merged into the Society of Company and Commercial Accountants in 1974)
I A C P	International Association of Chiefs of Police
I A C P A P	International Association for Child Psychiatry and Allied Professions
I A C Q	Instituto Argentino de Control de la Calidad (Argentina) (Institute for Quality Control)
I A D O	Iran Agriculture Development Organization (Iran)
I A F	Immobilizing Accelerating Factor
I A G L P	International Association of Great Lakes Ports (representing 16 United States and 5 Canadian ports)

I A G U S P	Instituto de Astronomía e Geofisica da Universidade de São Paulo (Brazil) (Sao Paulo University Institute of Astronomy and Geophysics)
I A L	International Association of Theoretical and Applied Limnology
I A M / T M D	Institute of Administrative Management/Telecommunications Managers Division
I A M F E	International Association on Mechanization of Field Experiments (Norway)
I A M L	International Association of Music Librarians
I A M L A N Z	International Association of Music Librarians, Australia/New Zealand Branch
I A P	International Academy of Proctology
I A P - V O *Strany*	Istrebitel'naya Aviatsiya P-VO *Strany* (USSR) (Air Force of Anti-Aircraft Defence of the Homeland)
I A P A	Inter-American Press Association
I A P H A	International Association of Port and Harbour Authoritie
I A P S	International Affiliation of Planning Societies
	International Association for the Properties of Steam (USA)
I A Q R	Indian Association for Quality and Reliability (India)
I A R P	Indian Association for Radiation Protection (India)
I A R U	International Amateur Radio Union
I A S	Institute of Accounting Staff
	Interactive Application System
	prefix to numbered series of International Accounting Standards issued by IASC (of ICCAP)
I A S G	Inflation Accounting Steering Group
I A S L	Illinois Association of School Librarians (USA)
	International Association for the Study of the Liver (Belgium)
I A S P	International Association of Scholarly Publishers
I A V R S	International Audiovisual Resource Service (sponsored by UNESCO)
I B	Industrialised Building
I B A	International Bauxite Association
I B A A	Independent Bankers Association of America (USA)
I B A L S	Interactive Balancing through Simulation
I B B Y	International Board on Books for Young People
I B C	Intermediate Bulk Container

88

I B E	Inventory By Exception
I B E S	Integrated Building and Equipment Scheduling
I B K	Institut für Bauen mit Kunststoffen (Germany) (Institute for Building with Plastics)
I B K C	Infectious Bovine Keratoconjunctivitis
I B O L S	Integrated Business-Oriented Language Support
I B P G R	International Board for Plant Genetic Resources (of CGIAR)
I B R	Infectious Bovine Rhinotracheitis
I B V L	Instituut voor Bewaring van Landbowprodukten (Netherlands) (Institute for Storage and Processing of Agricultural Produce)
I C A	International Chiropractors Association (USA) International Congress on Acoustics
I C A A	International Council on Alcohol and Addictions (Switzerland)
I C A E S	International Congress of Anthropological and Ethnological Sciences
I C A E W	Institute of Chartered Accountants in England and Wales
I C A F I	International Commission of Agriculture and Food Industries
I C A I	Institute of Chartered Accountants in Ireland
I C A P S	Integrated (Aircraft) Carrier Acoustic Prediction System
I C A S	Institute of Chartered Accountants in Scotland
I C A T S	Intermediate Capacity Automated Telecommunications System (of AFCS (USAF))
I C A W	International Conference on Automation in Warehousing
I C B A	International Community of Booksellers Associations (Australia)
I C B L	International Conference on the Biology of Lipids
I C B P	International Council for Bird Preservation
I C C	Information Center Complex (Oak Ridge National Laboratory (USA))
I C C A D	International Centre for Computer Aided Design
I C C A P	International Co-ordination Committee for the Accountancy Profession (to be succeeded by the International Federation of Accountants in 1977)

I C C A S	International Conference on Computer Applications in the Automation of Shipyard Operation and Ship Design
I C C C	IEEE (USA) Conference on Computer Communications
I C C H	International Conference on Computers and the Humanities
I C C O	International Carpet Classification Organization (Belgium)
I C D	Initiative Communications Deception
I C D B	Integrated Corporated Data Base
I C D O	International Civil Defence Organization (Switzerland)
I C D R G	International Contact Dermatitis Research Group
I C E	IOMTR Committee for Europe
I C E C A P	Infrared Chemistry Experiments—Coordinated Auroral Program (part of HAES program sponsored by the Defense Nuclear Agency (USDOD))
I C E E	Iranian Conference on Electrical Engineering (Iran)
I C E F	International Conferences on Environmental Future
I C E L	International Council of Environmental Law (Germany)
I C E S A	International Conference on Environmental Sensing and Assessment
I C E T	Institute for the Certification of Engineering Technicians (USA)
I C F	International Cultural Foundation
I C H T	International Committee on Haemostasis and Thrombosis
I C I E	International Centre for Industry and the Environment
I C I P E	International Centre of Insect Physiology and Ecology (Kenya)
I C I S	International Conference on Ion Sources
I C L C U A	*ICL* Computer Users Association
I C M	Improved Conventional Munitions
	International Conference on the Mechanical Behaviour of Metals
I C M A	Institut de Cercetari pentree Mecanizarea (Romania) (Mechanisation of Agriculture Research Institute)
	Institute of Cost and Management Accountants
	International City Management Association (USA)
I C M C	International Congress on Metallic Corrosion

I C M F	Indian Cotton Mills Federation (India)
I C M I S	Integrated Computerized Management Information System
I C O N	Interactive Creation of NASTRAN
I C O O	Iraqi Company for Oil Operations (Iraq)
I Corr T	Institution of Corrosion Technology (amalgamated with CAPA in 1975 to form ICST)
I C P	International Institute of Cellular and Molecular Pathology (Belgium)
I C P P	Interactive Computer Presentation Panel (an international research and development program between the USA and the Federal Republic of Germany)
I C P P	International Conference on the Internal and External Protection of Pipes
I C P S	International Congress of Photographic Science
I C R A	International Centre for Research in Accounting (Lancaster University)
I C R I S A T	International Crops Research Institute for the Semi-Arid Tropics (India)
I C S	Integrated Conning System
	Intra-cranial Stimulation
I C S C	Interim Communications Satellite Commission (the Board of Governors of INTELSAT)
	International Civil Service Commission (of UN)
I C S T	Institute for Computer Sciences and Technology (of NBS (USA))
	Institution of Corrosion Science and Technology
I C T	Institution of Corrosion Technology (amalgamated with CAPA in 1975 to form ICST)
I C T B	International Customs Tariffs Bureau
I C T E D	International Co-operation in the field of Transport Economics Documentation (of ECMT (OECD))
I C T F	International Conference on Thin Films
I C T S	International Congress on Transplantation
I C U S	International Conference on the Unity of the Sciences
I C V	Intracellular Virus
I C W A	International Coil Winding Association
I D A	Iminodiacetic Acid
I D A B	Industrial Advisory Board
I D C	Imperial Defence College (now RCDS)

I D C	Information Dissemination Committee (of S-CS (IEEE) (USA))
	Inter-departmental Committee on Publicity for Engineering and Technology (of government departments, the CBI, industry and the nationalised industries)
I D D	Insulin-Dependent Diabetes
I D E	Israel Desalination Engineering Ltd. (Israel)
I D E A S	Integrated Design and Analysis System
I D E N	Interactive Data Entry Network
I D M	Institute of Defence Management (India)
I D M A	Indian Drug Manufacturers Association (India)
I D M S	Integrated Database Management System
I D N E	Inertial-Doppler Navigation Equipment
I E A	Institute of Economic Affairs
	International Energy Agency (of OECD)
I E Aust	Institution of Engineers, Australia
I E C	Information Exchange Centre (of CISTI (Canada))
I E C E	Institute of Electronics and Communication Engineers (Japan)
I E C E C	Inter-society Energy Conversion Engineering Conference (of ASME, IEEE, and AIChE (USA))
I E C E J	Institute of Electronics and Communication Engineers of Japan (Japan)
I E D	Integrated Environmental Design
I E E F	Ion-Exchange-Evaporation-Filter
I E E J	Institute of Electrical Engineers of Japan (Japan)
I E I	Institution of Engineers of Ireland
I E O P	Immunoelectroosmophoresis
I E P	International Education Project (of the American Council on Education (USA))
I E S U A	Institut de l'Energie Solaire de l'Université d'Alger (Algeria) (Institute of Solar Energy of the University of Algiers)
I F	Immunofluorescence
I F A	International Federation of Airworthiness
I F A C / I F I P S O C O C O	IFAC/IFIP Symposium on Software for Computer Control
I F A C P R P	IFAC Conference on Instrumentation and Automation in the Paper, Rubber and Plastics Industries

I F A D	International Fund for Agricultural Development
I F A N	International Federation for the Application of Standards
I F A T	Indirect Fluorescent Antibody Test
I F A T E	International Federation of Airworthiness Technology and Engineering (now International Federation of Airworthiness)
I F A W P C A	International Federation of Asian and Western Pacific Contractors Associations
I F C C	International Federation of Clinical Chemistry
I F C S	Improved (Artillery) Fire Control System
I F E B S	Integrated Foreign Exchange and Banking System
I F F C O	Indian Farmers Fertiliser Co-operative Ltd (India) (partly government owned)
I F H T M	International Federation for the Heat Treatment of Materials
I F I A	International Fence Industry Association (USA)
I F I A S	International Federation of Institutes for Advanced Studies (Sweden)
I F M A	International Foodservice Manufacturers Association (USA)
I F M E	International Federation of Municipal Engineers
I F M I	Irish Federation of Marine Industries (Eire)
I F N	Institut Français de Navigation (France) (French Institute of Navigation)
I F O V	Instantaneous Field-Of-View
I F P M M	International Federation of Purchasing and Materials Management
I F R A	Inca-Fiej Research Association (Germany)
I F R C	International Fusion Research Council
I F S	International Foundation for Science (Sweden)
I F S M A	International Federation of Ship Master Associations
I F S S E C	International Fire, Security and Safety Exhibition and Conference
I F T o M M	International Federation for the Theory of Machines and Mechanisms
I G A T	Iranian Gas Truck Pipeline (of National Iranian Oil Company) (between Iran and USSR)
I G B S	International Gas Bearings Symposium
I G C	International Geological Congress
I G C A	Industrial Gas Cleaning Association

I G D	Institute of Grocery Distribution
I G D S	Iodine Generating and Dispensing System
I G E R	Institut National de Gestion et d'Économie Rurale (France) (National Institute of Rural Management and Economy)
I g G	Immunoglobulin G
I G G C I	International Geological/Geophysical Cruise Inventory (of World Data Center-A (USA))
I G S N 71	International Gravity Standardization Net 1971
I G T D S	Interactive Graphic Transit Design System
I G Tech E	Institution of General Technician Engineers
I H A	Indirect Haemagglutination test
I H A T	Indirect Haemagglutination Test
I H D	Ischaemic Heart Disease
I H M	Institute of Housing Managers
I H P	Isostatic Hot Pressing
I H S	Indian Health Service (of HEW (USA))
I H S S	Integrated Hydrographic Survey System
I H V E	Institution of Heating and Ventilating Engineers (became CIBS in 1976)
I I A	Institute of Internal Auditors (headquarters in USA)
I I A C	Industrial Injuries Advisory Council
I I A F	Iranian Imperial Air Force (Iran)
I I F T	Indian Institute of Foreign Trade (India)
I I H S	Insurance Institute for Highway Safety (USA)
I I I C	International Irrigation Information Centre (Israel)
I I N	Istituto Italiano di Navigazione (Italy) (Italian Institute of Navigation)
I I P	Istituto Italiano del Plastici (Italy) (Italian Institute for Plastic Materials)
I I S	Institute of Industrial Supervisors (later Institute of Supervisory Managers)
I K R D	Inverse Kinetics Rod Drop
I L A	Illinois Library Association (USA)
	Insurance Logistics Automated
I L A C I F	Latin America Institute of Auditing Sciences
I L A M A	International Life-saving Appliance Manufacturers Association
I L B	In-shore Life Boat
I L C A	International Livestock Centre for Africa (Kenya)

94

I L E P	International Federation of Anti-Leprosy Associations
I L L I N E T	Illinois Library and Information Network (USA)
I L L I P	*Illinois (University* (USA)) Integer Programming code
I L L O D I E - A I F	*Illinois (University* (USA)) Logical Design by Implicit Enumeration using the All-interconnection Inequality Formulation
I L M	Insulin-Like Material
I L R	Instituut voor Landbowtechniek en Rationalisatie (Netherlands) (Institute for Agricultural Techniques and Planning)
I L R A D	International Laboratory for Research on Animal Disease (Kenya)
I L R I	International Institute for Land Reclamation and Improvement (Netherlands)
I L S A M	International Language for Servicing And Maintenance
I L T	Interferometric Landmark Tracker
I M	Infectious Mononucleosis
I M / F M	Intensity Modulated/Frequency Modulated
I M A	Indonesian Mining Association (Indonesia)
	Industrial Medical Association (USA) (became AOMA in 1974)
	International Mohair Association
I M A C	Integrated Microwave Amplifier Converter
I M A D	Integrated Multi-sensor Airborne Survey
I M B L M S	Integrated Medical and Behavioral Laboratory Measurement System (a program of NASA (USA))
I M D G	International Maritime Dangerous Goods Code
I M E R	Instytut Mechanizacji i Elektrypikacji Rolnictwa (Poland) (Institute for Mechanization and Electrification of Agriculture)
I M F R A D	Integrated Multiple Frequency Radar
I M G	International Modular Group (of CIB)
I M H E	Institutional Management in Higher Education (a programme of OECD)
I M I	Industria Macchine Idrauliche (Italy)
I M I N O C O	Iranian Marine International Oil Company (Iran) (partly government owned)
I M L S	Institute of Medical Laboratory Sciences
I M M A P I	International Meeting of Medical Advisers in the Pharmaceutical Industry

I M O	International Meteorological Organization
I M O S	Federal Interagency Task Force on Inadvertent Modification of the Statosphere (USA)
I M P	Instrumental Match Prediction
I M P A C T	Intensive Matched Probation and After-Care Treatment
I M P C	International Mineral Processing Congress
I M P O S	Interactive Multi-Programming Operating System
I M P R E S S	Inter-disciplinary Machine Processing for Research and Education in the Social Sciences
I M Q	Istituto Italiano del Marchio de Qualità (Italy) (Italian Institution for Quality Branding)
I M R A	International Market Research Association
I M S	Index Management System
	Inertial Measuring Set
	Institute of Manpower Studies (Sussex University)
	Integrated Manufacturing System
	International Magnetospheric Study
I M S L	International Mathematical and Statistical Library (software)
I M T	Independent Model Triangulation
I M T A	Indiana Motor Truck Association (USA)
	Institute of Municipal Treasurers and Accountants (South Africa)
I M T E C	International Manpower Training for Educational Change (a branch of CERI (OECD))
I M X	Inquiry Message Exchange
I N	Institute of Navigation (USA)
I N A A	Instrumental Neutron Activation Analysis
I N C	Institut National de la Consommation (France) (National Institute on Consumer Affairs)
I N C A	Inventory Control and Analysis
I N C E	Institute of Noise Control Engineering (USA)
I N C E F	Institutul de Cercetari Forestiere (Romania) (Institute of Forestry Research)
I N C I R S	International Communication Information Retrieval System (Florida University (USA))
I N C I T E	Instructional Notation for Computer-controlled Inspection and Test Equipment
I N C P E N	Industry Committee for Packaging and the Environmer

I N C R A	International Copper Research Association (USA)
I N D A	International Non-wovens and Disposables Association
I N D A C	Industrial Data Acquisition and Control
I N D I	International Neutron Dosimetry Intercomparison (a project of ICRUM)
I N D I S	Industrial Information System (of UNIDO)
I N D O	Intermediate Neglect of Differential Overlap
I N E C E L	Instituto Ecuatoriano de Electrificación (Ecuador) (Institute of Electrification)
I N E L	Idaho National Engineering Laboratory (of ERDA (USA))
I N H I G E O	International Committee on the History of the Geological Sciences
I N I B O N	Institut Nacnoj Informacii i Fundamental'naja Biblioteka po Obscestvennym Naukam (USSR) (Institute of Scientific Information and Main Library of the Social Sciences)
I N L A	International Nuclear Law Association (Belgium)
I N L A W	Infantry Laser Weapon
I N N	Instituto Nacional de Normalización (Chile) (National Standards Institute)
I N O C	Iraq National Oil Company (Iran) (government owned)
In P	Indium Phosphide
I N P A D O C	International Patent Documentation Centre (Austria)
I N P E	Instituto Nacional de Pesquisas Espaciais (Brazil) (National Institute for Space Research)
I N P I	Institut National de la Propriété Industrielle (France) (National Institute of Industrial Patents)
I N S	Immigration and Naturalization Service (of the Department of Justice (USA))
I N S I G H T	Interactive System for Investigation by Graphics of Hydrological Trends
I N S I T E	Institutional Space Inventory Technique System
I N S P E C	Information Services in Physics, Electro-technology, Computers and Control (of IEE)
I N S P E C T	Infra-red System for Printed Circuit Testing

I N S T A A R	Institute of Arctic and Alpine Research (Colorado University (USA))
Inst P	Institute of Physics
Inst Pet	Institute of Petroleum
Inst P S	Institute of Purchasing and Supply
I N T A	Instituto Nacional de Tecnología Agropecuaria (Argentina) (National Institute of Agriculture and Farmstock Technology)
I N T A C T	Inter-modal Air Cargo Test (a joint project of the US government and Industry)
I N T A S A F C O N	International Tanker Safety Conference
I N T E L C A M	Société des Télécommunications Internationales du Cameroun (Cameroun)
I N T E R - NOISE	International Conference on Noise Control Engineering
I N T E R A N	International Conference on the Analysis of Geological Materials
INTER-EXPERT	International Association of Experts
I N T E R F A C E	Internationally Recognized Format for Automatic Commercial Exchange (of SITPRO)
INTERFAST	International Industrial Fastener Engineering Exhibition and Conference
INTEROCEAN	International Conference and Exhibition for Marine Technology
I N T U C	Indian National Trade Union Congress (India)
I O A	International Omega Association (USA)
I O C C	Interstate Oil Compact Commission (USA)
I O D E	IOC (UNESCO) Working Committee on International Oceanographic Data Exchange
I O E	Institute of Offshore Engineering (Heriot-Watt University)
I O L	Institute Of Librarians (India)
I O M	Institute Of Medicine (of National Academy of Sciences (USA))
I O O C	International Conference on Integrated Optics and Optical Fibre Communication
I O P E C	International Oil Pollution Exhibition and Conference
I O S A	Irish Offshore Services Association (Eire)
I O T & E	Initial Operational Test and Evaluation
I P	Integer Programming

I P A	Independent Publishers Association (Canada) (became ACP in 1976)
	International Paediatric Association (France)
I P A C	Independent Petroleum Association of Canada (Canada)
	Iran Pan-American Oil Company (Iran) (partly government owned)
	Isopropyl Acetate
I P A C K	International Packaging Material Suppliers Association
I P A C S	Integrated Power/Attitude Control System
I P A I	International Primary Aluminum Institute (USA)
I P B	Inventions Promotion Board (India) (merged into NRDC in 1973)
I P C	International Photographic Council (USA)
I P C A	International Passengers Consumer Association (disbanded in 1974)
I P C S	Image Photon Counting System
I P D	Instituto de Pesquisas e Desenvolvimento (of CTA (Brazil) (Institute for Research and Development)
I P D / T A S	Improved Point Defence/Target Acquisition
I P D A	International Periodical Distributors Association (USA)
I P E A C S	Instituto de Pesquisa Agropecuaria do Centrul Sul (Brazil) (South Centre Research Institute in Agriculture and Farmstock)
I P G	Information Policy Group (of OECD)
I P I C S	Initial Production and Information Control System
I P I E C A	International Petroleum Industry Environmental Conservation Association
I P M	Integrated Pest Management
I P M S	International Plastic Modellers Society
	Isopropylmethane Sulphonate
I P O	Instituut voor Perceptie Onderzoek (Netherlands) (Institute for Perception Research)
	International Projects Office (of NATO)
I P O D	International Phase of Ocean Drilling (of JOIDES)
I P P T A	Indian Pulp and Paper Technical Association (India)
I P P V	Intermittent Positive-Pressure Ventilation
I P R	Instituto de Pesquisas Rodoviarias (Brazil) (Institute of Highway Research)
I P R A	International Peace Research Association (Norway)
	International Public Relations Association
I P R O	International Pallet Recycling Organisation

I P S	Inertial Positioning Systems
	Institute of Polymer Science (Akron University (USA))
I P W S O M	Institute of Practitioners in Work Study, Organisation and Methods
I Q R P	Interactive Query and Report Processor
I R	Industrial Relations
I R A	Information Retrieval using APL (ie A Programming Language)
	International Reading Association (USA)
I R A C	Integrated Random Access Channel
I R A N O R	Instituto Nacional de Racionalización y Normalización (Spain) (National Institute of Standardization)
I R A P	Interagency Radiological Assistance Plan (USA)
I R A S	Infra-Red Measuring Astronomical Satellite
I R B T	Intelligent Remote Batch Terminal
I R C A M	Institute for Research and Coordination into Acoustics and Music (France)
I R C C D	Infra-Red Charge-Coupled Device
I R C S	International Research Communications System
I R C T	Institut de Recherches du Coton et des Textiles Exotiques (France) (Cotton and Tropical Textiles Institute)
I R D M	Illuminated Runway Distance Marker
I R D S	Idiopathic Respiratory Distress Syndrome
I R D U	Infra-Red Detection Unit
I R E N E	Indicating Random Electronic Numbering Equipment (of Central Bank of the Philippines) (serves the same purpose as ERNIE in the United Kingdom)
I R E Q	Institute of Research Quebec (Canada) (of Quebec Hydro-Electric Commission)
I R G	International Research Group on Wear of Engineering Materials
I R H O	Institute de Recherches pour les Huiles et Oleagineux (France) (Oils and Oil Seeds Research Institute)
I R I	Institution of the Rubber Industry (amalgamated into PRI in 1975)
I R I S	Industrial Relations Information System
I R L C	Illinois Regional Library Council (USA)
I R M M H	Institute of Research into Mental and Multiple Handicap
I R M R A	Indian Rubber Manufacturers Research Association

100

I R O P C O	Iranian Offshore Petroleum Company (Iran) (partly government owned)
I R R	Integral Rocket-Ramjet
I R R / S S M	Integral Rocket-Ramjet Surface-to-Surface Missile
I R S	Indian Register of Shipping (India)
	International Referral System (of the UN Environment Programme)
I R T	Institute for Rapid Transit (USA) (merged into APTA in 1974)
I S A A	Institute of Shops Acts Administration
I S A D C	Interim Standard Airborne Digital Computer
I S A G A	International Simulation And Gaming Association
I S A H M	International Society for Animal and Human Mycology
I S A P	Interactive Survey Analysis Package
I S A T A	International Symposium on Automotive Technology and Automation
I S A V V T	International Symposium on the Aerodynamics and Ventilation of Vehicle Tunnels
I S B D (M)	International Standard Bibliographic Description for Monographic Publications
I S B D (N B M)	International Standard Bibliographic Description for Non-Book Materials
I S B D (S)	International Standard Bibliographic Description for Serials
I S C R E	International Symposium on Chemical Reaction Engineering
I S C S	International Symposium on Cooling Systems
I S D S / I C	International Centre of the International Serials Data System (of UNESCO)
I S D T	International Symposium on Dredging Technology
I S E E	International Sun Earth Explorer
I S E F	International Science and Engineering Fair (USA) (designed to popularize science in high schools and administered by Science Service, a non-profit organization)
I S I	Information Sciences Institute (Southern California University (USA))
I S I R	International Society for Invertebrate Reproduction
I S I S	International Species Inventory System (at the Minnesota Zoological Garden and sponsored by the American Association of Zoological Parks and Aquariums)

I S I T	Intensifier Silicon Intensifier Target
I S L W G	International Shipping Legislation Working Group (of UNCTAD)
I S M	Institute of Sports Medicine
	Interstellar Matter
I S Ma C	Industrial Safety Management Centre (Glasgow College of Technology)
I S M L S	Interim-Standard Microwave Landing System
I S M S	Inherently Safe Mining Systems
I S O C C	Input System for Operator Connected Calls
I S O D O C	International Centre for Standards in Information and Documentation (of ISO)
I S O N	Isolation Network
I S P O	International Society for Prosthetics and Orthotics
I S Q A	Israel Society for Quality Assurance (Israel)
I S R I	Israel Shipping Research Institute (Israel)
I S R R	International Symposium on Roofs and Roofing
I S R S A	International Synthetic Rubber Safety Association
I S S	International Switching Symposium
	Ion Scattering Spectroscopy
I S S L S	International Symposium on Subscriber Loops and Services
I S S M	Incompletely Specified Sequential Machine
I S S M S	Integrated Support Services Management System (US A
I S S O L	International Society for the Study of the Origin of Lif
I S V A	Incorporated Society of Valuers and Auctioneers
I T A	International Tin Agreement (an organisation)
	International Tunnelling Association
I T C	International Thyroid Conference
I T C A	International Typographic Composition Association (USA)
I T C C	International Technical Cooperation Centre (of the Association of Engineers and Architects (Israel))
I T C M	Integrated Tactical Counter-Measures
I T C U	International Technological Collaboration Unit (of the Dept of Trade)
I T E	Institute of Television Engineers (Japan)
	Institute of Terrestrial Ecology (of the Natural Environment Research Council)
I T E C	International Total Energy Congress

I T E D	Integrated Trajectory Error Display
I T F	Institut Textile de France (France) (Textile Institute of France)
I T R U	Industrial Training Research Unit (University College, London)
I U A T	International Union Against Tuberculosis (France)
I U E	International Ultraviolet Explorer
I U I E C	Inter-University Institute of Engineering Control
I U I S	International Union of Immulogical Societies
I U M I	International Union of Maritime Insurance
I U S S P	International Union for the Scientific Study of Population (Belgium)
I V R	Instrumented Visual Range
I V S	Integrated Versaplot Software
	Instituto Venezolano de los Seguros Sociales (Venezuela) (Venezuelan Institute of the Social Security Services)
I W C S	International Wire and Cable Symposium
I W P A	International Word Processing Association
I W P P A	Independent Waste Paper Processors Association
I W S O M	Institute of Practitioners in Work Study, Organisation and Methods
I W S P	Institute of Work Study Practitioners (merged with The Organisation and Methods Society in 1975 to form the Institute of Practitioners in Work Study, Organisation and Methods)

J

J - S I I D S	Joint-Services (USDOD) Interior Intruder Detection System
J A C A	Japan Air Cleaning Association (Japan)
J A D P U	Joint Automatic Data Processing Unit (of the Home Office and London Metropolitan Police)
J A I M S	Japan-America Institute of Management Science (Hawaii)
J A M S A T	Japan Radio Amateur Satellite Corporation
J A P E X	Japan Petroleum Exploration Company (Japan)
J A R S	Journalisation And Recovery System
J A S	Japan Agricultural Standards (Japan)
	Japan Association of Shipbuilders (Japan)

J A T C A	Joinery And Timber Construction Association (of NFBT
J A W S	Jet Advance Warning System
J B P A	Japan Book Publishers Association (Japan)
J C A P	Joint Conventional Ammunition Panel (USDOD)
J C I I	Japan Camera and Optical Instruments Inspection and Testing Institute (Japan)
J C M C	Joint Conference on Medical Conventions
J C O	Joint Consultative Organisation for Research and Development in Agriculture and Food (of MAFF, Agricultural Reseach Council and Dept of Agriculture and Fisheries of Scotland)
J C P D S	Joint Committee on Powder Diffraction Standards (USA) (an international organization)
J D S	Job Diagnosis Survey
J E M	Jet Engine Modulation
J E N C	Joint Emergency National Committee for the building industry
J E O L	Japan Electron Optics Laboratory (Japan) (a company)
J E P O S S	*Javelin (Canadian Javelin Ltd)* Experimental Protection Oil Sands System
J E T	Joint European Torus (a project of EURATOM)
J F S	Jet Fuel Starter
J H	Juvenile Hormone
J I B P	Japan International Biological Programme
J I E	Junior Institution of Engineers (became Institution of General Technician Engineers, 1971)
J I E A	Japan Industrial Explosives Association (Japan)
J L A	Jamaica Library Association
J L O	Joint Liaison Organization (of RIBA, IOB, RICS, ICE, IEE, IHVE, IMechE, IStructE and RTPI)
J M I	Japan Machinery and Metal Inspection Institute (Japan)
J M P A B	Joint Materiel Priotities and Allocation Board (USDOD)
J M T B A	Japan Machine Tool Builders Association (Japan)
J N T O	Japan National Tourist Organization (Japan)
J O E R A	Japan Optical Engineering Research Association (Japan)
J O I D E S	Joint Oceanographic Institutions for Deep Earth Sampling (now an international project though still mainly funded by NSF (USA))
J O L	Job Organisation Language

J O N S D A P	Joint North Sea Data Acquisition Project
J O N S I S	Joint North Sea Information Systems (an informal group from scientific institutes in Belgium, Germany, Great Britain, Netherlands and Sweden to undertake JONSDAP during IDOE)
J O N S W A P	Joint North Sea Wave Project
J O T	Junction Optimisation Technique
J P L	Jet Propulsion Laboratory (California Institute of Technology) (operated for NASA (USA))
J R I A	Japan Rubber Industry Association
J S C	*Lyndon B Johnson* Space Center (of NASA (USA))
J S G	Joint Space Group (consisting of UKISC and DOI)
J S I A	Japan Software Industry Association (Japan)
J S L E	Japan Society of Lubrication Engineers (Japan)
J S S A	Japan Student Science Awards
J T C	Japan Tobacco Corporation (Japan)
J T C G/A L N N O	Joint Technical Coordinating Group for Air Launched Non-Nuclear Ordnance (USDOD)
J T G G / A S	Joint Technical Coordinating Group on Aircraft Survivability (USDOD)
J T D E	Joint Technology Demonstrator Engine
J T I D S	Joint (USAF and USN) Tactical Information Distribution System
J W P A C	Joint Waste Paper Advisory Council

K

K A M E D O	Swedish Organizing Committee for Disaster Medicine (Sweden)
K C L A	Known Coal Leasing Area (USA)
K E P	Key-Entry Processing
K E R M I	Kereskedelmi Minosgelle Norzo Intezet (Hungary) (Authority for Information Labelling)
K G R A	Known Geothermal Resource Area (USA)
K I N S Y M	Kinematic Synthesis
K I S R	Kuwait Institute for Science Research (Kuwait)
K L H	Keyhole Limpet Haemocyanin
K M S	Kansas Medical Society (USA)
K N P C	Kuwait National Petroleum Company (Kuwait)
K N V D	Koninklijk Nederlands Verbond van Drukkerijen (Netherlands) (Royal Netherlands Printing Assoc)

K O P	Kansallis-Osake-Pankii (Finland) (national bank)
K O R D I	Korean Ocean Research and Development Institute (South Korea)
K S A	Eidgenossisches Kommission für die Sicherheit von Atomlagen (Switzerland) (Federal Commission for the Safety of Nuclear Power Plants)
K S H	Kozponti Statisztikai Hivatel (Hungary) (Central Statistical Office)
K S S	Eidgenossisches Kommission zur Stahlenschutz (Switzerland) (Federal Commission for Radiation Protection)
K T B L	Kuratorium für Technik und Bauwesen in der Land- wirtschaft (Germany) (Council for Agricultural Engineering and Farm Building)
K W U C	Keyword and Universal Decimal Classification

L

L A	Linoleic Acid
L A A F	Libyan Arab Air Force (Libya)
L A B R V	Large Ballistic Re-entry Vehicle
L A C	Laboratory Accreditation Committee (of AIHA (USA))
	List of Assessed Contractors (issued by MOD)
L A C A C	Latin American Civil Aviation Commission
L A C A T E	Low Atmospheric Composition And Temperature Experiment
L A C I E	Large Area Crop Inventory Experiment (of USDA, NAS and NOAA (USA)) (aboard the second Earth Resources Technology Satellite
L A C I R S	Latin American Communication Information Retrieval System (of INCIRS (of University of Florida (USA))
L A C V	Lighter, Amphibious, Air Cushion Vehicle
L A D D	Low Altitude Drogue Delivery
L A D D E R	Life Assurance Direct Entry and Retrieval
L A D I E S	*Los Alamos (Scientific Laboratory)* (USA) Digital Image Enhancement Software
L A D I R	Low-cost Arrays for Detection of Infra-Red
L A G B	Linguistics Association of Great Britain
L A G E O	Laser Geodynamic Satellite
L A H A W S	Laser Homing and Warning System

106

L A I	Latex Agglutination-Inhibition
L A I R S	Labor Agreement Information Retrieval System (of USCSC)
L A L A	Linoleic Acid-Like Activity
L A L S D	Language for Automated Logic and System Design
L A L U C	Local Authority Land Use Classification system
L A M M A	Laser Microprobe Mass Analyser
L A M P	Logic Analyser for Maintenance Planner
L A M S	Land Acquisition and Management Scheme
L A M S A C	Local Authorities Management Services And Computer Committee (merged with LBMSU in 1975) (name of merged organisation to be retained)
L A N D S A T	previously known as Earth Resources Technology Satellite (ERTS)
L A N T S A R	Atlantic International Air and Surface Search and Rescue Seminar
L A P C O	Lavan Petroleum Company (Iran) (partly government owned)
L A R A M	Line-Addressable Random-Access Memory
L A R C	Leukocyte Automatic Recognition Computer
	Library Automation Research and Consulting Association (USA) (now the Library Information Science Division of the World Information Systems Exchange)
L A R I A T	Laser Radar Intelligence Acquisition Technology
L A S	Look-out Aiming Sight
L A S C O T	Large Screen Colour Television
L A S E O R S	London and South Eastern Operational Research Society
L A S I	Landing-Site Indicator
L A S L	Los Alamos (New Mexico) Scientific Laboratory (of ERDA (USA))
L A S S I W	Low Airspeed Sensing and Indicating Equipment
L A T A R	Laser-Augmented Target Acquisition and Recognition system
L A V M	LORAN Automatic Vehicle Monitoring
L B A	Lifting-Body-Airship
	London Boroughs Association
L B I R	Laser Beam Image Reproducer
L B M S U	London Boroughs Management Service Unit (merged with LAMSAC in 1975)
L B R	Laser Beam Recorder
L B T	Light-Beam Transmissometer

L C	Liquid-Crystal
	Localised Corrosion
	Locus Coaruleus
L C A C M	Liaison Committee of Architects of the *Common Market*
L C C I	London Chamber of Commerce and Industry
L C F S P R	Last Come, First Served Preemptive Resumé
L C G	Load Classification Group
L C G T / I G S	Low Cost Graphics Terminal/Interactive Graphics System
L C L	Lymphoblastoid Cell Line
L C L S C	Life-Cycle Logistic Support Cost
L C M S	Life Cycle Management System
	Low Cost Modular Spacecraft
L C S	Laboratory of Computer Science (Massachusetts General Hospital (USA))
L C S O	Low Cost Systems Office (of NASA (USA))
L C V	Low Calorific Value
L C X T	Large Cosmic X-ray Telescope
L D	Lymphocyte Defined
L D A	Land Development Aircraft
	Lymphocyte Dependent Antibody
L D D O	Long-Distance Diesel Oil
L D L	Loudness Discomfort Level
L D O	Light Diesel Oil
L E A H S	Life-time Evaluation and Analysis of Heterogeneous System
L E C	London Education Classification
L E C A	Light European Combat Aircraft
L E E	Laser Energy Evaluator
L E F T A	Labour (ie) (The Labour Party) Economic, Finance and Taxation Association
L E M	Leukocytic Endogenous Mediator
L E N D S	Library Extends Catalog Access and New Delivery System (of Georgia Institute of Technology (USA))
L E Q	Equivalent Continuous Sound Level
L E R C	Laramie Energy Research Center (of ERDA (USA))
L F R E D	Liquid-Fuelled Ramjet Engine
L G B	Laser Guided Bomb
L G C	Laboratory of the Government Chemist (now of DoI)

L G V	Lymphogranuloma Venereum
L H A	Landing Helicopter Assault ship (now known as General Purpose Amphibious Assault)
L H D	Load-Haul-Dump machinery
L H R	Long-term Heart Rate
L H R H	Luteinising Hormone-Releasing Hormone
L I A	Laser Institute of America (USA)
	Lead Industries Association (USA)
L I F E	Laser Induced Fluorescence of the Environment
L I L A	Life Insurance Logistics Automated
L I M	Line Insulation Monitor
	Line Interface Module
	Liquid Injection Moulding
L I N O C	Linear Optical Coincidence
L I N S	Laser -gyro Inertial Navigation System
L I Q S S	Liquid Steady State
L I Q T	Liquid Transient
L I S	Laser Isotope Separation
L I S A	Lead-In-Steel Analyser
L I S P B	Lithospheric Seismic Profile in Britain
L I T	Local Income Tax
L L A T I S	Low Light And Thermal Imaging Systems
L L C C A	Long Life Cycle Cost Avionics
L L R S	Laser Lightning Rod System
L M A	Laser-Microspectrochemical Analysis
L M C	Lymphocyte Mediated Cytotoxity
L M E	Liquid Metal Embrittlement
L M E C	Liquid Metal Engineering Centre (formerly of USAEC) (now of ERDA (USA))
L M I	Leucocyte Migration Inhibition
L M R U	Library Management Research Unit (University of Cambridge)
L N B	Large Navigation Buoy
L N R	Low Noise Receiver
L N T W T A	Low-Noise Travelling-Wave Tube Amplifier
L O B O	Lobe-On-Receive-Only
L O C M O S	Locally Oxidised Complementary Metal Oxide Semiconductor
L O D I F	Long Distance Infrared Flash Camera

L O F A R	Low-Frequency Omnidirectional Acoustic-frequency Analysis and Recording
L O G A L	Logical Algorithmic Language
L O G C	Logistics Center (US Army)
L O I S	Library Order Information System (of the Library of Congress (USA))
L O P	Limit of Proportionality
L O P S	*Lloyds (Register of Shipping)* Ocean Engineering Platform System
L O R A S	Low-Range Omni-directional Airspeed System
L O R D S	Logic and Register-Transfer Design System
L O R E	Land Ordnance Engineering Branch (of Canadian Armed Forces)
L O R I D S	Long Range Iranian Detection System (Iran)
L O S	Law of the Sea Conference
L O T I S	Logic, Timing and Sequencing
L P C G	Laser Planning and Co-ordination Group (of ERDA (USA))
L P D	Labelled Plan Display
L P I	Low-Probability-of-Intercept radar
L P L	List Processing Language
L P O	Liquid Phase Oxidation
L P S T T L	Low Power Schottky Transistor-Transistor Logic
L R - P A S S	*Lloyds (Register of Shipping)* Plan Appraised System for Ships
L R - S A F E	*Lloyds (Register of Shipping)* Ship Analysis using Finite Element
L R A A M	Long-Range Air-to-Air Missile
L R A C	Long-Run Average Cost Curve
L R B C	*Lloyds (Register of Shipping)* Building Certificate
L R C	Light, Rapid, Comfortable railway train
	Lipid Research Clinic (of NHLI (USA))
L R C C	Laboratoire de Recherches et de Control du Caoutchouc (France)
L R D	Labelled Radar Display
L R E S	Linear Rocket Engine System
L R I S	*Lloyds (Register of Shipping)* Industrial Services
L R M	Linear Regression Model
L R M G	Lockless Rifle/Machine Gun
L R M T R	Laser Ranger and Marked-Target Receiver

L R R S	Long-Range Radar Station
L R S	London Research Station (of the British Gas Corporation)
L R S I	Low-temperature Re-usable Surface Insulation
L R S M	Long Range Seismic Measurement
L R T	Light Rail Transit
L R V	Light Rail Vehicle
L S A	Laser-Supported Absorption
	London School of Accountancy
L S A C	Low-pressure Suction Air Conveyor
L S C	Linear Slope Controlled
L S D	Leadless Sealed Device
	Language for Systems Development
L S E B	Life Sciences and Biomedical Engineering Branch (of Aerospace Medical Association (USA))
L S I	Large Scale Integration
	Lateral Shear Interferometer
	Lunar Science Institute (operated by the Universities Space Research Association—a consortium of 43 universities (USA))
L S I S	Laser Scan Inspection System
L S M	Laboratory for the Structure of Matter (USN)
	Lancastrian School of Management (of the Lancashire Education Authority)
	Linear Synchronous Motor
L S R B	Linear Sound Ranging Base
L T A	Lighter-Than-Air
L T M	Laser Target Marker
	Low Thermal Mass
L T M R	Laser Target Marker/Ranger
L U C S	Land Use Cost Studies
L U M O	Lowest Unfilled Molecular Orbit
L V A	Landing Vehicle Assault
L V A S	Left Ventricular Assist System ("mechanical heart")
L V C E R I	Luncheon Voucher Catering Education Research Institute (Ealing Technical College, London)
L V D	Low Voltage Directive (of EEC)
L V F A	Low Velocity Friction Apparatus test
L V G O	Light Vacuum Gas Oil
L V N	Light Virgin Naphtha
L V R J	Low Volume Ramjet

L V W	Linked Vertical Well
L W C	Light Weight Coated Paper
L W D	Laser Welder/Driller
L W G R	Light-water-cooled, Graphite-moderated Reactor
L W I R	Long Wavelength Infra-Red
L W L D	Light Weight Laser Designator
L W P F	Long Wave Pass Filter
L W R	Light-water-cooled and moderated Reactor

M

M - D A S	Multispectral Data Analysis System
M & Q	prefix to numbered series of forms on Mines and Quarries (now issued by the Department of Energy)
M A	Maleic Anhydride
	prefix to numbered-dated series of Marine Standards issued by BSI
	Microscopic Agglutination
	Mill-Anneal
M A A	Medical Artists Association of Great Britain
M A A R M	Memory-Aided Anti-Radiation Missile
M A B	Man and Biosphere (a programme of UNESCO)
M A B S	Marine Automation-Bridge System
M A B S C	Management and Behavioral Science Center (University of Pennsylvania (USA))
M A C	Measurement and Analysis Centre
	Multifunctional Automobile Communication
M A C O S	Man: A Course of Study (a behavioural science course developed with NSF (USA) support)
M A D I S	Manual Aircraft Data Input System
M A F	Ministry of Agriculture and Forestry (Japan)
M A F V A	Miniature Armoured Fighting Vehicles Association
M A I N L I N E	Monitored Alarm Indication Line
M A L N	Minimum Air Low Noise
M A L O R	Mortar and Artillery Locating Radar
M A L S C E	Massachusetts Association of Land Surveyors and Civil Engineers (USA)
M A N F E P	*Manitoba (University*, Canada) Finite Element Programme
M A N I F I L E	*Manitoba (University*, Canada) File of World's Non-Ferrous Metallic Deposits

M A N M A M	Manufacturing Management
M A N T R A P	Machine and Network Transients Programme
M A O T	Medium Aperture Optical Telescope
M A P	Master Activity Programming
	Multibus Accounting Package
M A P D	Maximum Allowable Percent Defective
M A P D A	Mid-American Periodical Distributors Association (USA)
M A P P L E	Macro-Associative Processor Programming Language
M A P S	Manufacturing and Production System
	Minerals Analysis and Policy System (of Dept of the Interior (USA))
M A P W	Medical Association for Prevention of War
M A R	Minimum Acceptable Rate of Return
M A R B I	Machine-Readable Form of Bibliographic Information
M A R C	Manufacturers Association of Radiators and Convectors
M A R C C O	Master Real-time Circulation Controller
M A R C S	Marine Computer System
M A R K F E D	Punjab State Co-operative Supply and Marketing Federation (India)
M A R L I B	an information service based on the Institute of Marine Engineers Library
M A R O T S	Marine Orbital Technical Satellite
M A R P E X	Management of Repair Parts Expenditure system (US Army)
M A R R E S	Manual Radar Reconnaissance Exploitation System
M A R S	Magnetostatic Rate Sensor
	Mid-Air Retrieval System for drones (aircraft)
	Military Affiliate Radio Service (USA)
M A R S / S I P	Mohawk Access and Retrieval System/Self-Interpreting Programme generator
M A R S A S	Marine Search and Attack System (US Marine Corps)
M A S	Management *or* Managerial Appraisal System
M A S A R	Microwave Accurate Surface Antenna Reflector
M A S C	Multiplicative and Additive Signature Correction algorithm
M A S C O T	Modular Approach to Software Operation and Test
M A S S	Matrix Analysis Seismic Stress
	Multiple-Anvil Sliding System

M A S T	Michigan Alcoholism Screening Test
	Military Anti-Shock Trousers
M A S U	Multiple Acceleration Sensor Unit
M A T	Magyar Aluminiumipari Troszt (Hungary) (Hungarian Aluminium Corporation)
M A X N E T	Modular Application Executive for Computer Networks
M B S A	Model-Based System Analysis
M B S D	Multi-Barrel Smoke Discharger
M B T	Modified Boiling Test
M C A C	Measurement, Control and Automation Conference (representing Control and Automation Manufacturers Association, British Industrial Measuring and Control Apparatus Manufacturers Association, Electronic Engineering Association, and Scientific Instrument Manufacturers Association of Great Britain)
M C B	Metric Conversion Board (Australia)
M C B P	Muscle Calcium Binding Parvalbumin
M C C	Multilayer Ceramic Chip
M C D	Magnetic Crack Definer
M C E B	Military Communications Electronics Board (USDOD)
M C G S	Microwave Command Guidance System
M C I	Meal, Combat, Individual
	Multichip Integration
M C I D	Multi-purpose Concealed Intrusion Detection
M C L	Macro Creation Language
	Most Comfortable Level
M C M	Minimum Commitment Method
M C T	Manganese Cyclopentadienyltricarbonyl
M D	Marek's Disease
M D D	Machine Dependent Data
M D H	Minimum Descent Height
	Multidirectional Harassment
M D L	Modular Design Language
M D R S F	Multi-Dimensional Random Sea Facility (of Hydraulics Research Station)
M D S	Microprogrammme Design Support Subsystem
M E C A	Molecular Emission Cavity Analysis

114

M E C O M	Marine Engine Condition Monitor
M E C O N	Metallurgical and Engineering Consultants (India) Ltd (India) (a subsidiary of SAIL (India))
M E C U	Main Engine Electronic Control Unit
M E D	Multi-Effect Distillation
M E D E A	Multi-discipline Engineering Design Evaluation and Analysis System (a project of the US Army)
M E D I A	Modular Electronic Digital Instrumentation Assemblies
M E D I A T O R	Media Time Ordering and Reporting
M E D I N F O	Conference on Medical Informatics
M E L T A N	Mechanical Engineering Laboratory Thermal Analog Network
M E M A C	Machinery and Equipment Manufacturers Association of Canada (Canada)
M E M O	Maximising the Efficiency of Machine Operations (an advisory service of the Food, Drink and Tobacco Industry Training Board)
M E M T R B	Mechanical Engineering and Machine Tools Requirements Board (of DoI)
M E O	Manned Earth Observatory
M E R A D O	Mechanical Engineering Research and Development Organization (India)
M E R E S	Matrix of Environmental Residuals for Energy Systems
M E R L I N	Machine Readable Library Information
M E S A	Marine Ecosystems Analysis (a program of NOAA (USA))
	Mining Enforcement and Safety Administration (of Bureau of Mines (USA))
M E S H	A European Industrial Consortium (consisting of Aeritalia (Italy), ERNO (Germany), Fokker VFW (Netherlands), Hawker Siddeley Dynamics (UK), Matra (France) and SAAB-Scania (Sweden))
M E T C H E M	Metals/Materials, Fabricating and Testing Conference and Show for the Petrochemical Industry (USA)
M E T E	Multiple Engagement Test Environment
M E T T	Manned, Evasive Target Tank
M F	Mitogenic Factor
M F A	Multi-Fibre Arrangement (of GATT)
M F C	Membrane Fecal Coliform
M F C D	Modular Flare Chaff Dispenser

M F C S	Mathematical Foundations of Computer Science
M F P A	Monolithic Focal Plane Array
M F T	Microflocculation Test
M F T W	Machine-tool, Fixture, Tool and the Workpiece
M F U S Y S	Microfiche File Update System
M G F	Macrophage Growth Factor
M G I	Military Geographic Intelligence
M G M I	Mining, Geological and Metallurgical Institute (India)
M H B	Mueller-Hinton Broth
M H C	Major Histocompatibility Complex
M H G	Message Header Generator
M H I C	Microwave Hybrid Integrated Circuit
M H T U	Materials Handling Trials Unit (British Army)
M H V	Mouse Hepatitis Virus
M H W - R T G	Multi-Hundred-Watt Radioisotope Thermoelectric Generator
M I	Michelson Interferometer
M I A	Missile Intelligence Agency (US Army)
M I B A R	Multi-channel In-band Airborne Relay
M I C A	Man-computer Interaction in Commercial Applications (a part of HUSAT Loughborough University Research Group)
M I C R A D S	Microwave Radiation System
M I C R O S I D	Small Seismic Intrusion Detector
M I C S	Medical Instrument Calibration System
M I D	Microwave Division (of ISRO (India))
M I D A S	Materials for Industry Data and Applications Service (a materials advisory service of PERA)
	Meteorological Information and Dose Acquisition System
	MICOM (US Army) Digital Analysis Code
	Missile Detection Anti Surveillance (a project of USAF)
M I D C O M	Centre for the Development of the Metals Industry of Malaysia (Malaysia)
M I D M S	Machine Independent Data Management System
M I D O N A S	Military Documentation System (Dept of Defence (Switzerland))
M I D U	Mineral Investigation Drilling Unit (of Dept of Mines (Malaysia))
M I F	Migration-Inhibition Factor

116

M I F I L	Microwave Filter Design
M i G	Mikoyan-Gurevich
M I I A	Medical Intelligence and Information Agency (US Army)
M I I Z	Moscow Institute of Engineers of Land Use (USSR)
M I L E S	Multi-phenomenon Intrusion Line Sensor
M I M I C	Microfilm Information Master Image Converter
M I M S	*Mitrol* Industrial Management System
	Multiple Independent Manoeuvring Submunitions
M I N D	National Association for Mental Health
M I N D O	Modified Intermediate Neglect of Differential Overlap
M I N I	Heuristic Logic Minimization Technique
	Minicomputer Industry National Interchange (USA) (an association)
M I N I S I D	Manually Implanted Seismic Intrusion Detector
M I N O S	Mixed Integer Operational Scheduling
M I N P O S T E L	Ministry of Posts and Telecommunications (became Broadcast Dept of the Home Office, 1974)
M I P S	Modular Integrated Pallet System
M I R	Ministère de l'Industrie et de la Recherche (France) (Ministry of Industry and Research)
M I R A C	Microfilmed Reports and Accounts
M I R A D S	*Marshall (George C Marshall)* Space Flight Center (NASA (USA)) Information Retrieval and Display System
M I R S	Multi-purpose Infra-Red Sight
M I R V	Multiple Independently-targeted Re-entry Vehicle
M I S E R	Management Information System for Expenditure Reporting
	Methodology of Industrial System Energy Requirements (a project of ETSU (Dept of Energy))
	Moorfields (Eye Hospital, London) Information System Exception Reporting
M I S I	Multi-path Inter-symbol Interference
M I S S	Multi-Input-Safety-Shutdown-System
M I S T E R	Mobile Integrated System Trainer, Evaluator and Recorder
M I U	Maharishi International University (USA)
M L A	Manitoba Library Association (Canada)
	Mississippi Library Association (USA)

M L P W B	Multi-Layer Printed Wiring Board
M L R	Minimum Lending Rate
	Mixed Lymphocyte Reaction
	Mortar (Weapon) Locating Radar
M M	Macromodule
M M A D	Mass Median Aerodynamic Diameter
M M A J	Metal Mining Agency of Japan (Japan)
M M A S	Manufacturing Management Accounting Systems
M M C	Methylmercuric Chloride
	Monopolies and Mergers Commission
M M D	Mass Median Diameter
M M F R	Maximum Mid-expiratory Flow Rate
M M I	Macrophage Migration Inhibition
M M I J	Mining and Metallurgical Institute of Japan (Japan)
M M I S	Medicaid Management Information System
M M L E S	Map-Match Location-Estimation System
M M M A	Metalforming Machinery Makers Association
M M R	Method of Mixed Ranges
M M M R P V	Modular Multi-Mission Remotely Piloted Vehicle
M M S	Microfiche Management System
M M T	Multiple-Mirror Telescope
M N C	Medical Neurosecretory Brain Cells
M N L S	Modified New Least Squares
M O A T	Missile On Aircraft Test
M O B A	Mobility Operations for Built-up Areas (a project of US Army)
M O C	Minimal Oxygen Consumption
	Modular Organisation Charting
M O C B	Minimum Oil Circuit Breaker
M O D E	Mid-Ocean Dynamic Experiment (of American and British Universities)
M O D S	Medically Orientated Data System (of FDA (USA))
M O D U S	Modular One Dynamic User System
M o F	Ministry of Finance (Japan)
M O L D S	North American Conference on the Modernization of Land Data Systems
M O L P	Multiple Objective Linear Programming
M O P S Y	Multi-programming Operating System
M O R	Mandatory Occurrence Reporting

M O R S	Midland Operational Research Society
M O S P O	Mobile Satellite Photometric Observatory (of NASA (USA))
M O S S	Modelling Systems
M O S S T	Ministry of State for Science and Technology (Canada)
M O S T	*Maynard (H B Maynard & Co Ltd)* Operation Sequence Technique
	Micromation (Ltd) Output Software Translator
M O T	Ministry of Transport (Canada)
M O T A T	Museum of Transport and Technology (New Zealand)
M O U	Memorandum Of Understanding
M O V I M S	Motor Vehicle Information Management System
M O W D	Ministry of Works and Development (New Zealand)
M O W O S	*Meteorological Office* Weather Observing System
M P A	Mortar Producers Association
M P A D	Maximum Permissible Annual Dose
M P A I	Maximum Permissible Annual Intake
M P C	Mother-of-Pearl Clouds
M P C A G	Military Parts Control Advisory Group (USDOD)
M P D	Mean Population Doubling
M P E S	Mathematical, Physical and Engineering Science (a directorate of NSF (USA))
M P F W	Multi-shot Portable Flame Weapon
M P G S	Micro Programme Generating System
M P I	Multiphoton Ionization
M P L	Melamine Paper Laminate
M P M	Message Processing Module
M P M I	Magazine and Paperback Marketing Institute (USA)
M P P M	Materials-Process-Product Model
M P Q	Manpower Planning Quotas
M P S	Mathematical Programming System
M P T	Ministry of Posts and Telecommunications (became Broadcast Department of the Home Office in 1974)
M P T	prefix to numbered series issued by the Radio Regulatory Department of the Home Office and published by HMSO
M Q V	Ministère de la Qualité de la Vie (France) (Ministry of the Quality of Life)
M R A A M	Medium-Range Air-to-Air Missile
M R B	Magnetospheric Radio Burst

119

M R B	Motorized Rifle Battalion
M R C	Medical Research Council (Canada)
M R C A	Multi-Role Combat Aircraft (now called *"Tornado"*)
M R D O S	Mapped Real-time Disc Operating System
M R E	Modern Ramjet Engine
M R F	Mesencephalic Reticular Formation
M R F I T	Multiple Risk Factor Intervention Trial for coronary heart disease (of NHLI (USA))
M R I	Meal, Ready-to-eat, Individual (military rationing)
M R L	Multiple Rocket Launcher
m R N A	Messenger Ribonucleic Acid
M R P	Materials Requirements Planning
M R R D B	Malaysian Rubber Research and Development Board
M R S	Midlands Research Station (of the British Gas Corporation)
M R S A	Medium Range Surveillance Aircraft
M R T	Mean Radiant Temperature
M R T P	Monopolies and Restrictive Trade Practices Commission (India)
M S	The Metals Society
M S A	Manchester Society of Architects
M S A C 2	Milwaukee (USA) Symposium on Automatic Computation and Control
M S A T	Marine Services Association of Texas (USA)
M S B L S	Microwave Scanning Beam Landing System
M S C	Manpower Services Commission
M S C E	Magnetic-Strip Credit Card
M S C I C	Maryland State Colleges Information Center (USA)
M S D	Marine Sanitation Devices
M S D S	Multi-Spectral Scanner and Data System
M S I	Medium Scale Integration
M S I R I	Mauritius Sugar Industry Research Institute (Mauritius)
M S P S	Multiphase Serial-Parallel-Serial Storage
M S R	Mechanical Strain Recorder
M S R C E	Multi-carrier Station Radio Control Equipment
M S S	Mass Storage System
	Multi-Spectral Scanner *or* Sensor
M S S M	Multiple-Sine-Slit Microdensitometer
M S S N Y	Medical Society of the State of New York (USA)

M S T	Monolithic System Technology
M S T C	Management Systems Training Council (formerly the O & M Training Council)
M S U S M	Medical Society of the United States and Mexico
M S V	Multi-purpose Submersible Vessel
M T / S T	Magnetic Tape Selectric Typewriter
M T A	Microwave Transistor Amplifier
M T B M A	Mean-Time Between Maintenance-Action
M T B T	Miniature Thermal Bar Torch
M T C S	Minimum Core Teleprocessing Control System
	Minimum Telecommunications System
M T L	Merged Transistor Logic
	Mixed Thermoluminescence
M T M C	Military Traffic Management Command (US Army)
M T N	Multilaterial Trade Negotiations
M T P	Microtuble Protein
M 2 S	Modular Multiband Scanner
M T S T	Magnetic Tape Selectric Typewriter
	Maximal Treadmill Stress Time
M U A	Mail Users Association
M U C I A	Midwest Universities Consortium for International Activities (USA)
M U D D	Multisource Unified Data Distribution
M U L E	Modular Universal Laser Equipment
M U L E S	Missouri (USA) Uniform Law Enforcement System
M U L Q U A L	Multiple Goal Water Quality Model
M U L S	Minnesota (University) (USA) Union List of Serials
M U L T E W S	Multiple Target Electronic Warfare System
M U R F A A M C E	Mutual Reduction of Forces and Armaments and Associated Measures in Central Europe (negotiations between NATO and the Warsaw Treaty Organisation)
M U S T A R D	Modernisation of Units for Steelmaking At *River Don* (River Don Works, Sheffield of the British Steel Corporation)
M U S T R A C	Multiple-Simultaneous-Target Steerable Telemetry Tracking system
M U T T	Military Utility Tactical Truck
M U V I N	Multi-Unit Vibration Impact Neutralizer
M U X	Multiplexing

M V E	Murray Valley Encephalitis
M V R O	Minimum-Variance Reduced-Order
M V S	Multiple Virtual Storages
M W D	Ministry of Works and Development (New Zealand)
M W S	Magnetic Weapon Sensor
M W V	Mineralolwirtschaftsverband (Germany) (Oil Industry Association)

N

N A A Q S	National Ambient Air Quality Standards (of EPA (USA))
N A B	National Apex Body (India)
N A B C	National Association of Building Centres
N A C	Natal Associated Collieries (South Africa)
N A C E	National Advisory Committee on Electronics (India)
N A C E D	National Advisory Council on the Employment of the Disabled
N A C H A	National Automated Clearing House Association (USA)
N A C I L A	National Council of Indian Library Associations (India) (became FILA in 1975)
N A C L	Nippon Aviotronics Company Ltd (Japan)
N A C O S H	National Advisory Committee on Occupational Safety and Health (of Dept of Labor (USA))
N A C R O	National Association for the Care and Resettlement of Offenders
N A C S	National Association of College Stores (USA)
N A D E E C	NATO Defence Electronic Environment Committee
N A D F A S	National Association of Design and Fine Art Societies
N A D O T	North Atlantic Deepwater Oil Terminal
N A G	Numerical Algorithms Group (a non-profit company formed by Nottingham, Birmingham, Manchester, Leeds and Oxford Universities for data processing service internationally to industry and universities)
N A G P M	National Association of Grained Plate Makers (USA)
N A H F O	National Association of Hospital Fire Officers
N A H T	National Association of Head Teachers
N A I M	Number Allocation and Inspection Module
N A I T	Northern Alberta Institute of Technology (Canada)
N A L	National Acoustics Laboratory (Australia)
N A M A	National Automatic Merchandising Association (USA)

N A M D I	National Marine Data Inventory (replaced by ROSCOP of the World Data Center-A, Oceanography (USA)
N A M R A D	Non-Atomic Military Research And Development (a sub-committee of NATO)
N A N A	Northwest Alaska Natives Association (USA)
N A P C	Non-Adherent Peritoneal Cells
N A P C A	National Association of Pipe Coating Applicators (USA)
N A P I M	National Association of Printing Ink Manufacturers (USA)
N A P L	National Association of Printers and Lithographers (USA)
N A Q P	National Association of Quick Printers (USA)
N A R A C	National Association of Refrigeration and Conditioning Contractors (amalgamated with HVCA, 1974)
N A R F	Natural Axial Resonant Frequency
N A R I	National Association of Recycling Industries (USA)
N A R P A	National Air Rifle and Pistol Association
N A S	Northern Archaeological Society
N A S C P	North American Society for Corporate Planning (USA)
N A S D	*NKK (Nippon Kokan* (Japan)) Advanced Ship Design
N A S H A	North American Survival and Homesteading Association (Canada)
N A S N	National Aerometric Surveillance Network (of EPA (USA))
N A S Q A N	National Stream Quality Accounting Network (of the Geological Survey (USA))
N A S W M	National Association of Scottish Woollen Manufacturers
N A T I S	National Information Systems
N A V D A B	NAVSEA Ocean Environmental Acoustic Data Bank (USN)
N A V M A C S	Naval Modular Automated Communications Systems (USN)
N A V M A T	Naval Material Command (USN)
N A V O C E A N O	Naval Oceanographic Office (USN) (now part of the Defense Mapping Agency (USDOD))
N A V O C F O R M E D	Naval On-Call Force for the Mediterranean (of NATO)
N A V O R D	Naval Ordnance Systems Command (USN) (now absorbed into NAVSEA (USN))
N A V S	National Anti-Vivisection Society

N A V S E A	Naval Sea Systems Command (USN)
N A V S H I P S	Naval Ship Systems Command (USN) (now absorbed into NAVSEA (USN))
N A V S T A R	Navigation System using Time and Ranging
N A V T A C	*Nimrod* (Aircraft) Navigation Tactical
N A W E S A	Naval Weapons Engineering Support Activity (USN)
N A W K	National Association of Warehouse Keepers
N A Y E	National Association of Young Entrepreneurs (India)
N B C C A	National Business Council for Consumer Affairs (USA)
N B D	Negative Binomial Distribution
N B S T	National Board for Science and Technology (Eire)
N C A	National Commission on Agriculture (India)
	National Composition Association (of PIA (USA))
	Nonspecific Cross-reacting Antigen
N C A E	National College of Agricultural Engineering (became a School of the Cranfield Institute of Technology in 1975)
N C A R	National Center for Atmospheric Research (of UCAR (USA))
N C C	National Computer Conference (sponsored by AFIPS (USA))
	National Consumer Council
	Nature Conservancy Council (of DoE)
N C C L S	National Committee for Clinical Laboratory Standards (USA)
N C C R	National Center for Resource Recovery (USA)
N C D A D	National Council for Diplomas in Art and Design (amalgamated with CNAA in 1974)
N C E C A	National Council on Education for the Ceramic Arts (USA)
N C E F T	National Commission on Electronic Fund Transfers (USA)
N C F P	National Conference on Fluid Power (USA)
N C F S	Non-Contingent Foot-Shock
N C I C	National Cavity Insulation Council
N C I T	National Council on Inland Transport
N C J R S	National Criminal Justice Reference Service (of LEAA (Dept of Justice (USA))
N C P T	National Conference on Power Transmission (USA)

N C S	National Corrision Service (of Dept of Industry) (at NPL)
N C S L	National Conference of Standards Laboratories (USA)
N C S R	National Centre of Systems Reliability (of UKAEA)
	National Council for Scientific Research (Lebanon)
N C U F	National Computer Users Forum (secretariat at National Computing Centre)
N D A B	Numerical Data Advisory Board (Division of Chemistry and Chemical Technology of NAS/ NRC (USA))
N D B	National Delegates Board (of AGARD (NATO))
N D B O	NOAA Data Buoy Office (USA)
N D C	National Documentation Centre (of NRC (Sudan))
N D D O	Neglect of Diatomic Differential Overlap
N D M C	New Delhi Municipal Committee (India)
N D P	Net Domestic Product
N D P C A L	National Development Programme in Computer Assisted Learning
N D T A A	Non-Destructive Testing Association of Australia (Australia) (now AINDT)
N D T S	Non-Destructive Testing Society of Great Britain (became part of the British Institute of Non-Destructive Testing in 1976)
N E A	Net Energy Analysis
N.E A C H	New England (USA) Automated Clearing House
N E A T	*NCR* Electronic Autocoding Technique
N E B	National Enterprise Board
N E C A P	*NASA* (USA) Energy-Cost Analysis Program
N E D A	National Electronics Development Association (New Zealand)
N E D E L A	Network Definition Language
N E I C	National Energy Information Center (of Federal Energy Agency (USA))
N E I S S	National Electronic Injury Surveillance Safety System (operated by CPSC (USA))
N E G I S T O R	Negative Resistor
N E L	National Engineering Laboratory (previously of DTI, now of DoI)

N E L D I C	*Nippon (Electric Company)* (Japan) Electric Layout Design System for Integrated Circuits
N E O R M P	North-East Ohio Regional Medical Program (USA)
N E P A	National Electric Power Authority (Nigeria)
N E P D B	Navy Environmental Protection Data Base (USN) (now NEPSS)
N E P S S	Naval Environmental Protection Support Service (USN)
N E Q C C	North East Quality Control Conference (USA)
N E S O	Navy Environmental Support Office (of NEPSS (USN))
N E T A N A L	Network Analysis
N E T E	Naval Engineering Test Establishment (of the Canadian Armed Forces)
N E W S C O M P	Newspaper Composition
N E W S T E C	Newspaper Society Technical Conference and Exhibition
N F A	New Fighter Aircraft
N F C G	National Federation of Consumer Groups
N F C P G	National Federation of Catholic Physicians Guilds (USA)
N F D M	Non-Fat Dry Milk
N F D S	National Fire Data Center (of NFPCA (USA))
N F P C A	National Fire Prevention and Control Administration (Dept of Commerce (USA))
N F R S	National Fire Reference (of NFPCA (USA))
N F T	Nutrient Film Technique
N F T A	Niagara Frontier Transportation Authority (USA)
N G L	Natural Gas Liquids
N G O	Non-Governmental Organisation having relationship with the United Nations
N G S	National Geodetic Survey (geodetic program of the National Ocean Survey of NOAA (USA))
N G S D C	National Geophysical and Solar-terrestrial Data Center (of EDS (NOAA) (USA))
N G T E	National Gas Turbine Establishment (now of MoD (PE))
N H G A	National Hang Gliding Association
N H M A	National Housewares Manufacturers Association (USA)
N H O	Northern Hemisphere Observatory (on the island of La Palma in the Canaries)

N H R E	National Hail Research Experiment (of the National Center for Atmospheric Research (USA))
N H S	Normal Human Sera
N I	The Nautical Institute
	Neutralization Index
N I A	National Institute on Aging (of NIH (HEW) (USA))
N I A A A	National Institute for Alcoholism and Alcohol Abuse (of ADAMHA (USA))
N I C O N	Association of Northern Irish Consultants International
N I D A	National Institute for Drug Abuse (of ADAMHA (USA))
	National Investment and Development Authority (Papua New Guinea)
N I E C C	National Industrial Energy Conservation Council (Dept of Commerce (USA))
N I G R O	Northern Ireland General Register Office
N I H B C	Northern Ireland House Building Council
N I I G A I K	Novosibirsk Institute of Engineers of Geodesy, Aerial Surveys and Cartography (USSR)
N I I P	National Institute of Industrial Psychology (reconstituted in 1974)
N I L E C J	National Institute of Law Enforcement and Criminal Justice (Dept of Justice (USA))
N I M T S M	Nauchonolzsledovatelsci Institut po Mechanizatiziva, Tractorno i Selskostopansko (Bulgaria) (Research Institute of Mechanization, Tractor and Agricultural Machinery Construction)
N I P A	National Institute of Public Administration (Bangladesh)
N I P G	Nederlands Instituut voor Praeventieve Gneeskunde (of TNO) (Netherlands) (Netherlands Institute for Preventive Medicine)
N I P H L	Noise-Induced Permanent Hearing Loss
N I P T S	Noise-Induced Permanent Threshold Shift
N I R T	National Iranian Radio and Television (Iran)
N I S C	National Industrial Space Committee (succeeded by UKISC in 1975)
N I S C O N	National Industrial Safety Conference
N I S O	National Industrial Safety Organisation (Eire)
N J S H S	National Junior Science and Humanities Symposium (USA)

N K K	Nippon Kokan (Japan)
N L / 1	Non-programmer Language 1
N L E T S	National Law Enforcement Telecommunications System (USA)
N L M E	Non-Linear Material Effect
N L S	National Library of Scotland
	New Least Squares
	No-Load Start
N L U C	National Land Use Classification system
N M A	National Microfilm Association (USA) (title change to National Micrographics Association in 1975)
N M D A	National Metal Decorators Association (USA)
N M I A	National Meteorological Institute of Athens (Greece)
N M L A	New Mexico Library Association (USA)
N O P S	National Ocean Policy Study (a special Staff group of the US Senate Committee on Commerce)
N O R - L U C S	*Northern Software Consultants* Library Updating and Compiling System
N O R A S I S	Northern Ohio Chapter of ASIS (USA)
N O R D E L	Nordic Electricity Union
N O R G R A I N	North American Grain Charter (USA)
N O R M A L	*Nova (Data General NOVA* Minicomputers) Real-time Macro Language
N O R S	Northern (Maritime) Offshore Resources Study Group (Edinburgh University)
N O S C	Naval Ordnance Systems Command (USN) (now merged into NAVSEA)
N O T A M S	Notices to Airmen
N P A	National Pipeline Authority (Australia)
N P C	National Peanut Council (USA)
N P C C	National Projects Construction Corporation (India) (Government owned)
N P D E S	National Pollution Discharge Elimination Scheme (of EPA (USA))
N P D N	Nordic (Denmark, Finland, Iceland, Norway and Sweden) Public Data Network
N P D O	Non-Profit Distributing Organization
N P G	Nuclear Planning Group (of NDAC (NATO))
N P I	National Productivity Institute (South Africa)

N P L	National Physical Laboratory (formerly of DTI, now of DoI)
N P R C G	Nuclear Public Relations Contact Group (Italy)
N P R D S	Nuclear Plant Reliability Data System (of ANSI (USA))
N P R L	National Physical Research Laboratory (of CSIR (South Africa))
N P V	Nuclear-Polyhedrosis Virus
N Q R	Nuclear Quadruple Resonance
N R A	National Renderers Association (USA)
N R A C	National Research Advisory Council (New Zealand)
N R C	Nuclear Regulatory Commission (USA)
N R D C	National Resources Defense Council (USA)
N R M G	Nederlands Rekenmachine Genootschap (Netherlands)
N R O	National Reconnaissance Office (USA)
N R P C	National Railroad Passenger Corporation (USA) (a quasi-governmental agency)
N R R L	Norsk Radio Relae Liga (Norway) (Norwegian Amateur Radio Relay League)
N S	Neuroelectric Society (USA)
N S B	National Standards Board (Ghana)
N S C	National Seeds Corporation (India)
N S D C	National Serials Data Centre (part of the Bibliographic Services Division of the British Library)
N S E	Nigerian Society of Engineers (Nigeria)
N S E S G	North Sea Environmental Study Group (of seven offshore operators and MAFF)
N S I	Norsk Senter for Informatikk (Norway) (Norwegian Center for Information)
N S I C	National Small Industries Corporation (India)
N S L	National Science Library (Canada) (now part of CISTI)
N S M	New Smoking Material
N S N	NATO Stock Number
N S O S G	North Sea Oceanographic Study Group (of seventeen offshore operators)
N S R A	National Small-bore Rifle Association
N S R C	Natural Science Research Council (Canada)
N S W C	Naval Surface Weapons Center (USN)
N S W P T C	New South Wales Public Transport Commission (Australia)

N T B	Non-Tariff Barriers
N T C	National Terotechnology Centre (of DoI) (operated at Electrical Research Association)
N T D S C	Nondestructive Testing Data Support Center (administered by Defense Supply Agency (USDOD) and operated at the Southwest Research Institute)
N T I A C	Nondestructive Testing Information and Analysis Center (previously operated by AMMRC (US Army)) (now administered by Defense Supply Agency (USDOD) and operated at the Southwest Research Institute)
N T L	Natural Thermoluminescence
N T L S	Non-transposed Loop Sensor
N T S - I	Navigation Technology Satellite One
N T S K	Nordiska Tele-Satelit Kommitten (Nordic Committee for Satellite Telecommunications)
N U R E	National Uranium Resource Evaluation (a program of ERDA (USA))
N U T I S	Numerical and Textual Information System
N V D	Night Viewing Device
N V E B W	Non-Vacuum Electron Beam Welding
N V T	Norwegian Variable Time artillery fuze
N W D C	Navigation/Weapon Delivery Computer
N W L	Naval Weapons Laboratory (USN) (now NSWC (USN))
N W O R G	North Western Operational Research Group
N W R C	Naval War Research Center (US Navy)
N W W A	National Water Wells Association (USA)
N Y M A C	National Young Managers Advisory Committee (of BIM)
N Y R G	New York Rubber Group (USA)
N Y S N I	New York State Nutrition Institute (USA)
N Z B C	New Zealand Broadcasting Corporation (New Zealand) (disbanded 1975)
	New Zealand Book Council (New Zealand)
N Z P C I	New Zealand Prestressed Concrete Institute (New Zealand)
N Z S G	Non-Zero-Sum Game

O

O A C	Oceanic Affairs Committee (of ABOI, BMEC, BNCOE, CBMPE, SUT and UEG)

O A P W L	Overall Power Watt Level
O A S I S	Ohio (Chapters) of the American Society for Information Science (USA)
	Operational Automated Ship's Information System
	Orders, Accounting, Stock, Invoicing and Statistics
O A S P	Over-All Sound Pressure level
O A S P L	Over-All Sound Pressure Level
O B M	Oxygen-Bottom *Maxhutte (Eisenwerk-Gesellschaft Maiximilianshutte)*
O B O E	Offshore Buoy Observing Equipment
O B V	Octane Blending Value
O C A M	Organisation Commune Africaine et Mauricienne (Afro-Maurician Common Organisation)
O C C & D C	Oregon Coastal Conservation and Development Commission (USA)
O C D	Office of Civil Defense (USA) (now Defense Civil Preparedness Agency (joint agency of DOD and NASA (USA))
O C G	Österreichische Computer Gesellschaft (Austria) (Austrian Computer Society)
O C I M F	Oil Companies International Marine Forum (a group of 45 oil firms and tanker owners)
O C L	Operator Control Language
O C M	Oil Content Monitor
O C R D	Office of the Chief of Research and Development (US Army) (replaced by ODCSRA in 1974)
O C Z M	Office of Coastal Zone Management (of NOAA (USA))
O D A	Optical Diffraction Analysis
	Overseas Development Administration (of the Foreign and Commonwealth Office) (became Ministry of Overseas Development in 1974– usually abbreviated as ODM)
O D C S R D A	Office of the Deputy Chief of Staff for Research, Development and Acquisition (US Army)
O D M	Ministry of Overseas Development (re-established in 1974 as a separate and independent Department)
O D S	Oxide Dispersion-Strengthened
O D T	Odour Detection Threshold
O E A	Office of Economic Adjustment (of Office of the Assistant Secretary of Defense (USA))

O E C	Office of Energy Conservation (of NBS (Dept of Commerce (USA))
O E M	Optical Electron Microscope
O E P	Office of Energy R & D Policy (USA)
O E Q	Order of Engineers of Quebec (Canada)
O E S	Bureau for Oceans and International Environmental and Scientific Affairs (of the State Dept (USA))
O E T B	Offshore Energy Technology Board (of Dept of Energy)
O F D	Optical Fire Director
O F F I	Orszagos Fordito es Forditashitelesito Iroda (Hungary) (National Office for Translations and Attestations)
O F F I N T A C	Offshore Installations Technical Advisory Committee
O F I N T A C	Offshore Installations Technical Advisory Committee
O F P P	Office of Federal Procurement Policy (USA) (in the Office of Management and Budget)
O F T	Office of Fair Trading
O G C	Office of General Counsel (of EPA (USA))
O G D C	Oil and Gas Development Corporation (Pakistan) (government owned)
O G I	Österreichische Gesellschaft für Informatik (Austria) (Austrian Society for Information Processing)
O G T T	Oral Glucose Tolerance Test
O H S P A C	Occupational Health/Safety Programs Accreditation Commission (USA)
O H T	Overheating Temperature
O I C A	Ontario Institute of Chartered Accountants (Canada)
O I I	Office of Invention and Innovation (NBS (USA)) (disbanded 1975)
O I W P	Oil Industry Working Party (of IEA (OECD))
O K	Optical Klystron
O L A	Ohio Library Association (USA)
	Ontario Library Association (Canada)
O L A F	*Operand (Data Processing) Lattice File*
O L C C	Optimum Life Cycle Costing
O L F	On-Line Filing
O L M R	Office of Labor-Management Relations (of USCSC)
	Organic Liquid Moderated Reactor
O M C	Office of Munitions Control (of State Department (USA))

O M C B	Ocean Materials Criteria Branch (of Naval Research Laboratory (USN))
O M I T	Orinthine-decarboxylase, Motility, Indole, Trytophan-deaminase
O M P	Organometallic Polymers
O M S	The Organisation and Methods Society (merged with the Institute of Work Study Practitioners in 1975 to form the Institute of Practitioners in Work Study, Organisation and Methods)
O M T	Orthomode Transducer
O M T C	Organisation and Methods Training Council (now the Management Systems Training Council)
O O L H M D	Optimized Optical Link Helmet-Mounted Display
O O P	Off-line Orthophoto Printer
O P	Office of Preparedness (General Services Adminis-tration (USA))
O P C	Optimization-Prediction System
	Organic Photoconductor
O P C C	Oil and Petrochemical Contractors Committee (of CBMPE)
O P E	Oxidation Pond Effluents
O P G	Overseas Projects Group (of BOTB)
O P O L	Offshore Pollution Liability Agreement
O P O M P	Overall Planning and Optimization and Machining Processes
O P P	Office of Pesticide Programs (of EPA (USA))
O P P I	Organisation of Pharmaceutical Producers of India (India)
O P R A D	Operations Research and Development Management
O P S	Optical Power Spectrum
O P S P A	Oleandomycin-Polymyxin-Sulphadiazine-Perfringens Agar
O P T R A K	Optical Tracking and Ranging Kit
O P U S	An Organisation for Promoting the Understanding of Society (formed in 1975 by The Tavistock Institute of Human Relations and The Industrial Society)
O P U S	*(The) Open University* System
O P W	Office of Public Works (Eire)
O Q L	On-Line Query Language

O R A C L E	Optical Reception of Announcements by Coded Line Electronics
O R B I T	Order Billing Inventory Technique
O R C S	Organic Rankine-Cycle System
O R E	Office de Recherches et d'Essais (of UIC) (Office of Research and Testing)
O R E S	Office of Research and Engineering Services (Kentucky University (USA))
O R G S	Operational Research Group of Scotland
O R I C	*Oak Ridge (National Laboratory)* (ERDA (USA)) Isochronous Cyclotron
O R I O N	On-line Retrieval of Information Over a Network
O R M A K	*Oak Ridge (National Laboratory)* (ERDA (USA)) Tokamak
O R N L	Oak Ridge (National Laboratory) (now of ERDA (USA)) (name changed to Holifield National Laboratory in 1974 and back again to Oak Ridge National Laboratory in 1976)
O R T	Odour Recognition Threshold
O R T F	Organisation Radio Télévision Française (France) (disbanded 1974)
O R V	Off-Road Vehicle
O S A H R C	Occupational Safety and Health Review Commission (USA)
O S A S	Offshore Advisory Service (of THE (of BSI))
O S C A R	On-line System for Controlling Activities and Resources
O S C O	Oil Service Company of Iran (Iran) (a multi-national consortium)
O S D	Ocean Sciences Division (of NRL (USN))
O S D O C	Over-the-Shore Discharge of Container Ships (a project of the US Army)
O S E	Office of Science Education (of AAAS (USA))
O S E B	Orissa State Electricity Board (India)
O S F L A G	Offshore Structures Fluid Loading Advisory Group (of the National Physical Laboratory)
O S G K	Österreichische Studiengesellschaft für Kibernetik (Austria) (Austrian Society for Cybernetic Studies)
O S M V T	Operating System with the option of Multiprogramming with a Variable number of Tasks

O S O	Offshore Supplies Office (of the Department of Energy)
O S P R D S	Oblate Spheroids
O S R	Office of Scientific Research (USAF)
O S R P A	Offices, Shops and Railway Premises Act of 1963
O S T	Objectives, Strategies, and Tactics
O S T I	Office of Scientific and Technical Information (of DES) (became Research and Development Department of the British Library in 1974)
O S U K	Opthalmological Societies of the United Kingdom
O S W	Office of Saline Water (Dept of the Interior (USA)) (now part of the Office of Water Research and Technology)
O T	Ortho Tolidine
O T A R	Overseas Tariffs and Regulations (a section of the Dept of Trade)
O T C	One-Time Carbon paper
O T D	Ocean Technology Division (of Naval Research Laboratory (USN))
O T E C	Ocean Thermal Energy Conversion
O T H - B	Over The Horizon Back-scatter
O T H - F	Over The Horizon Forward-scatter
O T I U	Overseas Technical Information Unit (of DTI) (now of DoI)
O T S	Orbital Technical Satellite
O T U	Operational Taxonomic Unit
O T W	Over-the-Wing externally-blown jet flap
O U	The Open University
O U L C S	Ontario Universities Library Cooperative System (Canada)
O V E	Österreichischer Verband für Elektrotechnik (Austria) (Austrian Society for Electro-technology)
O V T R	Operational Video Tape Recorder
O W R T	Office of Water Research and Technology (Dept of the Interior (USA))
O W S	Ocean Weather Ship
	Oil Water Separator
O X I M	Oxide-Isolated Monolithic technology

P

P-VO	Protivo-vozdushnaya Oborona (Strany) (USSR) (Anti-Aircraft Defence (Force) of the Homeland)
PA	Phthalic Anhydride
	Pressure Anomaly
	prefix to numbered series of Business Monitors issued by the Business Statistics Office of the Department of Industry and published by HMSO
	Publishers Association
PABST	Primary Adhesively Bonded Structure
PAC	Perturbation Angular Correlation
	Powder Air Conveyor
	Private Aviation Committee (of CAA)
	Productivity Advisory Council (South Africa)
PAC-FACS	Programmed Appropriation Commitments - Fixed Asset Control System
PACE	Planning And Control made Easy
	Processing And Control Element
PACOS	Package Operating System
PACT	Programmable Automatic Continuity Tester
PACX	Private Automatic Computer Exchange
PAD	Pressure Anomaly Difference
	Primary Afferent Depolarization
PAECT	Pollution Abatement and Environmental Control Technology
PAF	Pakistan Air Force (Pakistan)
PAHOCENDES	Pan-American Health Organization Center for Development Studies
PAILS	Projectile Airburst and Impact Location System
PALE	Pelvis And Legs Elevating seat
PALMS	Propulsion Alarm and Monitoring System
PAMA	Professional Aviation Maintenance Association (USA)
PAMF	Programmable Analogue Matched Filter
PAMIRASAT	Passive Microwave Radiometer Satellite
PAMS	Plan Analysis and Modeling System
PANAFTEL	Pan-African Telecommunication Network
PANDIT	Produce an Adjusted Nuclear Data Input Tape
PANEES	Professional Association of Naval Electronics Engineers and Scientists (USA)
PANPA	Pacific Area Newspaper Production Association (Australia)

P A N S D O C	Pakistan National Scientific and Technical Documentation Centre (Pakistan) (now PASTIC)
P A N S I P	Propulsion and Airframe Structural Integration Programme
P A N S Y	Programme Analysis System
P A P	Pulmonary Arterial Pressure
P A P A	Parallax Aircraft Parking Aid
P A P I	Precision Path Indicator
P A P T E	(The) President's Advisory Panel on Timber and the Environment (USA)
P A Q	Position Analysis Questionnaire
P A R C S	(Car/Automobile) Parking and Revenue Control System
P A R M	Precision Anti-Radiation Missile
P A R S	Private Aircraft Reporting System (of FAA (USA))
P A R V O	Professional and Academic Regional Visits Organisation
P A S	Para-aminosalicylic Acid
	Periodic Acid-Schiff
	Photo-acoustic Spectroscopy
P A S S	Prototype Artillery Sub-system
P A S T I C	Pakistan Scientific and Technological Information Centre (Pakistan)
P A T	Programmable Automatic Tester
P A T R A C	Planning And Transportation Research Advisory Council
P A T S	Philippine Aeronautics Training School (Philippines)
	Portable Acoustic Tracking System
	Predicasts (*Incorporated* (USA)) Abstract Terminal Service
P A U L	PROSPER Alphanumeric User Language
P B A S	Post Block Aerial Surveying
P B C	Peripheral Bus Computer
P B E I S T	Planning Board for European Inland Surface Transport (a NATO civil emergency planning agency)
P B F	Permalloy-Bar File
P B G C	Pension Benefit Guaranty Corporation (of Dept of Labor (USA))
P B N A	Phenyl Beta-naphthylamine
P B S	Public Broadcasting Service (USA)

P B T	Polybutylene Terephthalate
P C	Phosphorylcreatine
	Pitting Corrosion
	Polymer Concrete
P C B	Point-Contact Breakdown
P C C	Philippine Cotton Corporation (Philippines)
	Polymer Cement Concrete
P C C D	Peristaltic Charge-Coupled Device
P C D D S	Private Circuit Digital Data Service
P C E	Pyrometric Cone Equivalent
P C I E	Period of Central Inspiratory Excitability
P C M A	Post Card Manufacturers Association (USA)
P C M B	Parachloro-Mercury Benzoic acid
P C N	Parent Country Nationals
P C T	Patent Cooperation Treaty
P D	Potential Difference
P D A	Potato Dextrose Agar
P D E	Phosphodiesterase
P D E S	Pulse-Doppler Elevation Scan
P D H	Pyruvate Dehydrogenase
P D I N	Pusat Dokumentasi Ilmiah Nasional (Indonesia) (Scientific and Technical Documentation Centre)
P D I S	Pusat Dokumentasi Ilmu-Ilmu Sosial (Indonesia) (Social Sciences Documentation Centre)
P D M	Pulse Duration Modulation Modem
P D M S	Polydimethylsiloxane
P D N E S	Pulse-Doppler Non-Elevation Scan
P D P	Plasma Display Panel
P D V	Pyrotechnic Development Vehicle
P D X	Poloidal Divertor Experiment (at the Plasma Physics Laboratory of Princeton University (USA))
P E	Phosphatidylethanolamine
P E B	Phototype Environment Buoy
P E C I	Projects and Equipment Corporation of India (India)
P E E	Photoelectric Emission
P E E T P A C K	Process Engineering Evaluation Techniques Package
P E G	Petrochemical Energy Group (an *ad hoc* group of several major chemical companies in the USA)
P E I	Planning Executives Institute (USA)

P E K	Pig Embryo Kidney
P E L	Physics and Engineering Laboratory (of DSIR (New Zealand))
P E L S S	Precision Emitter Location Strike System
P E M	Protein-Energy Malnutrition
P E M E C	International Plant Engineering and Maintenance Exhibition and Conference
P E M V	Pea Enation Mosaic Virus
P E N S A D	Pensions Administration system
P E P	Partitioned Emulation Programme
	Positron-Electron Project (of Stanford University and California University (USA))
P E P C O	Committee on Professional Education for Publishing (of AAP (USA))
P E R	Professional and Executive Recruitment (a service of the Manpower Services Commission) (previously of the Dept of Employment)
P E R F	Planetary Entry Radiation Facility (of Langley Research Center (NASA) (USA))
P E R S I S	Personnel Information System
P E R T V S	Perimeter Television System
P E T	Pentaerythritol Tetrastearate
	Potential Evapotranspiration
	Pre-Eclamptic Toxaemia
P E T A N S	Petroleum Training Association North Sea (sponsored by the Petroleum Industry Training Board)
P E T C O C K	Proposal Evaluation Technique Conditioned on Contract Kind
P E T T	Project: Engineering and Technology for Tomorrow (a slogan of the Inter-departmental Committee on Publicity for Engineering and Technology)
P E V	Propeller-Excited Vibration
P F B	Petroleum Fims Bureau (ceased operation in 1974)
P F C	Plaque-Forming Cell
	Privately Financed Consumption
P F D F	Plutonium Fuel Development Facility (of PNC (Japan))
P F F	Plaque-Forming Factor
P F F F	Plutonium Fuel Fabrication Facility (of PNC (Japan))

P F I A B	(The) President's Foreign Intelligence Board (USA)
P F M	Pre-Finished Metal
P F S	Porous Friction Surface
P G	Patrol Gunboat
P G A	Phospho-glyceric Acid
P G K	Phosphoglycerate Kinase
P G M	Precision Guided Munitions
P G O	Pyrolysis Gas Oil
P G R V	Precision Guided Re-entry Vehicle
P H A	Passive Haemagglutination
P H I B	Phosphor-Inverted Bi-polar transistor device
P H I L I R A N	Phillips Petroleum Company (Iran) (partly government owned)
P H I L S O M	Periodical Holdings In the Library of the School Of Medicine network (based on Washington University School of Medicine (USA))
P H O C I S	Photogrammetric Circulatory Surveys
P H T	Passive Haemagglutination Test
P H W R	Pressurized Heavy-water-moderated and cooled Reactor
P I	Plastics Institute (amalgamated into PRI in 1975)
P I A	Peripheral Interface Adaptor
P I B	Polytechnic Institute of Brooklyn (USA) (now PINY (USA))
P I C	Polymer-Impregnated Concrete
	Positive-Impedance Converter
	Production Inventory Control
	Pulse Indicating Cartridge
P I D	Polarization Image Detector
P I D A	Payload Installation and Deployment Aid
P I D C	Parameter Inventory Display System (maintained by NODC (NOAA) (USA))
P I E	Photo-Induced Electrochromism
P I F	British Paper and Board Industry Federation
P I L L S	Particulate Instrumentation by Laser Light Scattering
P I M A	Paper Industry Management Association (USA)
Pi Mc	Particle Measurement Computer
P I M P	Programme for Interactive Multiple Process simulation

P I M R	Przemyslowy Instytut Maszn Rolniczych (Poland) (Institute of Agricultural Machinery)
P I N S	Palletized Inertial Navigation System
P I N Y	Polytechnic Institute of New York (USA)
P I P	Pipe Inspection Programme
P I P I T	Peripheral Interface and Programme Interrupt Translator
P I R L	PRISM (Personnel Record Information System for Management) Information Retrieval Language
P I S C E S	Production Information Stocks and Cost Enquiry System
P I T	Physical Inventory Taking
P I T A S	Petroleum Industry Training Association Scotland
P I V S	Particle-Induced Visual Sensations
P J A	Pipe Jacking Association
P L A	Phospholipase A
	Programmed Logic Array
P L A N	Programming Language *Nineteen hundred* computer
P L A N E S	Programmed Language-based Enquiry System
P L A R S	Position Locating And Reporting System
P L C	Programmable Logic Controller
P L E M	Pipeline End Manifold
P L E X	Plant Experimentation
P L L S	Portable Landing Light System
P L M	Planned Lighting Maintenance
P L P	Plastic Lined Pipe
	Pyridoxal Phosphate
P L R	Public Lending Right
P L R S	Position Location Reporting System
P L T	*Princeton* (Plasma Physics Laboratory, Princeton University (USA)) Large Torus
P L U S S	*USS Point Loma* Unmanned Search System
P M	prefix to numbered series of Business Monitor Quarterly Statistics issued by Business Statistics Office of Dept of Industry and published by HMSO
P M A	Petroleum and Minerals Authority (Australia)
	Polyurethane Manufacturers Association (USA)
	Produce Marketing Association (USA)

P M A C	Purchasing Management Association of Canada (Canada)
P M B O	Participative Management By Objectives
P M C	Project Management Corporation (USA) (a non-profit corporation organised to manage CRBRP (USA))
P M D	Project-based Management Development
P M D C	Pakistan Minerals Development Corporation (Pakistan) (government owned)
P M D S	Projected Map Display Set
P M E L	Pacific Marine Environmental Laboratory (of ERL (NOAA (USA))
P M I R D	Passive Microwave Intercept Receiver Display
P M N	Polymorphonuclear
	Polymorphonuclear Neutrophils
P M O S	P-channel Metal Oxide Semiconductor
P M R	Pacific Missile Range (USN)
	Pressure Modulated Radiometer
P M S	Processors, Memories and Switches
P M S P	Plant Modelling System Programme
P N A	Project Network Analysis
P N E R L	Pacific Northwest Environmental Research Laboratory (of EPA (USA))
P N G	Papua-New Guinea
P N I	Pulsed Neutron Interrogation
P N I T C	Pacific Northwest International Trade Council (USA)
P N K A	Protein Induced by Vitamin K Absence and Antagonists
P N O C	Philippine National Oil Company (Philippines) (government owned)
P N V S	Pilots Night Vision System
P O A C	International Conference on Port and Ocean Engineering under Arctic Conditions
P O C	Public Oil Company (Sudan)
P O E	Polyoxyethylene
P O G O	Pre-Oxidation Gettering of the Other side
	Problem-Oriented Graphics Operation
P O L A N G	Polarization Angle
P O L A R S	Pathology On-line Logging And Reporting System
P O L K A	Petroleum, Oil and Lubricants Out-of-Kilter Algorithm

P O M	Polyoxymethylene
P O P	Palletizing Optimization Programme
	Perceived Outcome Potential
P O P A	Panel On Public Affairs (of the American Physical Society (USA))
P O Q	Period Order Quantity
P O W E R	Programmed Off-line Waste Reduction
P O W T E C H	International Powder and Granular Technology and Bulk Solids Exhibition and Conference
P O Y	Pre-Oriented Yarn
P P	Protoporphyrin
P P A	Printing Platemakers Association (USA)
P P C	Predicted Propagation Correction
P P D	Petroleum Production Division (of Dept of Energy)
P P D C	Polymer Products Development Centre (of RAPRA)
P P D I	Pilots Projected Display Indicator
P P L C	Patients Protection Law Committee
P P O M	Particulate Polycyclic Organic Matter
P P Q	Polyphenylquinoxaline
P P S A	Pan-Pacific Surgical Association
P Q	prefix to numbered series of Business Monitors issued by Business Statistics Office of the Dept of Industry and published by HMSO
P Q E	Post-Qualification Education
P R	Proton Resonance
P R A G M A	Processing Routines Aided by Graphics for Manipulation of Arrays
P R A M	Productivity, Reliability, Availability and Maintainability
	Propelled Ascent Mine
P R C	Polysulphide Rubber Compound
P R D P E C	Power Reactor Development Programme Evaluation Committee (of AECL (Canada))
P R D S	Processed Radar Display System
P R E V A N	Precompiler for Vector Analysis
P R I	Plastics and Rubber Institute
P R O' I N'	International Product Innovation Congress and Exhibition
P R O C S I M	Processor Simulation language
P R O I	Project Return On Investment

P R O J A C S	Project Analysis and Control System
P R O M	Pockel's Readout Optical Modulator
P R O M S T R A	Production Methods and Stress Research Association (Netherlands)
P R O N T O	Programmable Network Telecommunications Operating system
P R P	Platelet-Rich Plasma
	Polyribophosphate
P R P P	Phosphoribosyl Pyrophosphate
P R T	Petroleum Revenue Tax
P S	Polystyrol
P S A	Philosophy of Science Association
P S B	Public Service Board (Australia)
P S C C	Paper Stock Conservation Committee (of American Paper Institute (USA))
P S E	Psychological Stress Analyser (a 'lie detector')
P S I	Page Survival Index
P S I D C	Punjab State Industrial Development Corporation (India)
P S M	People for Self Management (USA) (an organisation)
P S M A	Pressure Sensitive Manufacturers Association
P S M M	Patrol Ship Multi-Mission
P S P A	Professional Sports Photographers Association
P S P R D S	Prolate Spheroids
P S Q L	Process Screening Quality Level
P S R	Pain Sensitivity Range
P S S C	Public Service Satellite Consortium (USA)
P S S T	Public Sector Standardization Team (of government departments, nationalised industries and local authorities)
P S T H	Peristimulus Time Histogram
P S T I A C	Pavements and Soil Trafficability Information Analysis Center (US Army)
P S V	Polished-Stone Value
P T A	Polytungsten Anions
P T C	Public Transport Commission (New South Wales (Australia))
P T D A	Power Transmission Distributors Association (USA)
P T D L	Programmable Tapped Delay Line
P T T I	Precise Time and Time Interval

P T U	Propylthiouracil
P U C F	Polyurethane-Coated Fabric
P U L S A R	Pulsating Star
P U N	Plasma Urea Nitrogen
P U S	Passive Ultrasonic Sensor
P U S H	Public Use Sample Helper
P V C C F	Polyvinyl Chloride-Coated Fabric
P V D	Peripheral Vascular Disease
	Physical Vapour Deposition
P V H	Propane-Vacuum-Hydrogen
P V M	Point Visibility Meter
	Process Evaluation Module
P V P	Prototype-Validation Phase
	Pulmonary Vascular Resistance
P V Q	Personal Value Questionnaire
P V R	Portable, Volume-controlled Respirator
P V S	Personal Value System
P W A	Papierwerke Waldhof Aschaffenburg Aktiengesell- schaft (Germany)
P W L	Power Watt Level
P W R	Pressurized Light-water-moderated and cooled Reactor
P X L	Patrol, Experimental Land-based aircraft
P Z C	Point of Zero Charge

Q

Q – B O P	Quiet, Quick, Quality Basic Oxygen Process
Q A F C O	Qatar Fertilizer Company (Qatar) (state is a majority shareholder)
Q A L D	Quality Assurance Liaison Division (of Defense Nuclear Agency (USDOD))
Q A M	Quality Assurance Monitor
Q A S	Question Answering System
Q C G A T	Quite Clean General Aviation Turbofan (a project of NASA (USA))
Q C M	Quick-Connects for bulkhead Mounting
Q C R T	Quick Change Real-Time
Q D T A	Quantitative Differential Thermal Analysis
Q E P	Quality Evaluation Program (of the College of American Pathologists (USA))

Q G P O	Qatar General Petroleum Organisation (Qatar)
Q I E	Quantitative Immunoelectrophoresis
Q L I I	Quasi-Linear Intensity Interferometer
Q M	Quantum Mechanics
Q M E	Queueing Matrix Evaluation
Q P R	prefix to numbered series of Quality Procedural Requirements issued by MoD
Q S	Quadraphonic Stereo
Q S R A	Quiet Short-haul Research Aircraft
Q T M	prefix to numbered series of Quality Technical Memoranda issued by MoD
Q T R	Quality Technical Requirement (of MoD)
Qu A D	Quality Assurance Department (of BSI)
Q U E S T A R	Quantitative Utility Evaluation Suggesting Targets for the Allocation of Resources
Q U I D S	Quick Interactive Documentation System
Q W G / C D	Quadripartite Working Group on Combat Development (representative of the American, British, Canadian and Australian Armies)

R

R & R R	Range and Range Rate
R A	Radar Altimeter
	Recrystallization-Anneal
	Relaxation Allowance
R A A F	Royal Australian Air Force (Australia)
R A A P	Residue Arithmetic Associative Processor
	Resource Allocation And Planning system
R A C	Radiometric Area Correlator
	Relative Address Coding
	Rhomboidal Air Controller
	Rubber Association of Canada (Canada)
R A C E S	Radio Amateur Communication Emergency Services (USA)
R A D A R	Receivable Accounts Data-entry And Retrieval
R A D C A P	*Rome Air Development Center* (USAF) Associative Array Processor
R A D C O L S	*Rome Air Development Center* (USAF) On-Line Simulator

146

R A D I	Retail Alarm for Display and Intruder
R A D M A P	Radiological Monitoring Assessment Prediction system
R A D R U	Rapid Access Data Retrieval Unit
R A D S	Radar Alphanumeric Display Sub-system
R A e C	Royal Aero Club of the United Kingdom
R A F G S A	Royal Air Force Gliding and Soaring Association
R A I D S	Real-time AUTODIN Interface and Distribution System (USDOD)
R A I R	Ram Augmented Inter-stellar Rocket
R A L I	Resource and Land Information program (of the United States Geological Survey)
R A M	Rancho Anthropomorphic Manipulator
	RF (radio frequency) Absorbing Material
	Rolling Airframe Missile
R A M - D	Reliability And Maintainability-Dependability
R A M I S	Rapid Access Management Information System
R A M I T	Rate-Aided Manually Initiated Tracking
R A M S	Remote Arctic Measuring System buoy
R A N	Royal Australian Navy (Australia)
R A N C	Radar Attenuation, Noise and Clutter
R A N S A	Royal Australian Naval Sailing Association (Australia)
R A N T	Re-entry Antenna Test
R A O T	Rocker Arm Oiling Time
R A P	Radiological Assistance Program (of ERDA (USA))
	Reactive Atmosphere Process
	Reliable Acoustic Path sonar
R A P I D	Register for the Ascertainment and Prevention of Inherited Diseases (of the Medical Research Council)
	Remote Automatic Parts Input for Dealers
R A P P O R T	Rapid Alert Programmed, Power management of Radar Targets
R A P S	Radar Automatic Plotting System
R A S A R	Resource Allocation System for Agricultural Research
R A S E	Rapid Automatic Sweep Equipment
R A T A S	Research And Technical Advisory Services (a department of Lloyd's Register of Shipping)

147

R A T E R	*Raytheon* Acoustic Test and Evaluation Range
R A T F O R	Rational FORTRAN
R A T P	Régie Autonome des Transports Parisiens (France)
R A V E	Research Aircraft for Visual Environment (a project of ECOM (US Army))
R B C	Rotating Beam Ceilometer
R B O C	Rapid Bloom Off-board Chaff
R B O T	Rotating Bomb Oxidation Test
R B S	Rutherford Back-Scattering
R B S N	Reaction Bonded Silicon Nitride
R B T	Rose Bengal Test
R C	Replacement Cost accounting
R C A	Regional Cooperative Agreement for Research, Development and Training related to Nuclear Science and Technology in South and Southeast Asia, the Pacific and the Far East
	Replacement Cost Accounting
R C D S	Royal College of Defence Studies
R C H M (E)	Royal Commission on Historical Monuments (England)
R C M	Red Cell Mass
	Royal College of Midwives
R C N	Reticulum Cell Neoplasms
	Royal College of Nursing
R C P I	Royal College of Physicians of Ireland
R C S I	Royal College of Surgeons of Ireland
R D A	Radioactive Dentine Abrasion
	Railway Development Association
R D I	Recommended Daily intake
R D N	Resource Decision Network
R D P	Radar Detector Processor
R D S	Research Defence Society
	Respiratory Distress Syndrome
R D T & E	Research, Development, Test and Engineering
R E A	Right Ear Advantage
R E A M	Rapid Excavating And Mining
R E A M S	*Ramond (Albert Ramond and Associates Incorporated* (USA)) Electronically Applied Maintenance Standards
R E C	Rural Electrification Corporation (India)
R E C A	Repetitive Element Column Analysis

R E C A T	Reduced Energy Consumption of the Air Trans-portation system (a study by NASA (USA))
R E D Y	Re-circulation Dialysate machine
R E F	Railway Engineers Forum (of the Institutions of Civil, Mechanical, Electrical and Railway Signal Engineers)
R E G A L	Remote Generalised Application Language
R E I N S	Radar Equipped Inertial Navigation System
R E L I P O S I S	Research Liaison Panel On Scientific Information Services (of the British Gas Corporation)
R E M C O	Reference Materials Council Committee (of ISO)
R E M P A	Reference Materials Party (of ISO)
R E M S C O N	Conference and Exhibition on Remote Supervisory and Control Systems
R E M U S	Routine for Executive Multi-Unit Simulation
R E N S	Reconnaissance Electronic Warfare and Naval Intelligence System
R E P C O N	Rain Repellant and Surface Conditioner
R E P L A C	Symposium on Reinforced Plastics Process against Corrosion
R E P S	Repetitive Electromagnetic Pulse Simulator
R E S C A M	Regional Centre for Education in Science and Mathematics (of SEAMEO)
R E T R A	Radio, Electrical and Television Retailers Association
R 4	Recovery and Reuse of Refuse Resources (a program of USN)
R F / I R	Radio Frequency/Infra-Red
R F A	Royal Fleet Auxiliary
R F I	Remote File Inquiry
R F S	Radio Frequency Surveillance
R F S / E C M	Radio Frequency Surveillance/Electronic Counter Measures
R F V	Regressing Friend Virus
R H C S A	Regional Hospitals Consultants and Specialists Association (became HCSA in April 1974)
R H L	Rectangular Hysteresis Loop
R I B	Rijksinkoopbureau (Netherlands) (Government Purchasing Office)

R I D E	Rail International Design Environment (an *ad hoc* group of UIC)
R I E C	Research Institute for Estate Crops (Indonesia)
R I M	Reaction Injection Moulding
R I N	Royal Institute of Navigation
R I P	Radioisotope Precipitation
R I Q S	Remote Information Query System (of North-western University (USA))
R I S O S	Research In Secured Operating Systems (a project of ARPA (USDOD))
R I T A	*Rand (Corporation)* (USA) Intelligent Terminal Agent
R I T E S	*Rail India* Technical and Economics Services (India)
R I W	Reliability Improvement Warranty
R J A F	Royal Jordanian Air Force (Jordan)
R L	prefix to dated-numbered series of reports issued by Redstone Arsenal (US Army)
R L G	Research Libraries Group (USA) (comprising the research libraries of New York Public Library, the libraries of Columbia, Harvard and Yale universities)
R M C	Rotation Modulation Collimator
R M D	Research Management Division (of DoE)
R M I	Rack Manufacturers Institute (USA)
R M R S	Rocky Mountain Radiological Society
R M S C	Royal Marines Sailing Club
R N L I	Royal National Life-boat Institute
R N S A	Royal Naval Sailing Association
R N Z A F	Royal New Zealand Air Force
R O D A R	(Helicopter) Rotor Blade Radar
R O D S I M	*J. S. N. Rodriguez* and *N. E. Simons* computer programme
R O M A N	Remotely Operated Mobile Manipulator
R O M B I	Results of Marine Biological Investigations (maintained by NODC (NOAA) (USA))
R O O I	Return On Original Investment
R O S A	Recording Optical Spectrum Analyzer
R O S C O P	Report of Observations/Samples Collected by Oceanographic Programs (of World Data Center-A, Oceanography (USA))

R O S E	Residuum Oil Supercritical Extraction
R O T S A L	Rotate and Scale
R P	prefix to numbered series of Reference Papers issued by the Electricity Council
R P E	Ratings of Perceived Exertion
	Rocket Propulsion Establishment (now of MoD)
R P E A	Retarding Potential and Electrostatic Analyzer
R P H	Remotely Piloted Helicopter
R P H A	Reversed Passive Haemagglutination
R P I	Retail Price Index
R P M	Reinforced Plastic Matrix
R P M B	Remotely Piloted Mini-Blimp
R P N	Reverse Polish Notation logic
R P P I T B	Rubber and Plastics Processing Industry Training Board
R P R	Rapid Plasma Reagin
R P W	Ranked Positional Weight
R R E	Royal Radar Establishment (MoD) (became RSRE in 1976)
R R I D	Reverse Radial Immunodiffusion
R R I M	Rubber Research Institute of Malaysia (Malaysia)
R R R	Rapid Runway Repair
R R U	Road Research Unit (of NRB (New Zealand))
R S A A	Remote Sensing Association of Australia (Australia)
R S A F	Royal Saudi Air Force (Saudi Arabia)
R S I	Radial Shear Interferometer
R S M A D	Remote Sensing and Meteorological Division (of ISRO (India))
R S O	Rectified Skew Orthomorphic
	Relativistic and Spin-Orbit
R S R E	Radar and Signals Research Establishment (MoD) (part at Baldock and part at Christchurch)
R S S	Remote Sensing Society
	Resource Security System
R S S L	*Raytheon (Company)* Scientific Simulation Language
R T D / C C S	Resources and Technical Services Division/Cataloging and Classification Section (of the American Library Association (USA))
R T L	Register Transfer Language
R T P R	Reference Theta-Pinch Reactor
R T P S	Real-time Telemetry Processing System

R T R A	Radio and Television Retailers Association (name changed to RETRA in April 1976)
R T S A	Retail Trading Standards Association
R T T V	Real Time Television
R U A G	Refrigeration and Unit Air Conditioning Group (of HVCA)
R U C A	Rijksuniversitair Centrum Antwerpen (Belgium) (State University Centre of Antwerp)
R U U	Ryksuniversiteit Utrecht (Netherlands) (State University, Utrecht)
R V	Recreational Vehicle
R V F	Rate Variance Formula
R V I A	Recreational Vehicle Institute of America (USA)
R V P	Radar Video Preprocessor
R V S N	Raketny Voiska Strategicheskovo Naznacheniya (USSR) (Strategic Rocket Forces)
R W C	Round Wire Cable
R W R	Radar Warning Receiver

S

S - Cubed	Serial Signalling Scheme
S / O	Solvent to Oil ratio
S A	Slide Agglutination
S A A	Single Article Announcement (a current awareness service of the American Chemical Society (USA))
	Society of American Archivists (USA)
	South Atlantic Anomaly
S A A C	Simulator for Air-to-Air Combat
S A A F	South African Air Force (South Africa)
S A A M	Simulation, Analysis And Modelling
S A B	South American Blastomycosis
S A B H A T A	Sand and Ballast Hauliers and Allied Trades Alliance
S A C	Space Applications Centre (of ISRO (India))
	Submerged Air Cushion
S A C A R T S	Semi-Automated Cartographic System
S A C C M	Slow Access Charge-Coupled Memory
S A C E	Systems Acceptance Check-out Equipment
S A C E U R	Supreme Allied Commander Europe (of NATO)
S A C M A	Société Anonyme de Construction de Moteurs Aéronautiques (France)

S A C N A S	Society for the Advancement of Chicano and Native American Scientists (USA)
S A D A R	Société Anonyme d'Appareillage Radioéléctrique (France)
S A D C	Singapore Air Defence Command (Singapore)
S A D E	Sensitive Acoustic Detection Equipment
S A E B	Spacecraft Assembly and Encapsulation Building (of NASA (USA))
S A E S T	Society for the Advancement of Electrochemical Science and Technology (India)
S A E W	Ships Advanced Electronic Warfare
S A F	Singapore Air Force (Singapore)
S A F C A	Safeguard Communication Agency (of USASTRATCOM) (became BMDCA (of USACC) in 1975)
S A F E	System for Automated Flight Efficiency
S A F E O R D	Safety of Explosive Ordnance Databank (of NWL (USN))
S A F E R	Société d'Amenagement Foncier et d'Établissement Rural (France)
S A G T	Systematic Approach to Group Technology
S A I F	South African Institute of Foundrymen (South Africa)
S A I L	Structural Analysis Input Language
S A I L S	Software Adaptable Integrated Logic System
S A I M	South African Institute of Management (South Africa)
S A I M C	South African Institute for Measurement and Control (South Africa)
S A I M E N A	South African Institute of Marine Engineers and Naval Architects (South Africa)
S A I M R	South African Institute of Medical Research (South Africa)
S A I N T	Systems Analysis of Integrated Network of Tasks
S A I T	Service d'Analyse de l'Information Technologique (of CRIQ (Canada)) (Technological Information Analysis Service)
S A J	Shipbuilders Association of Japan (Japan)
S A L I N E T	Satellite Library Information Network (a consortium of libraries, a library school, and regional agencies with headquarters at Denver Graduate School of Librarianship (USA))

153

S A L M	Single Anchor Leg Mooring
S A L R	Saturated Adiabatic Lapse Rate
S A M	S-Adenosyl-Methionine
	Scanning Auger Microprobe
	Sequential Access Method
	Simple Automated Movement
S A M A N T H A	System for the Automated Management of Text from a Hierarchical Arrangement
S A M E C S	Structural Analysis Method for Evaluation of Complex Structures
S A M I	System Acquisition Management Inspection system (of AFISC (USAF))
S A M I R	Société Anonyme Moroccaine de l'Industrie du Raffinage (Morocco)
S A M M	Semi-Automatic Measuring Machine
S A M S	Stratospheric And Mesopheric Sounder
S A M S O N	Strategic Automatic Message Switching Operational Network (of the Canadian Armed Forces)
S A N A E	South African National Antartic Expedition
S A N C O T	South African National Committee on Tunnelling (South Africa)
S A O D A P	Special Action Office for Drug Abuse Prevention (of the Office of the President (USA))
S A P	Simplified Astro Platten
S A R	Stable Auroral Red arcs
S A R B I C A	Southeast Asian Regional Branch of the International Council on Archives
S A R I E	Selective Automatic Radar Identification Equipment
S A R U	Systems Analysis Research Unit (of DoE)
S A S	Statistical Analysis System
S A S A	South African Sugar Association (South Africa)
S A S I	Society of Air Safety Investigators
S A S I S	Semi-Automatic Speaker Identification System
S A S O	Saudi Arabia Standards Organization (Saudi Arabia)
S A T	Systematic Assertive Therapy
S A T S I M	Saturation Countermeasures Simulator
S A W	Seeking, Asking and Written questionnaire
	Society of Architects in Wales
	Squad Automatic Weapon
S A W D	Surface Acoustic Wave Device

S A W M A	Soil and Water Management Association
S A W O	Surface Acoustic Wave Oscillator
S A W S	Satellite Attack Warning System
	Squad Automatic Weapon System
S A W T R I	South African Wool and Textile Research Institute (of CSIR (South Africa))
S A X	Strong Anion Exchange
S B A	School Bookshop Association
	Small Businesses Association
S B C	Small Business Computer
S B G G E D D	Schottky-Barrier Gate Gunn-Effect Digital Device
S B G I	Society of British Gas Industries
S B O	Specific Behavioural Objectives
S B P	Sugar Beet Pulp
S B S C	Schottky Barrier Solar Cell
S C A	Small Calibre Ammunition
	Society of Commercial Accountants (merged into SCCA in 1974)
	Supersonic Cruise Aircraft
S C A C	South Carolina Aeronautics Commission (USA)
S C A L A	Society of Chief Architects of Local Authorities
S C A M S	Scanning Microwave Spectrometer
S C A N	Southern California Answering Network (administered by California State Library (USA))
S C A N T I E	Submersible Craft Acoustic Navigation and Track Indication Equipment
S C A O	Standing Conference on Atlantic Organisations
S C A R	Supersonic Cruise Airplane Research (a project of NASA (USA))
S C A R E	Sensor Control Anti-Anti-Radiation Missile Radar Evaluation
S C A T H A	Spacecraft Charging At High Altitudes
S C A T S	Standard Coal Aerosol Test
S C A U L W A	Standing Conference of African University Libraries, Western Area (Ghana)
S C B F	Spinal Cord Blood Flow
S C C	Signal Channel Controller
S C C A	Society of Company and Commercial Accountants (formed in 1974 by the merger of the Institute of Company Accountants, Society of Commercial Accountants, and Cost Accountants Association)

S C C D	Surface-Channel Charge-Couple Device
S C C O P	State Consulting Company for Oil Projects (Iraq)
S C D S	Shipboard Chaff Decoy System
S C E	Sister Chromatid Exchanges
	Stratified Charge Engine
S C E T	Scottish Council for Educational Technology
S C H O L A R	*Schering (Corporation)* Oriented Literature Analysis and Retrieval system
S C I	Science of Creative Intelligence
S C I E N C E	Société des Consultants Indépendants et Neutres de la Communauté Européenne (Belgium)
S C I M P	Self-Contained Imaging Micro-Profiler
S C L	Scottish Central Library (merged with National Library of Scotland in 1974 to form National Library of Scotland Lending Services)
	System Chart Language
S C L E R A	Santa Catalina Laboratory for Experimental Relativity and Astrometry (the name of a telescope designed and operated by Professor Henry Hill and Carl Zanoni)
S C M	Samarium Cobalt Magnet
	Soluble Cytotoxic Mediator
	Steam-Cure Mortar
	Strategic Cruise Missile
S C M A I	Staff Committee on Mediation, Arbitration, and Inquiry (of the American Library Association (USA)
S C O D S	Standing Committee on Ocean Data Stations (of NERC
S C O L C A P	Scottish Libraries Co-operative Automation Project
S Con Me L	Standing Conference for Mediterranean Librarians
S C O P E	Standing Conference on Overseas Placements and Exchanges
	System for Computing Operational Probability Equations
S C O P E S	Squad Combat Operations Exercise (Simulation) (US Army)
S C O R E	System Capability Over Requirement Evaluation
S C O R E S	Scenario Oriented Recurring Evaluation System (US Army)
S C O R P I O	Subject Content-Oriented Retriever for Processing Information On-line

S C O T	Shell Claus Off-gas Treating
S C O T B E C	Scottish Business Education Council
S C P	Single Cell Protein
S C P C	Single-Channel-per-Carrier
S C P E A	Southern California Professional Engineering Association (USA)
S C P V	Silkworm Cytoplasmic Polyhedrosis Virus
S C R I P T	*Stanford (University)* (USA) Computerized Researcher Information Profile Technique
S C S	Sea Control Ship (now called VSTOL Support Ship)
	Society for Computer Simulation (USA)
S C T L	Schottky Coupled Transistor Logic
S C T T	Submarine Command Team Trainer
S C X	Strong Cation Exchange
S D	Serologically Defined
	Systems Design
	prefix to numbered series of Business Monitor Quarterly Statistics on Service and Distribution issued by Business Statistics Office of Dept of Industry and published by HMSO
S D A	Scottish Development Agency
S D B	Society for Developmental Biology (USA)
S D C	Signal Data Converter
S D F	Standard Data Format
S D H	Succinic Dehydrogenase
S D L C	Synchronous Data Link Communications
	Synchronous Data Link Control
S D M A / S S-T D M A	Space Division Multiple Access/Spacecraft Switched Time Division Multiple Access
S E A	Soluble Egg Antigen
	Statistical Energy Analysis
S E A C	South Eastern Architects Consortium (reconstituted 1974—formerly South East Authorities Collaboration)
S E A M	Servicios de Equipos Agricolas Mecanizados (Chile) (Mechanized Agricultural Equipment Service)
S E A M E O	South-East Asian Ministers of Education Organization
S E A M E S	South-East Asian Ministers of Education Secretariat (Thailand)
S E A R C C	South-East Asia Regional Computer Conference

S E A S S M C	*SHARE* (USA) European Association Symbolic Mathematical Computation
S E A S A T	Ocean Survey Satellite
S E A T O	South-East Asia Treaty Organization (ceased military activities in 1973 and phasing out all other activities by 1978)
S E B	Surface Effect Boat
S E C A	Southern Educational Communications Association (USA)
S E C L F	Station d'Essais Combustibles et Lubrifiants de la Flotte (of the French Navy)
S E C M A	Stock Exchange Computer Managers Association
S E C T	Service des Équipements de Champs de Tir (of DRME (France))
S E D I S	Surface Emitter Detection, Identification System
S E E	Société des Electriciens, des Electoniciens et des Radioéléctriciens (France) (Society of Electrical, Electronics and Radio Technicians)
S E G	Society of Exploration Geophysicists (USA)
S E G A I P	Self Gated In-water Photography
S E L	Sensitized-Erythrocyte-Lysis
S E L D A M	Selective Data Management system
S E L D O M	Selective Dissemination of MARC (a service of Saskatchewan University (Canada))
S E L C A L L	Selective Calling
S E L E A C	Standard Elementary Abstract Computer
S E M	Singularity Expansion Method
	System Extension Module
S E M A	Storage Equipment Manufacturers Association
S E M D A	Surveying Equipment Manufacturers and Dealers Association
S E M K O	Svenska Elecktriska Materielkontrollanstalten (Sweden) (Swedish Institute for Testing and Approval of Electrical Equipment)
S E M P	Self Erecting Marine Platform
S E N A	Servicio Nacional de Aprendizaje (Colombia) (State sponsored organization for professional training)
S E O	Satellite for Earth Observations
S E O S	Synchronous Earth Observation Satellite

158

S E P D	Scottish Economic Planning Department
S E P P	Société d'Étude de la Prévision et de la Planification (Switzerland) (Society for the Study of Futures)
S E Q	Standing Group on Emergency Questions (of IEA (OECD))
S E R	Sociaal Economische Raad (Netherlands) (Economic and Social Council)
S E R A	Socialist Environment and Resources Association
S E R I	Solar Energy Research Institute (USA)
S E R L	Services Electronic Research Laboratory (MoD) (became Radar and Signals Research Establishment (Baldock) (of MoD) in 1976)
S E S	Service des Études Scientifiques (Algeria) (Scientific Studies Service)
S E S A M E	Severe Environmental Storms and Mesoscale Experiment
S E S O	Ship Environmental Support Office (of NEPSS (USN))
S E S T	Short Effective Service Time
S E T E P	Science and Engineering Technician Education Program (of NSF (USA))
S E T P	Society of Experimental Test Pilots (USA)
S E U	Subjective Expected Utility
S E W	Shipboard Electronics Warfare
	Surface Electromagnetic Wave
S E W I D	Surface Electromagnetic Wave Integrated Optics
S E W M A	Simple Exponentially Weighted Moving-Average
S F A	Serum Folate
S F A I	Steel Furnace Association of India (India)
S F C	Scottish Film Council (now the Scottish Council for Educational Technology)
S F C I	State Farms Corporation of India (India)
S F E N	Société Française d'Énergie Nucléaire (France) (French Nuclear Energy Society)
S F G A	Single Floating-Gate Amplifier
S F I S	Small Firms Information Service (of DoI)
S F O L D S	Ship Form On-Line Design System
S F P	Société Française de Photogrammétrie (France) (French Society of Photogrammetry)

S F R L	Spin-Flip Raman Laser
S F S	Society of Fleet Supervisors (USA)
S F T P	Science For The People (an association in USA)
S F V	Semliki Forest Virus
S G D	prefix to numbered series of reports on Solar-Geophysical Data issued by the National Geophysical and Solar-Tessestrial Data Center (USA)
S G F	Sveriges Gummitekniska Forening (Sweden) (Swedish Rubber Industry Association)
S G P A	Scottish General Publishers Association
S G S R	Society for General Systems Research (USA)
S H A	Software Houses Association (merged into Computer Services Association, 1975)
S H A G	Simplified High-Accuracy Guidance
S H A L E	Stand-off, High Altitude, Long Endurance
S H A P E	*Stevens* and *Harrison* Adaptive Parameter Estimation
S H E L F	Super-Hardened Extremely Low Frequency
S H I E	Surface Helmholtz Integral Equation
S H I E L D	*Sylvania* High Intelligence Electronic Defence
S H O R A D S	Short-Range, All-weather Air-Defence System
S H W	prefix to numbered series on Safety, Health and Welfare (now issued by HSE and published by HMSO)
S I A	Secretariat of Industrial Approvals (India)
S I A M	Self-Initiated Anti-aircraft Munition
S I C A V	Sociétés d'Investissement à Capital Variable (France)
S I C D O C	Special Interest Committee on Systems Documentation (of ACM (USA))
S I C O F A A	System of Cooperation Among the American Air Forces
S I C O M I	Sociétés Immobilières pour le Commerce et l'Industrie (France)
S I C S O F T	Special Interest Committee on Software Engineering (of ACM (USA))
S I D	Society for Investigative Dermatology (USA)
	SWIFT (Society for Worldwide Interbank Financial Telecommunications) Interface Devices
S I D I N S A	Siderurgia Integrada SA (Argentina)
S I D S	Sudden Infant Death Syndrome

S I E C	Scottish Industrial Estates Corporation (of the Dept of Industry)
S I E C U S	Sex Information and Education Council of the United States (USA)
S I F E	Society of Industrial Furnace Engineers
S I F E T	Società Italiana di Fotogrammetria e Topografia (Italy) (Italian Society of Photogrammetry and Topography)
S I G	Schweizerische Industrie Gesellschaft (Switzerland)
S I G s	Special Interest Groups
S I G s of A S I S (USA)	
A H	Arts and Humanities
A L P	Automated Language Processing
B S S	Behavioral and Social Sciences
B C	Biological and Chemical Information Systems
C B	Costs, Budgeting and Economics
C R	Classification Research
E D	Education for Information Science
F S	Foundations of Information Science
I A C	Information Analysis Centers
I P	Information Publishing
I S E	Information Services to Education
L A N	Library Automation and Networks
L A W	Law and Information Technology
M G T	Management Information Activities
M R	Medical Records
N D B	Numerical Data Bases
N P M	Non-Print Media
P P I	Public-Private Interface
R T	Reprographic Technology
S D I	Selective Dissemination of Information
T I S	Technology, Information and Society
U O I	User On-line Interaction
S I G A C T	Special Interest Group on Automata and Computability Theory (of ACM (USA))
S I G A R C H	Special Interest Group on Architecture of Computer Systems (of ACM (USA))
S I G A R T	Special Interest Group on Artificial Intelligence (of ACM (USA))

161

S I G B D P	Special Interest Group on Business Data Processing (of ACM (USA))
S I G B I O	Special Interest Group on Biomedical Computing Of ACM (USA))
S I G C A P H	Special Interest Group on Computers and the Physically Handicapped (of ACM (USA))
S I G C A S	Special Interest Group on Computers and Society (of ACM (USA))
S I G C O M M	Special Interest Group on Data Communication (of ACM (USA))
S I G C O S I M	Special Interest Group on Computer Systems Installation Management (of ACM (USA))
S I G C P R	Special Interest Group on Computer Personnel Research (of ACM (USA))
S I G C S E	Special Interest Group on Computer Science Education (of ACM (USA))
S I G C U E	Special Interest Group on Computer Uses in Education (of ACM (USA))
S I G D A	Special Interest Group on Design Automation (of ACM (USA))
S I G G R A P H	Special Interest Group on Computer Graphics (of ACM (USA))
S I G I R	Special Interest Group on Information Retrieval (of ACM (USA))
S I G L A S H	Special Interest Group on Language Analysis and Studies in the Humanities (of ACM (USA))
S I G L I G U N	Signal Light Gun
S I G M A P	Special Interest Group on Mathematical Programming (of ACM (USA))
S I G M E T R I C S	Special Interest Group on Measurement Evaluation (of ACM (USA))
S I G M I C R O	Special Interest Group on Microprogramming (of ACM (USA))
S I G M I N I	Special Interest Group on Minicomputers (of ACM (USA))
S I G M O D	Special Interest Group on Management of Data (of ACM (USA))
S I G N U M	Special Interest Group on Numerical Mathematics (of ACM (USA))

S I G O P S	Special Interest Group on Operating Systems (of ACM (USA))
S I G P L A N	Special Interest Group on Programming Languages of ACM (USA))
S I G S A M	Special Interest Group on Symbolic and Algebraic Manipulation (of ACM (USA))
S I G S I M	Special Interest Group on Simulation (of ACM (USA))
S I G S O C	Special Interest Group on Social and Behavioral Science Computing (of ACM (USA))
S I G U C C	Special Interest Group on University Computing Centers (of ACM (USA))
S I L	System Implementation Language
S I L O S	Side Looking Sonar
S I M	Servicio Industrial de la Marina (Peru)
S I M A	Scientific Instrument Manufacturers Association of Great Britain (federated into BEAMA in 1975)
	Secondary Ion Mass Analyser
	Southern India Millowners Association (India)
S I M G	Societas Internationalis Medicinae Generalis
S I M P	Satellite Interface Message Processor
S I M S	*SIAM* (USA) Institute for Mathematics and Society
	Surface-to-Air Missile Intercept Missile System
S I M S T R A T	Simulation/Strategy
S I N D B A D	Systematic Investigation of Diver Behaviour At Depth
S I P	Sea Ice Penetrometer
	Silicon-on-Insulator and Polysilicon
	Submerged Injection Process
S I P O S	Semi-Insulating Polycrystalline Silicon
S I R	Shipboard Intercept Receiver
	Sports Institute for Research (University of Windsor (Canada))
S I R C S	Ship-board Intermediate Range Combat System
S I R E	Satellite Infra-Red Experiment (of USAF)
S I R E P	*Sira (Institute)* Evaluation Panel
S I R I P	Société Irano-Italienne des Pétroles (Iran)

S I R T F	Shuttle Infra-Red Telescope Facility
S I S	School of Information Studies (Syracuse University (USA))
	System Interrupt Supervisor
S I S G A C	Scottish Industrial Safety Group Advisory Council
S I S I	Short Increment Sensitivity Index
S I S T A C	Scottish Industrial Safety Training Advisory Council
S I T E	Shipboard Information, Training and Entertainment
S K C S R	Statni Knihovna Ceskoslovenske Socialisticke Republik (Czechoslovakia) (State Library of the Czechoslovak Socialist Republic)
S K F	Svenska Kullagerfabriken (Sweden)
S L A B	Static Lifting Aerodynamic Body
S L A D O	System Library Activity Dynamic Optimiser
S L C	Sound Level Conversion
	Streamline Curvature
S L C F	Société Le Chauffage Français (France)
S L C M	Sea-Launched Cruise Missile
S L E	St. Louis Encephalitis
S L I C E	*Surrey (University)* Library Interactive Circulation Experiment
S L I M	Store Labour and Inventory Management
S L L A	Sri Lanka Library Association (Sri Lanka)
S L M	Single-Level Masking
S L M S	Selective Level Measuring Set
S L R	Stepped-Load-Resistor
S L R P	Society for Long Range Planning
S L S	School of Library Science (Case Western Reserve University (USA))
	School of Library Science (Kent State University (USA))
	School of Library Science (University of Kentucky (USA))
	School of Library Science (Syracuse University (USA)) (became School of Information Studies in 1974)
S L S E N Y	School Librarians of Southeastern New York (USA)
S L T	Standing group on Long Term Cooperation (of IEA (OECD))

S L U G	Superconducting Low-inductance Undulatory Galvanometer
S L U M T	Slacked Unconstrained Minimization Technique
S L U T T	Surface Launched Underwater Transponder Target
S L V C	Super Linear Variable Capacitor
S M	Styrene Monomer
S M A C	Sequential Multiple Analysis plus Computer
	Simulation Model of Automobile Collisions
	Simultaneous Multichannel Analyser plus Computer
S M B	Side Marker Board
S M C A	Suckling Mouse Cataract Agent
S M C L	Southeastern Massachusetts Cooperating Libraries (USA)
S M D	Soil Moisture Deficit
S M E C	Snowy Mountains Engineering Corporation (Australia) (a public corporation)
S M E S	Superconducting Magnetic Energy Storage
S M F	Systems Management Facility
S M H E A	Snowy Mountains Hydro Electric Authority (Australia)
S M I	Supermarket Institute (USA)
S M I A C	Soil Mechanics Information Analysis Center (US Army)
S M I T E S	State-Municipal Income Tax Evaluation System
S M L S	Searborne Mobile Logistic System
S M O N	Subacute Myelo-Optico-Neuropathy
S M O P S	School of Maritime Operations (Royal Navy)
S M O R N	Specialist Meeting on Reactor Noise
S M O R O M S	Summer Meeting Of the Royal Meteorological Society
S M P S	Switched-Mode Power Supply
S M R E	Safety in Mines Research Establishment (of DTI) (later of Dept of Energy but now of the Health and Safety Executive)
S M S	Software Monitoring System
S M T D	Synchronous Mode-locked Tunable Dye laser
S M T R B	Ship and Marine Technology Requirements Board (of Dept of Industry)
S M T S	Symposium on Marine Traffic Systems

S M X	Sulphamethoxazole
S N	Serum Neutralization
	Society for Neuroscience (USA)
S N A	Systems Network Architecture
S N A P	Subroutines for Natural Actuarial Processing
S N A R C	Short Nickel Line Accumulating Register Calculator
S N E F C A	Syndicat National des Entreprises du Froid et du Conditionnement de l'Air (France)
S N M	Special Nuclear Materials
S N O E	Smart Noise Equipment
S N P A	Southern Newspaper Publishers Association (USA)
S N U P P S	Standardized Nuclear Unit Power Plant System (a project of five electric utility companies in the USA)
S N V B A	Scottish National Vehicle Builders Association
S O A A	State of the Art Advancement
S O A S I S	Southern Ohio Chapter of ASIS (USA)
SODEPADOM	Société pour le Développement des Papiers Domestiques (France)
S O F	Succinic Oxidase Factor
S O F I R A N	Société Française des Pétroles d'Iran (Iran)
SOFRATOME	Société Française d'Études et de Réalisation Nucléaires (France)
S O F T	Signature Of Fragmented Tanks
S O L	Systems Optimization Laboratory (Stanford University (USA))
S O L A C E	Sales Order and Ledger Accounting using the *Computerline (Bureau Services)* Environment
S O L I N E T	Southeastern Library Network (USA)
S O L I T	Society of Library and Information Technicians (USA)
S O M	Standing Group on Oil Markets (of IEA (OECD)) Stand-Off Missile
S O M M	Stand-Off Modular Missile
S O N D E	Society of Non-Destructive Examination (became part of the British Institute of Non-Destructive Testing in 1976)
S O N I C	Société Nationale des Industries de la Cellulose (Algeria) (a government agency)
S O O T	Solar Optical Observing Telescope

S O P	Study Organization Plan
S O R	Sequential Occupancy Release
S O R D I D	Summary of Reported Defects, Incidents and Delays
S O R G	Southern Operational Research Group
S O S	SPSS Over-ride System
S O T A S	Stand-Off Target Acquisition System
S P A	Stimulation-Produced Analagesia
S P A C E S	Scheduling Package and Computer Evaluation, Schools
S P A D	Self Protection Aid Device
S P A I	Screen Printing Association International (USA)
S P A L	Stabilized Platform Airborne Laser
S P A R	Space Processing Applications Rocket (a project of NASA (USA))
	Store Port Allocation Register
	Submersible Pipe Alignment Rig
S P A R E	Error-tolerant and Reconfigurable Associative Processor with Self-repair (this is an inverse acronym)
S P A R M	Sparrow Anti-Radiation Missile
S P A U	Signal Processing Arithmetic Unit
S P C	Standard Product Concept
	Standing Group on Relation with Producers and other Consumer Countries (of IEA (OECD))
S P D	Surface Potential Difference
S P E	Signal Processing Element
	Society for Photographic Education
	Society of Petroleum Engineers (of AIME (USA))
S P E C	Speech Predictive Encoded Communications
	Systems and Procedures Exchange Center (of Association of Research Libraries (USA))
S P E E D	Simplified Profile Enlargement from Engineering Drawings
S P F	Science Policy Foundation
S P I C E	Spacelab Payload Integration and Co-ordination in Europe
S P I D A C	Specimen Input to Digital Automatic Computer
S P I R E	Space Inertial Reference Equipment
S P I R I T	Sales Processing Interactive Real-time Inventory Technique
S P I R T	Solar-Powered Isolated Radio Transceiver

S P L A D	Self-Propelled Light Air Defence gun
S P L A S H	Special Programme to List Amplitudes of Surges from Hurricanes
S P L C F	Sustained Peak Low-Cycle Fatigue
S P M	Single Point Moor *or* Mooring
	Solar Polar Monitor
S P N S	Standard Product Numbering System
S P R D	Science Policy Research Division (of the Library of Congress Congressional Research Service (USA))
S P R E A D	Spring Evaluation Analysis and Design
S P R I T E	Sequential Polling and Review of Interacting Teams of Experts
S P S	Separation Processes Service (of DoI) (operated by AERE (UKAEA) and Warren Spring Laboratory)
	Serial-Parallel-Serial Storage
S P S S	Statistical Package for the Social Sciences
S P T	Soldered Piezoelectric Transducer
	Strength-Probability-Time
S P T L	Superconducting Power Transmission Line
S P X	Stepped Piston Crossover
S Q U I R E	System for Quick Ultra-fiche-based Information Retrieval
S R A	Society of Research Administration (USA)
S R A C	Short-Run Average Cost Curve
S R B	Solid Rocket Booster
S R B C	Sheep Red Blood Cell
S R D	Single Radial Diffusion
S R D E	Signals Research and Development Establishment (of MINTECH and later of MOD) (became Radar and Signals Research Establishment (Christchurch) of MOD in 1976)
S R D T	Single Radial Diffusion Test
S R H	Single-Radial-Haemolysis
S R I	Serengeti Research Institute (Tanzania)
S R I F	Somatotropin Release Inhibiting Factor
S R S	Seat Reservation System
S R T O S	Special Real Time Operating System
S S	Scanning Spectrometer
	Sum of Squares
S S A	Solid State Amplifier

S S A P	Statement of Standard Accounting Practice
S S A S	Special Signal Analysis System
S S C	Shape Selective Cracking
	Southern Surgical Congress (USA)
	Spectroscopy Society of Canada (Canada)
S S C S	Strain Sensitive Cable Sensor
	Symposium on the Simulation of Computer Systems
S S D	Scientific Services Department (of CEGB)
	System for System Development
S S D S	Ship Structural Design System
S S E	Safe Shut-down Earthquake
S S E T	Steady State Emission Test
S S F	Smallest Serving Factor
S S G	Second Stage Graphitization
S S H R C	Social Sciences and Humanities Research Council (Canada)
S S I	Small Scale Integration
S S I D C	Small Scale Industries Development Corporation (India)
S S I S	*Squibb (E R Squibb & Sons Incorporated)* (USA)
	Science Information System
S S I T	Semi-Submarine Ice-breaking Tanker
S S O S	Severe Storm Observing Satellite
S S R - C A S	Secondary Surveillance Radar Collision Avoidance System
S S R A	Spread Spectrum Random Access
S S R C C	Social Science Research Council of Canada (Canada)
S S R P	Stanford Synchroton Radiation Project (of Stanford Linear Accelerator Center (USA))
S S R S	Society for Social Responsibility in Science (USA)
	Submarine Sand Recovery System
S S S	Serial Signalling Scheme
	Space Saver Spare tyre
S S S M	Standard Surface-to-Surface Missile
S S S R	Society for the Scientific Study of Religion (USA)
S S T	Safe-Secure Trailer road vehicle
	Shortest Service Time
S S T O	Single-Stage-to-Orbit
S S V	Semi-submersible Support Vessel
	Submarine Support Vessel

S S S W P	Seismology Society of the South West Pacific (New Zealand)
S T	Space Telescope (a project of NASA (USA))
S T A	Sail Training Association
S T A C	Sensor Transmitter Automatic Choke
S T A C S	Satellite Telemetry And Computer System
S T A G S	*S-Tank* (fighting vehicle) Agility and Survivability
S T A I	State-Trait Anxiety Inventory
S T A M	Statistical Analogue Monitor
S T A M P	Small Tactical Aerial Mobility Platform
S T A N	Statistical Analysis
S T A O	Science Teachers Association of Ontario (Canada)
S T A Q U A R E L	International Conference on the Application of Statistical Methods in Quality and Reliability Control
S T A R	Ship Tactical Airborne Remotely Piloted Vehicle String Array processor
S T A R P A H C	Space Technology Applied to Rural Papago (an Indian Reservation in Arizona (USA)) Advanced Health Care
S T A R S	Standard Time And Rate Setting
S T A T E C	Service Central de la Statistique et des Études Économiques (Luxembourg) (Statistical and Economic Studies Central Service)
S T A T U S	Subscriber Traffic and Telephone Utilisation System
S T C	Solar Thermal Commission
S T D	Sexually Transmitted Diseases
S T D S D	Solar-Terrestrial Data Services Division (of NGSDC (EDS) (NOAA) (USA))
S T E / I C E	Simplified Test Equipment for Internal Combustion Engines
S T E G	Simulated Time-base and Echo Generator
S T E L L A R	Star Tracker for Economical Long Life Attitude Reference
S T E M	System Trainer and Exercise Module
S T E P	System for Test and Plug
S T E P S	Strategy Evaluator and Planning-Production System
S T E W S	Shipboard Tactical Electronic Warfare System
S T F	Soluble Thymic Factor

S T G	Schiffbautechnische Gesellschaft (Germany)
S T I	Surface Transfer Impedance
S T I / S S	Scientific and Technical Information Systems and Services
S T I A	Scientific, Technological and International Affairs (a directorate of NSF (USA))
S T I C	Serum Trypsin Inhibitory Capacity
	Stodola In-Core Matrix
S T I S E C	Scientific and Technological Information Services Enquiry Committee (of the National Library of Australia (Australia))
S T L	Schottky Tansistor Logic
S T M	International Group of Scientific, Technical and Medical Publishers
S T O I C	Systematic Technique Of Incentive Contracting
S T O M P	Short-Term Off-shore Measurement Programme
S T O P	Storage Protection
S T O P S	Self-contained Tanker Off-loading Pump System
S T O R E S	Syntactic Trace Organized Retrospective Enquiry System
S T O U	Super Tractor Oil Universal
S T O V L	Short Take-Off with Vertical Landing
S T P	Service Time Prediction
	Special Trade Passenger ship
S T R A T C O M	Strategic Communications Command (US Army) (now Communications Command)
	Stratospheric-Composition (a program of four government agencies, ten government laboratories and private industry in the USA)
S T R E A K	Surfaces Technology Research in Energetics, Atomistics, and Kinetics (a discussion group of Dept of Metallurgy and Materials, City of London Polytechnic)
S T R N	Standard Technical Report Number
S T U M P	Submersible, Transportable Utility, Marine Pump
S T V P	Salinity, Temperature, Sound-Velocity and Pressure-sensing system
S U A	Serum Uric Acid
S U C	Society of University Cartographers

S U E R F	Société Universitaire Européenne de Recherches Fiancières (European University Society of Financial Research)
S U M E D	an oil pipeline from Ain Sokna on the Gulf of Suez to Sidi Kreir, west of Alexandria in Egypt
S U R T A S S	Surveillance Towed Array Sonar System
S U R V	Surface Viewing
S U S I E	Surface/Underwater Ship Intercept Equipment
S U S T A	Southern United States Trade Association (USA)
S V A	Schweizerische Vereinigung für Atomenergie (Switzerland) (Swiss Association for Atomic Energy)
S V D	Singular Value Decomposition
S V L T	Schweizerischer Verband für Landtechnik (Switzerland) (Swiss Association for Agricultural Technology)
S V P S F	Space Variant Point Spread Function
S V S	Society for Vascular Surgery (USA)
S W A L C A P	South West Academic Libraries Co-operative Automation Project
S W A P	Selective Wide Area Paging
S W A T	Special Weapons and Tactics Team
	Switching and Automata Theory
S W A T H	Small Waterplane Area Twin Hull
	Small-Wetted-Area Twin-Hull
S W B M	Still Water Bending Moments
S W L A	Southwestern Library Association (USA)
S W M	Standards, Weights and Measures Division (of Dept of Prices and Consumer Protection)
S W O R C C	Southwestern Ohio Regional Computer Center (of University of Cincinnati and Miami University, Ohio (USA))
S W O R D S	South Wales Operational Research Discussion Society
S W P F	Short Wave Pass Filter
S W S	Slow-Wave Sleep
S W U L S C P	South West University Libraries Systems Co-operation Project (now SWALCAP)
S Y M R A P	Symbolic Reliability Analysis Programme
S Y N C O N	Synergistic Convergence
S Z A	Solar Zenith Angle
S Z F	Schweizerische Vereinigung für Zukunftsforschung (Swiss Association for Futures Research)

172

S Z R	Sodium-cooled, Zirconium-hydride-moderated Reactor

T

T A	Terephthalic Acid
	Transactional Analysis
	Transition Altitude
T A A	Temporary Assistance Authority (Australia)
T A A S A	Tool And Alloy Steels Association (India)
T A C	Technical Advisory Committee (of CGIAR)
	Telemetry And Command
	Terrain Analysis Center (of ETL (US Army))
T A C C	Technology Assessment Consumerism Centre
T A C E L I S	Transportable Emitter Location and Identification System
T A C E L R O N	Tactical Electronic warfare
T A C J A M	Tactical Jammer *or* Jamming
T A C O M	Tank-Automotive Command (US Army) (in 1976 split into Tank-Automotive Materiel Readiness Command and Tank-Automotive Research and Development Command)
T A C O M E W S	Tactical Communications Electronic Warfare System
T A C O S	Tactical Airborne Countermeasures or Strike (a project of the USAF)
T A C 3	Target Recognition and Attack Multisensor, Automatic Carrier Landing System, Carrier Airborne Inertial Navigation System, Condor air-to-surface stand-off missile, Communication-Navigation-Identification (ie, TRAM, ACLS, CAINS, CONDOR, CNI)
T A C T	Total Audit Concept Technique
T A D	Traffic Analysis and Display
	Transaction Application Driver
T A D D S	Target Alert Data Display Set
T A E G	Training Analysis and Evaluation Group (USN)
T A G	Time Automated Grid system
	Towed Acoustic Generator
	Trans-Atlantic Geotraverse
T A G S	Tower Automated Ground Surveillance System
T A L	Tetra-alkyl Lead

173

T A L C	Tank-Automotive Logistics Command (US Army)
T A L I S M A N	Transfer Accounting and Lodgement for Investors, Stock Management for jobbers (of the London Stock Exchange)
T A L M A	Truck And Ladder Manufacturers Association
T A M	Towed Acoustic Monitor
T A M A	Training Aids Management Agency (US Army)
T A M P A	Tender Assist Minimum Platform Arrangement
T A M T U	Tanzania Agricultural Machinery Testing Unit (Tanzania)
T A P	Transient Analysis Programme
T A P A	Three-dimensional Antenna Pattern Analyzer
T A P S	Transform Adaptable Processing System
T A R O M	Transporturile Aeriene Romane (Romania) (Romanian National Airline)
T A S D C	Tank-Automotive Systems Development Center (US Army)
T A T	Tyrosine Amino Transferase
T A T P A C	Trans-Atlantic, Trans-Pacific (telecommunications network linking London, Montreal, New York, Sydney, Hong Kong and Tokyo)
T A W	Thrust Augmented Wing
T B A B	Tryptose Blood Agar Base
T B E	Tick-borne Encephalitis
T B L	Transitional Butterworth-Legendre filters
T B R	Treasury Bill Rate
T B T O	Tributyl Tin Oxide
T B W	Time-Bandwidth
T C A	Telecommunications Association (USA)
T C C	Telecommunications Corporation (Jordan)
	Transitional Cell Carcinoma
T C C S	*Texaco* Controlled Combustion System
T C D	Ternary Coded Decimal
	Trinity College, Dublin (Eire)
T C L	Transfer Chemical Laser
T C M A	Tufted Carpet Manufacturers Association (merged into BCMA in 1976)
T C O M	Tethered Communications
T C S	Torpedo Control System
T C S A	Tetrachlorosalicylanilide

174

T C S E V	Twin-Cushion Surface Effect Vehicle
T C T	Two-Component Tokamak
	Two Component Torus
T C T S	Trans-Canada Telephone System (Canada) (a consortium of eight telecommunications companies)
T C V	Terminal Configured Vehicle
T D	Thoracic Duct
T D B	Toxicology Data Bank (of National Library of Medicine (USA))
T D B C	Two-Dimensional Bragg Cell
T D L	Topographic Developments Laboratory (US Army)
T D L R	Terminal Descent Landing Radar
T D M	Time Domain Metrology
T D M G	Telegraph and Data Message Generator
T D O L	Tetradecanol
T D S	Transaction Driven System
T D S A	Telegraph and Data Signal Analyzer
T D S C C	Tidbinbilla Deep Space Communication Complex (Australia)
T E A	Triethanolamine
T E A M	The European-Atlantic Movement
T E A S	Total Engine Air System
T E C H N I - C A T O M E	Société Technique pour l'Énergie Atomique (France)
T E C H N I C H A R	Association pour le Perfectionnement Technique des Appareils Domestiques d'utilisation du Charbon (Belgium) (Association for the Technical Approval of Coal Using Domestic Appliances)
T E C H N I C O L	Association pour le Perfectionnement Technique des Appareils Domestiques d'utilisation des Combustibles Liquides (Belgium) (Association for the Technical Approval of Oil Burning Domestic Appliances)
T E D	Transferred Electron Device
T E D S	Tactical Electronic Decoy System
T E L B R A S	Telecomunicacoes Brasileiras SA (Brazil)
T E M P S	Transportable Electro-Magnetic Pulse Simulator
T E N	Toxic Epidermal Necrolysis

T E N	Trans-Europ-Night
T E O S S	Tactical Emitter Operational Support System (a project of USAF)
T E P	Transparent Electro-photographic Process
	Transparent Electro-Photography
T E P I G E N	Computer-controlled Television Picture Generation system
T E R A	Total Energy Resource Analysis
T E R C O	Telephone Rationalisation by Computer
T E R N	Terminal and En-Route Navigation
T E R P E S	Tactical Electronic Reconnaissance Processing and Evaluation System
T E S L A	Committee on Technical Standards for Library Automation (of the American Library Association Automation Division (USA))
T E S Y	Terminal Editing System
T E T A M	Tactical Effectiveness Testing of Antitank Guided Missiles (a project of the US Army)
T E T J C	Tribology Education and Training Joint Committee (secretariat provided by IMechE)
T E T M T U	Tetramethyl Thiourea
T E U R E M	CCITT Regional Tariff Group for Europe and the Mediterranean Basin
T E W A C	Totally Enclosed All-Water-Cooled
T E W D S	Tactical Electronic Warfare Defence System
T E W S	Tactical Electronic Warfare Suite (in a military aircraft)
	Tactical Electronic Warfare System
T E X T E L	Trinidad and Tobago External Telecommunications Con▌
T F I O	Thin Film Integrated Optics
T F T R	Tokamak Fusion Test Reactor
T G S	Thermal Growing Season
T H A	Total Hydrocarbon Analyzer
T H C - C R C	Tetrahydrocannabinol Cross-Reacting-Cannabinoids
T H E M E	The Hydrogen Economy Miami Energy (a conference)
T H I N G S	Three-dimensional Input of Graphical Solids
T H R O E	Tessaral Harmonic Resonance of Orbital Elements
T H T	Tetrahydrothiopen
T H U S	*TRADA* Home Unit System
T I A	Transient Ischaemic Attack

T I B	Technical Intelligence Branch (of the National Coal Board
T I D E D A	Time Dependent Data Analysis
T I E	The Institute of Ecology (USA)
	Total Interlibrary Exchange (of the California Library Network) (USA)
T I F I	Technology Insight Foundation Incorporated (a non-profit educational corporation relating to computer technology)
T I F R	Total Investment For Return
T I G E R	Telephone Information Gathering for Evaluation and Review
T I G T	Turbine Inlet Gas Temperature
T I M	Test-bed for Individual Modules
	Triose Phosphate Isomerase
T I M A T I O N	Time Navigation artificial satellite
T I N F O	Tieteellisen Informoinnin Neuvosto (Finland) (Council for Scientific and Research Libraries)
T I P	Telephone Information Processing
	Total Isomerization Process
T I P S	Telemetry Integrated Processing System
T I R - F P L	Total Internal Reflection - Face Pumped Laser
T I R S	Thermal Infra-Red Scanner
T I S	Technical Information Service (of NRC (Canada))
T I S C	Technology Information Sources Center (of Southern California counties (USA))
T I S I	Thai Industrial Standards Institute (Thailand)
T I T U S	Textile Information Treatment Users Service
T I X I	Turret Integrated Xenon Illuminator
T J S	Tactical Jamming System
T L	Transition Level
T L D	Thermoluminescent Detector
T L E	Thin Layer Electrochemistry
T L I	Tank Liquid Level Indicator
T L P	Tension Leg Platform
T L V	Tracked Levitated Vehicle
T M	Transcendental Meditation
T M I	Transition-Metal-Ion
T M P	Thermo-mechanical Pulp *or* Pulping
	Trimethoprim

T M P	Trimethoprim-sulpha-methoxazole
T M S	Transmatic Money Service
T M S b	Trimethylstibine
T N C	Troponin C
T N I	Troponin I
T N I - A U	Tentara Nasional Indonesia—Angkatan Udara (Indonesia) (Indonesian Armed Forces—Air Force)
T N P	Trinitrophenol
T N P G	The Nuclear Power Group Limited (functions transferred to NNC in 1975)
T N R I S	Transportation Noise Research Information Service (Dept of Transportation (USA))
T N T	Troponin T
T O C P	Triorthocresyl Phosphate
T O L C C S	Trends in On-Line Computer Control Systems
T O M	Transparent Office Manager
T O M B	Technical Organizational Memory Bank
T O P A Z	Technique for the Optimum Placement of Activities in Zones
T O P C O P S	The Ottawa (Canada) Police Computerized On-line Processing System
T O P S	Task Oriented Processing System
	Training Opportunities Scheme (of the Dept of Employment) (since 1974 operated by TSA of the Manpower Services Commission)
T O P S T A R	The Officer Personnel System, the Army Reserve (US Army Reserve)
T O R	Teletype On Radio
T O S	Text Organizing System
T O S A R	Topological representation of Synthetic and Analytical Relations of concepts
T O U	Tractor Oils Universal
T P	Tryptophan Pyrrolase
T P B P C	Triphenyl Benzl Phosphonium Chloride
T P E	Trypsin-Protein Esterase
T P H A	Treponema Pallidum Haemagglutination
T P I	Treponema Pallidum Immobilisation
T P P	Thiamine Pyrophosphate
T P T	Total Plasma Tryptophan
T P T O	Tripropyl Tin Oxide

T P U	Thermoplastic Urethanes
	Transverse Propulsion Unit
T R	Thermoplastic Rubber
T R A C E	Total Risk Assessing Cost Estimate
T R A C S	Telemetry Receiver Acoustic Command System
	Total Royalty Accounting and Copyright Systems
T R A M	Target Recognition and Attack Multi-sensor
T R A N S A N A	TRADOC Systems Analysis Activity (US Army)
T R A N S Y T	Traffic Network Study Tool
T R C	Technology Reports Centre (of DTI) (transferred to Dept of Industry in 1974)
	Telegram Retransmission Centre (of the British Post Office)
T R C H I I	Tanned Red Cell Haemagglutination Inhibition Immunoasay
T R E M C A R D S	Transport Emergency Cards
T R I B	Tire Retread Information Bureau (USA)
T R I C O N	Tri-Service Container program (USDOD)
T R I M T U	Trimethyl Thiourea
T R I S N E T	National Network of Transportation Research Information Services (of Dept of Transportation (USA))
T R I S T A N	Tri-Ring Intersecting Storage Accelerators in Nippon
T R M S	Technical Requirements Management System
T R O S C O M	Troop Support Command (US Army)
T R S B	Time Reference Scanning Beam
T S A	Training Services Agency (of Dept of Employment) (transferred to the Manpower Services Commission in 1974)
T S A R	Time Scanned Array Radar
T S C	Tryptose-Sulphite-Cycloserine
T S D	Time-Span-of-Discretion
T S R	Temperature-Sensitive Resistor
T S S	Tangential Signal Sensitivity
T S S A	Tumour-Specific Surface Antigen
T S U	Thermosetting Urethanes
T T & C	Tracking, Telemetry and Control
T T A C	Telemetry, Tracking And Command
T T F	Tetrathiafulvalene
T T N S	TOW Thermal Night Sight
T T P	Time-Temperature Parameter

T T R I	Telecommunication Technical Training and Research Institute (Egypt)
T T U	Through-Transmission Ultrasonic testing
T T X	Tritated Tetrodotoxin
T U T F	Technology Use Task Force (of Los Angeles Area Chamber of Commerce (USA))
T V C	Transient Voltage Counter
T V G	Television Video Generator
T V I D	Television Identification of personnel
T V M	Target-via-Missile
T V R	Temperature Voltage Ramp
T V S U	Television Sight Unit
T W A	Thames Water Authority
T Y G	Trypticase-Yeast-Glucose
T Z M	Titanium-Zirconium-Molybdenum

U

U A	The Underwater Association
U A E	United Arab Emirates
U A R R S I	Universal Aerial Refuelling Receptacle Slipway Installation
U A R T	Universal Asychronous Receiver/Transmitter
U A S I F	Union des Associations Scientifiques et Industrielles Françaises (France) (Union of French Scientific and Industrial Associations)
U A X	Unit Automatic Exchange
U A Z – E E S	University of Arizona, Engineering Experiment Station (USA)
U B	Urine Bilirubin
U B I N E P S	Union Bank of India – NAYE Entrepreneurship Promotion Scheme (India)
U B I P	Ubiquitous Immunopoietic Polypeptide
U C	University of Cincinnati (USA)
U C B - I L R	University of California at Berkeley, Institute of Library Research (USA)
U C C	Underclad Cracking
	University College, Cork (Eire)
U C C E G A	Union des Chambres de Commerce et Établissements Gestionnaires d'Aéroports (France) (Union of Chambers of Commerce and Organisations Managing Regional Airports)

U C D	University College, Dublin (Eire)
U C G	University College, Galway (Eire)
U C H C I S	Urban Comprehensive Health Care Information System
U C M M	Universidad Católica Madre y Maestra (Dominican Republic)
U C O R	Uranium Enrichment Corporation (South Africa)
U C R N	Unique Consignment Reference Number (of SITPRO)
U F O	Un-Filtered Oil
U G 3RD	Upgraded Third Generation System for air traffic control
U D A M	Universal Digital of Avionics Module
U D I L	University Directors of Industrial Liaison
U E L	Upper Explosive Limit
U E P M D	Union Européenne des Practiciences en Médécine Dentaire (of the EEC) (European Union of Practitioners of Dental Medicine)
U F I P T E	Union Franco-Ibérique pour la Production et le Transport de l'Électricité (Franco-Spanish Union for the Production and Transmission of Electricity)
U F T A A	Universal Federation of Travel Agents Associations
U H E	Ultra-High Efficiency lamp
U H M W P E	Ultra-High Molecular Weight Polyethylene
U I N F	Union Internationale de la Navigation Fluviale (Belgium) (International Union for Inland Waterways Navigation)
U K C A	United Kingdom CAMAC Association
U K H S	United Kingdom Hovercraft Society
U K I S C	United Kingdom Industrial Space Committee (of SBAC, Electronic Engineering Association and Telecommunications Engineering and Manufacturing Association)
U K L F S	United Kingdom Low Flying System
U K S M T	United Kingdom Sea Mist Test
U L A	Uncommitted Logic Array
U L C	Underwriters Laboratories of Canada (Canada)
U L C C	Ultra-Large Crude Carrier
U L I	Ultra-Low Interstitial
U L P Z	Upper Limits for the Prescriptive Zone

U M D	Unitized Microwave Device
U M I	Utah Management Institute (Utah University (USA))
U M M L	Union Médicale de la Méditérranée Latine (Latin-Mediterranean Medical Union)
U M R C C	Universities Mobile Radio Research Corporation (a consortium formed by Bath, Birmingham and Bristol Universities)
U M S	Ultrasonic Motion Sensor
	Unit for Manpower Studies (Dept of Employment)
U M V U E	Uniformly Minimum Variance Unbiased Estimator
U N C I T R A L	United Nations Commission on International Trade Law
U N C L O S	United Nations Conference on the Law of the Sea
U N D R O	United Nations Disaster Relief Office
U N E A S	Union of European Accountancy Students
U N E O	United Nations Emergency Operation
U N E P	United Nations Environment Programme (a UN agency)
U N I C I S	University of Calgary (Canada) Information Systems
U N I D R O I T	International Institute for the Unification of Private Law
U N I F E	Union of European Railway Industries
U N I H E D D	Universal Head-Down Display
U N I M S	*Univac* Information Management System
U N I P A R S E	Universal Parser
U N I S	*Univac* Industrial System
U N I S Y M	Unified Symbolic Standard Terminology for Mini Computer Instructions
U N L O S C	United Nations Law of the Sea Conference
U N O	University of New Orleans (USA)
U N P H U	Universidad Nacional Pedro Henriquez Urena (Dominican Republic)
U N S	Unified Numbering System of metals and alloys (of SAE (USA))
U N S O	United Nations Sahel Office (of UN) (Sahel countries are Cape Verdi, Chad, Gambia, Mali, Mauritania, Niger, Senegal and Upper Volta)
U P A S I	United Planters Association of South India (india)
U P C	Universal Product Code
U P M	Uninterruptible Power Module

U P R	Unsaturated Polyester Resin
U P S	Ultraviolet Photoelectron Spectra
U P S E B	Uttar Pradesh State Electricity Board (India)
U P S T C	Uttar Pradesh State Textile Corporation (India)
U R F	Union des Services Routiers des Chemins de Fer Européens (Union of European Railways Road Services)
U R L	User Requirements Language
U R R V S	Urban Rapid Rail Vehicle and Systems (a program of UMTA (DOT (USA))
U S A B	United States Activities Board (of IEEE (USA))
U S A C A A	United States Army Concepts Analysis Agency
U S A E C	United States Atomic Energy Commission (USA) (disbanded in 1974 and replaced by ERDA and the Nuclear Regulatory Commission)
U S A E N P G	United States Army Engineer Power Group
U S A F O	United States Army Field Office
U S A F S O	United States Air Force Southern Command
U S A F S T C	United States Army Foreign Science and Technology Center
U S A J P G	United States Army Jefferson Proving Ground
U S A M	Uniformly-Sampled-Autoregressive Moving average
U S A M C	United States Army Materiel Command (became DARCOM in 1976)
U S A M C - I T C	United States Army Materiel Command Interim Training Center
U S A M I D A	United States Army Major Item Data Agency
U S ASATCOM A	United States Army Satellite Communications Agency
U S A S C C	United States Army Strategic Communications Command (became United States Army Communications Command in 1973)
USATOPOCOM	United States Army Topographic Command (became Defense Mapping Agency Topographic Center in 1972)
U S A W C	United States Army War College
U S C S C	United States Civil Service Commission
U S E R C	United States Environment and Resources Council (USA)
U S F G C	United States Feed Grains Council (USA)
U S R A	United States Railway Association (USA)

U S I A S	Union Syndicale des Industries Aéronautiques et Spatiales (France) (Aerospace Industry Association) (became GIFAS in 1975)
U S I B	United States Intelligence Board (USA)
U S I C	Undersea Instrument Chamber
U S M M A	United States Merchant Marine Academy (of the Maritime Administration (USA))
U S N C / T A M	United States National Committee on Theoretical and Applied Mechanics (of NAS/NRC (USA))
U S N S A	United States Naval Sailing Association (USA)
U S R E D C O M	United States Readiness Command
U S S S T	United States Salt Spray Test
U S T I S	Ubiquitous Scientific and Technical Information System
U S U H S	Uniformed Services University of the Health Sciences (USDOD)
U T A C V	Urban Tracked Air Cushion Vehicle
U T C	Universal Time Coordinated
U T I	Unit Trust of India (India)
U T L A S	University of Toronto (Canada) Library Automation System (on-line network comprising Ontario and Quebec university libraries, and public and government libraries)
U T M	Universal Testing Machine
U T W	Under-the-Wing externally-blown jet flap
U V S	Universal Versaplot Software

V

V / H U D	Vertical/Head-Up Display
V - V S	Voenno-Vozdushniye Sily (USSR) (Air Forces of the USSR)
V A B D	Van Allen Belt Dosimeter
V A E	Vinyl Acetate-Ethylene
V A I	Vorticity Area Index
V A L T	VTOL Approach and Landing Technology
V A M P	Volume, Area and Mass Properties
V A N S	Value Added Network Service
V A R E S	*Vega (Precision Laboratories Incorporated)* (USA) Aircraft Radar Enhancing System

V A S	Vereniging van Accountancy-Studenten (Netherlands) (Society of Accountancy Students)
V A S C A	Electronic Valve and Semi-Conductor Association (ceased to operate in 1973) (member companies became direct members of the Electronic Components Board)
V A S T	System Vibration and Static Analysis
V A T S / S N A P	Video Augmented Tracking System/Single-seat Night Attack Programme
V A T T R	prefix to numbered series of reports issued by Value Added Tax Tribunals
V C E	Variable-Cycle Engine
V C H P	Variable Conductance Heat Pipe
V C I	Vapour-phase Corrosion Inhibitor
V C O D	Vertical Carrier Onboard Delivery
V D A	Verband der Automobilindustrie (Germany) (Automobile Industry Association)
V d B	Velocity Decibel
V D C	Vinylidene Chloride
V D C M	Vinylidene Chloride Monomer
V D I	Vehicle Deformation Index
V E R L A C	Vertical Ejection Launch Aero Reaction Control
V E S P E R	Vehicles, Equipment and Spares Provision, Economics and Repair
V E T	Vibrational-Energy Transfer
V E T M I S	Vehicle Technical Management Information System (of TACOM (US Army))
V F E T	Vertical Field-Effect Transistor
V F R	Vehicle-Fuel-Refinery
V G O	Vacuum Gas Oil
V H M W P E	Very High Molecular Weight Polyethylene
V I A R C O	Venezuelan International Airways Reservations Computerized system
V I B S	Vibration Sensor
V I C C I	Voice Initiated Cockpit Control and Integration
V I M S	Virginia Institute of Marine Science (USA)
V I P	Vasoactive Intestinal Peptide
V I R A	Vehicular Infra-Red Alarm
V I S A R	Visual Inspection System for the Analysis of Reports (a project of the Automobile Association)

V I S P A	Virtual Storage Productivity Aid
V I S S R	Visible and Infrared Spin Scan Radiometer
V K R	Video Kinescope Recording
V L C H V	Very Low Cost Harassment Vehicle
V L F	Vectored Lift Fighter
V L S I	Very Large Scale Integration
V N	Virtual Machine
V M H	Ventral Medial Hypothalamus
V M M	Virtual Machine Monitor
V M O S	V-groove Metal Oxide Semiconductor
V M S	Vertical Motion Simulator
V N A V	Volumetric (three-dimensional) Area Navigation
V O I C E S	Voice Operated Identification Computer Entry System
V O L V A R	Volume-Variety
V O N	Vereniging voor Oppervlaktetechnieken Metalen (Netherlands) (Metal Finishing Association)
V O T	Voice Onset Time
V P E	Vapour Phase Epitaxy
V P I R G	Vermont Public Interest Research Group (USA)
V P O	Vapour Phase Oxidation
V P R	Vacuum Pipette Rig
V R C A M S	Vehicle/Road Compatibility Analysis and Modification System
V R D S	Vacuum Residuum Desulphurizer
V R X	Virtual Resource Executive
V S	Vibration Sensor
	Virtual Storage
V S A N	Virtual Storage Access Method
V S C	Variable Speech Control
V S S	V/STOL Support Ship
V T A	Voenno-Transportnayaviatsiya (USSR) (the Air Transport Aviation – a group of the Soviet Air Force)
V T E	Visual Task Evaluation *or* Evaluator
V T G	Vehicle Technology Group (of IEEE (USA))
V T U	Vibrating Tie Under-cutter
V V T	Variable Valve Timing
V W D	Von Willebrand's Disease

186

V W F	Von Willebrand Factor
V W S	Ventilated Wet Suit

W

W A A V P	World Association for the Advancement of Veterinary Parasitology
W A C O	World Air Cargo Organisation
W A E S	Workshop on Alternative Energy Strategies
W A F	Wrap-Around-Fin
W A I S	*(David) Wechsler* Adult Intelligence Scale
W A M P	Wire Antenna Modeling Programme
W A O	Wet-Air Oxidation
W A P	Worst-case circuit Analysis Programme
W A P R I	World Association of Pulp and Papermaking Research Institutes
W A R D A	West African Rice Development Association
W A S C A L	Wide Angle Scanning Array Lens antenna
W A S P	Wave Adaptive Semi-submersible Platform
	Weightless Analysis Sounding Probe
	Wien Automatic System Planning Package
	World Association of Societies of Anatomic and Clinical Pathology
W A T	World Airport Technology (an international association)
W A T G	Wave Activated Turbine Generator
W A T T e c	Welding and Testing Technology Exhibition and Conference (USA)
W B S E B	West Bengal State Electricity Board (India)
W C C	World Crafts Council (USA)
W C C I	World Council for Curriculum and Instruction
W C I A	Watch and Clock Importers Association
W C O T P	World Conference of Organizations of the Teaching Profession (Switzerland)
W C S R C	Wild Canid Survival and Research Center (USA)
W D M	World Development Movement
W E C P N L	Weighted Equivalent Continuous Perceived Noise Level
W E D A R	Weather Damage Reduction
W E E	Western Equine Encephalitis

187

W E L	Weapons Effects Laboratory (of WES (US Army))
W E R C	World Environment and Resources Council
W E S T I	*Westinghouse* Teleprocessing Interface System
W E W P	West Europe Working Party (of the Book Development Council)
W F S F	World Future Studies Federation (Italy)
W G C	World Gas Conference (an association)
W G P O R A	Western Gas Processors and Oil Refiners Association (USA)
W G S	World Geodetic System
W H E E L S	Special Analysis of Wheeled Vehicles Study Group (US Army)
W I B	Working-party on Instrument Behaviour
W I G E	"Wing-in-Ground" Effect
W I M A	Western Industrial Medical Association (USA)
W I M A	Wire Mesh Welding
W I S E	Wisconsin (USA) Regional Energy Model
W I S E	World Information Systems Exchange (USA)
W I T	Wire-in-Tube sensor
W L A	Welsh Library Association
W M A	Welding Manufacturers Association (federated in BEAMA in 1975)
	World Medical Association (HQ Secretariat now in France)
W M A C	Waste Management Advisory Council (of the Dept of Energy and Dept of Industry)
W M A R C	World Maritime Administrative Radio Conference
W N B A	Womens National Book Association (USA)
W N W D A	Welsh National Water Development Authority
W O G A	Western Oil and Gas Association (USA)
W O G S C	World Organisation of General Systems and Cybernetics
W O R D S	Western Operational Research Discussion Society
W P	Word Processing
W P A	World Psychiatric Association
W P R	Work Planning and Review
W P R L	Water Pollution Research Laboratory (absorbed into WRC, 1974)
W R A	Water Research Association (absorbed into WRC, 1974)

W R B	Water Resources Board (absorbed into WRC, 1974)
W R C	Water Research Centre
W R N E	Whiteshell Nuclear Research Establishment (of AECL (Canada))
W R R I	Water Resources Research Institute (New Mexico State University (USA))
W S A	Wasser und Schiffahrtsampt (Germany) (Water and Ships Canal Authority)
W S B	Wheat-Soy Blends
W S E V	Winged Surface Effect Vehicle
W S L	Warren Spring Laboratory (previously of DTI) (now of DoI)
W S O	World Simulation Organization
W T	Wealth Tax
W T B A	Water-Tube Boilermakers Association (federated in BEAMA, 1975)
W V A S	Wake-Vortex Avoidance System

X

X P D	Cross-Polarisation Discrimination
X P S	X-ray Photoemission Spectroscopy
X R D	X-Ray Diffraction

Y

Y A R D S	Yard Activity Reporting and Decision System
Y H O R G	Yorkshire and Humberside Operational Research Group
Y M P	Young Management Printers
Y P C S	Young Peoples Computer Society
Y P O	Young Presidents Organization (USA)
Y S	Yield of Strength

Z

Z B S	Zero Bias Schottky diode
Z I G	Zoster-Immune Globulin
Z P A	Zone of Polarising Activity

NOTAMS, NTS-1, NTSK,
OOLHMD, OTW, PAC, PAF,
PAMA, PANSIP, PAPA, PAPI,
PARS, PATS, PERF, PIDA,
PINS, PNVS, POLANG, PPDI,
PSSC, QCGAT, QCRT, QSRA,
R&RR, RAAF, RAeC, RAVE,
RECAT, REINS, RJAF, RNZAF,
RPMB, RRR, RSAF, SAAF,
SAC, SAEB, SAF, SAFE, SAIL,
SALINET, SAMECS, SASI, SAWS,
SBO, SCA, SCAC, SCAR,
SCATHA, SDMA/SS, SEASAT,
SEO, SEOS, SETP, SHALE,
SMB, SORDID, SPAR, SPICE,
SSOS, SSR-CAS, SSRA, SSTO,
STACS, STAMP, STOVL, TAC,
TAROM, TAW, TCOM, TCV,
TDLR, TDSCC, THROE,
TIMATION, TL, TNI-AU,
TRSB, TTAC, UCCEGA, UDAM,
UG3RD, UKISC, UKLFS,
UNIHEDD, USASATCOMA,
USIAS, UTW, V/HUD, V-VS,
VALT, VAMP, VIARCO,
VLCHV, VLF, VMS, VNAV,
VTA, WACO, WAF, WASP, WAT,
WVAS

Aerosols
CMD, FEA, MMAD

Agriculture
ABBA, AFT, AGLINET, AGREP,
AGRI/MECH, ALB, APC, ARDC,
ARMIS, ARPAC, ASETA, BAHPA,
BASAM, BAU, BCEAM, BML,
CANFARM, CARIS, CEEMA,
CEEMAT, CELOS, CEMAG, CGER,
CGIAR, CICA, CICH, CIGR,
CIMMYT, DEULA, DLG, EAGGF,
EUSAFEC, GSFC, HFRO, HGS,
IADO, IAMFE, IBVL, ICAFI,
ICMA, ICRISAT, IFAD, IFFCO,
IGER, ILCA, ILR, ILRAD, IMER,

IPEACS, IPM, IRHO, JAS, JCO,
KTBL, LACIE, MAF, NCA, NCAE,
NFT, NIMTSM, NSC, PIMR,
RASAR, RIEC, SEAM, SFCI,
SVLT, TAMTU, TGS, WARDA

Air Conditioning
ACAB, NARAC, RUAG, SNEFCA

Air Cushion Vehicles
CASPAR, LACV, LVA, SAC,
TCSEV, UKHS, UTACV

Air Pollution
AIRMAP, APCA, APRG, AQCR,
ARPEGE, IGCA, JACA, MIDAS,
NAAQS, NASN

Aluminium
AAMA, AFCMA, CIOA, CIRA,
IPAI, MAT

Animals
IAAPEA, ILRAD, NAVS, WCSRC

Archaeology
AIA, AINA, NAS

Architecture
AAMA, ACCESS, CAPPS, FAS,
FOSPLAN, GRASP, LCACM, MSA,
SAW, SCALA, SEAC, SPACES

Arctic & Antarctic Areas
GISP, INSTAAR, POAC, RAMS,
SANAE

Armament Research
ADC, ARMCOM

Associations, etc. for Science & Technology
ACESA, ADSS, AICRO, ALECSO, ASTEC, AWIS, CASTARAB, COSTED, CSRA, CSSP, CSTP, DSTO, DWT, EJCSC, ESF, ESRC, IFC, KISR, MIR, MOSST, NBST, NCSR, NRAC, NRC, NSRC, PSA, SES, SFTP, SPF, SSRS, STIA, UASIF

Astronomy & Astrophysics
ASP, GPS, HARES, HARIS, IAGUSP, ISEE, IUE, MMT, PULSAR, SAR, SCLERA, SZA

Atmospheric Physics
ASRC, GASP, IMOS, LACATE, NCAR, NHRE, SAMS, VABD

Atomic Energy
ACRS, AEB, AEC, AGR, ASLAB, ASLB, ATEN, ATWS, AUSTRIATOM, BIFN, BNDC, BWR, CFR, CIRNA, COCHASE, CRBRP, CRDM, CTR, DAEC, DERE, DITE, DMA, ENS, ENSEC, ERDA, ERG, ESC, FGCB, FNAL, FNP, FRAMATEG, FRTC, GCR, GNT, GT-HTGR, HANE, HTGR, HWGCR, HWLWR, IAB, IFRC, IKRD, INLA, JET, KSA, LASL, LEAHS, LIS, LPCG, LWGR, LWR, MISS, NPG, NPRCG, NPRDS, NRC, NURE, OLMR, ORIC, ORMAK, ORNL, PANDIT, PFDF, PFFF, PHWR, PMC, PRDPEC, PWR, RCA, SFEN, SMORN, SNM, SNUPPS, SOFRATOME, SSE, SSRP, SVA, SZR, TCT, TECHNICATOME, TFTR, TNPG, TRISTAN, UCOR, USAEC, WRNE

Automobile Engineering
AAPS, AAPSD, ADA, ADSYM, AECE, AFMS, BARBI, BTV, CEP,

CTMA, CVCC, EASS, EFE, ESTA, EVA, FMC, FWD, GAWR, GEA, HEI, HELP, IMTA, ORCS, RV, RVIA, SCE, SFS, SNVBA, SSET, STAC, TCCS, VDA, VDI, VISAR, VVT

Banking
BASE, BINS, CBCT, CHIPS, EIB, FIRP, FOCIS, IBAA, IFEBS, KOP, MLR, NACHA, NCEFT, NEACH, SID, TBR, TMS

Bauxite
IBA

Bearings
AFBMA, BSA, IGBS

Behavioural Sciences
BSRD, CST, EIT, MABSC, MACOS, SEU, TA, WAIS,

Binding
BIA

Biology
ASP, BIS, DBS, EMBL, GMBF, JIBP, SDB

Birds
ICBP

Bookselling
ABAA, AECB, CBA, ICBA

Bottling
CETIE

Brass
CABWA

Brewing
CAMRA

Broadcasting (see also Radio, Television)
NZBC, PBS

Building (see also
Civil Engineering, Construction)
ABCM, ANCE, AWWF, BCT,
BERU, BMP, BOSS, BSRIA,
CAPFCE, CARBS, CFIA, CIBS,
CONACS, DGAS, EDRA,
EURIMA, FOB, GLBSA, HDD,
HEBA, IB, IBES, IBK, IMG,
ISRR, JATCA, JENC, LUCS,
NABC, NCIC, NICON, NIHBC

Business Equipment
CBEMA

Cargo
ACAAI, WACO

Carpets
BCCS, BCITA, BCMA, FBCM,
ICCO, TCMA

Cartography (see Mapping)

Catering (see also Food)
CISCO, LVCERI

Cement
CAA, CMA, GRC, HAC, HACC,
HWM, MBT, SCM

Ceramics
CFRGC, CPC, HPSN, NCECA,
RBSN

Cheese
ASSIFONTE

Chemical Engineering
BCISC, CHEMSAFE, CISHEC,
CONCEPT, CSChE, DESCNET,
PEETPACK

Chemistry
ACS/DCI, ALWIN, ANQUE,
CNDO, CPL, ECDIN, INDO,
JCPDS, MINDO, NDDO, QIE,
SAA, TOSAR

Chromatography
COW, DAIGC, GC-MS, GCMS,
HPLC

Civil Engineering (see also
Building, Construction)
ASIS, CESMM, DICB, ECCS,
IFAWPCA, MALSE, MOWD,
MWD, OPW

Clocks and Watches
WCIA

Coal and Coke
ACCCI, APA, ATM, BCC, BCOA,
CMA, CMAL, KCLA, TIB

Colour
DCMA

Commerce (see Trade)

Computers (see Data
Processing)

Concrete
CTIAC, HACC, NZPCI, PC, PCC,
PIC

Conservation
ACF

Construction Engineering
(see also Building, Civil
Engineering)
ACCESS, AFF, BPA, CCOU,
CIAC, CIF, CPPG

Consumer Organisations
CPSC, CREDOC, DPCP, INC,
IPCA, NBCCA, NCC, NFCG

Containerisation (see
Packaging)

Copper
CABWA, CRFS, INCRA

Corrosion
BJG, CAB, CAPA, CAPCIS,
COIPM, CPAC, CRES, DCI,
ICMC, ICorrT, ICST, ICT, LC, NCS,
PC, REPLAC, VCI

Cosmetics
COLIPA

Cotton
(see Textiles)

Cranes (see also
Materials Handling)
CALM, CLM, CMAA

Cybernetics
OSGK, WOGSC

Data Processing
AAIMS, ABAS, ABC, ABCU,
ABLE, ACC, ACCOMP, ACDL,
ACL, ACM, ACOMPLIS, ACRE,
ACT, ACTSU, ACUG, ADABAS,
ADAL, ADAMHA, ADCIS, ADE,
ADOPT, ADPESO, ADSYM,
AREIMS, AFACO, AFAM, AFDSC,
AFLOSH, AFOS, AGILE,
AHAB, AICA, AID, AIDUS,
AIM, AIMS, AIP, AISB,
ALBANY, ALECS, ALMIDS,
ALQAS, AMCOS, AME,
AMMINET, AMPL, AMPP, ANA,
ANCIRS, AP, APCOM, APCS,
APDL, APET, APPLE, APROC,
APV, ARDI, ARIS, ARME,
ARMIS, ARPEGE, ARPL,
ARTEMIS, ASAP, ASAS, ASC,
ASEE/CoED, ASET, ASIS,
ASSET, ASTAP, ASTRA, ATEMIS,
ATSU, AUTCOM, AUTRAN,
AUTRANAV, BADADUQ, BAMP,
BARON, BASE, BASIL, BASS,
BCAP, BCSAA, BCUA, BDAM,
BINS, BIPS, BLEAP, BLOCS,
BOSS, BPS, BRITSHIPS,
BUDWSR, CABS, CAD, CADC,
CADC/CC, CADD, CADE, CADET,

CADSYS, CAE, CAIRS, CAL,
CALAS, CALB, CALP, CAM,
CAMAL, CAMEL, CAMOL,
CAMOS, CAN/OLE, CAN/SDI,
CANFARM, CAP, CAPABLE,
CAPER, CAPOSS, CAPPS, CAPS,
CARBS, CARDS, CARS, CAS,
CASC, CASCADE, CASCOMP,
CASH, CASOE, CASPERS, CAST,
CBCT, CBEMA, CCSEM, CECC,
CEDPA, CENTAC, CEPACS,
CHAM, CHDL, CHIPS, CIAG,
CICAS, CILA, CiMOS, CIMS, CLA,
CLAM, CLASS, CLASSIC, CLCCS,
CLEOPATRA, CLICS, CLIP,
CLISP, CLM, CLODS, CLOG,
CLSD, CMA, CMM, CMP,
COCHASE, COCS, CODAP,
COFAD, COLA, COLING,
COMFORT, COMICS, Comm/
ADP, COMPAC, COMPACS,
COMPASS, COMPEC, CONACS,
CONCAP, CONCEPT, CONRAD,
CONSER, CONTRAC, COPICS,
CORTEZ, COSBA, COSFAD,
COSMOS, COSSACK, CPARS,
CPC, CPDS, CPEUG, CPIC,
CRILA, CS, CSA, CSC, CSERB,
CSOCR, CT/Cosba, CTL, CUAG,
CUE, CUPID, CURE, DAISY,
DAMOS, DARIAS, DARMS,
DAS, DASI, DBAM, DBAWG,
DBDA, DBMS, DBOMP, DCDS,
DCS, DDCMP, DHLLP,
DIAM, DIMS, DIODE, DIS, DISC,
DLIMP, DMR, DOLARS, DOMINA,
DPC, DPS, DTE, DTOL, DTUC,
DUCE, DWIM, EATCS, ECI, ECSA,
ECTA, ECUBE, EDIT, EDOS/RJE,
EFTS, EIN, EMIS, EMS, ENDEX,
EPOCS, EPS, EQUATE, ETAADS,
EUROCOMP, EUROMICRO,
EZPERT, FACES, FACET, FACS,
FACT, FAIRS, FAP, FAST,
FATAR, FATS, FBOS, FEAMIS,
FECONS, FEDSIM, FICS, FILTAN,
FIRES-T, FISAR, FLANG,
FLAPS, FLEE, FLIP, FOCIS,
FOCS, FORTSIM, FOSPLAN,

FPS, FST, GADPET, GALS,
GASSS, GCL, GDMS, GEOMED,
GGE, GI, GINO F, GIPSSY, GIRL,
GLAD, GNC, GODAS, GOLD,
GLP-1, GRASP, GTMS, HCUA,
HDL, HEADS-UP, HELP, HILA,
HIPO, HISSG, HLL, HLSUA,
HMSS, HUDWAC, HUTCH, IBE,
IBES, IBOLS, ICCAD, ICCC,
ICDB, ICLCUA, ICMIS, ICON,
ICPP, ICS, ICST, IDEAS, IDEN,
IDMS, IFEBS, IGTDS, IHSS, ILA,
IMPOS, IMPRESS, IMS, IMSL,
IMX, INCA, INCITE, INDAC,
INSIGHT, INSITE, INTERFACE,
IPICS, IQRP, IRA, IRBT, ISADC,
ISAP, ISIS, IVS, JADPU, JARS,
JAWS, JOL, JOT, JSIA, KEP,
KINSYM, KWUC, LAAF,
LACAC, LADDER, LADIES,
LALSD, LARC, LCGT/IGS, LCS,
LEAHS, LILA, LINS, LIQSS,
LIQT, LOGAL, LOIS, LOPS,
LORDS, LOTIS, LPL, LR-PASS,
LR-SAFE, LUCS, MABS, MANFEP,
MANIFILE, MANMAN,
MANTRAP, MAP, MAPPLE,
MAPS, MARCCO, MARCS,
MARS/SIP, MASCOT, MASS,
MAXNET, MCL, MDD, MDH,
MDL, MDS, MEDEA, MEDIA,
MEDIATOR, MEDINFO,
MELTAN, MERLIN, MFUSYS,
MIDAS, MIDMS, MIFIL, MIMS,
MINI, MINOS, MIRAC, MIRADS,
MISER, MMAS, MMIS, MMS,
MODS, MODUS, MOPSY, MOSS,
MOST, MOVIMS, MPGS, MPS,
MSCIC, MSS, MT/ST, MTCS, MTST,
MULES, MVS, NACHA, NAG,
NASD, NCC, NCEFT, NCUF,
NDPCAL, NEACH, NEAT,
NEISS, NELDIC, NETANAL,
NEWSOMP, NL/1, NOR-LUCS,
NORMAL, NRMG, NUTIS,
NWDC, OCG, OCL, OGI, OLAF,
OLF, OPOMP, OPUS, OQL,
ORBIT, ORION, OSCAR, OSMVT,
OSPRDS, OTS, PAC-FACS, PACOS,
PALMS, PANDIT, PANSIP,
PANSY, PARCS, PATS, PAUL,
PBC, PEETPACK, PENSAD, PEP,
PERSIS, PHILSOM, PIMP, PIP,
PIPIT, PIRL, PISCES, PLAN,
PLANES, PMS, PMSP, PNA, POGO,
POLARS, POP, POWER, PRAGMA,
PREVAN, PROCSIM, PROJACS,
PRONTO, PSI, PSPRDS, PUSH,
QAM, QAS, QUIDS, RAAP, RADAR,
RADCAP, RADCOLS, RAMIS,
RAPID, RATFOR, REAMS, REGAL,
REMUS, RFI, RITA, RODSIM,
ROTSAL, RSS, RSSL, RTL, SAAM,
SAFE, SAFEORD, SAIL, SAM,
SAMANTHA, SAMECS, SAMSON,
SAS, SBC,SCHOLAR, SCL, SCOLAP,
SCOPE, SCORPIO, SCRIPT, SCS,
SDF, SDLC, SEARCC, SEAS SMC,
SECMA, SELDAM, SELEAC, SEM,
SFOLDS, SHA, SHAPE, SICDOC,
SICSOFT, SID, SIGACT, SIGARCH,
SIGART, SIGBDP, SIGBIO,
SIGCAPH, SIGCAS, SIGCOMM,
SIGCOSIM, SIGCPR, SIGCSE,
SIGCUE, SIGDA, SIGGRAPH,
SIGIR, SIGLASH, SIGMAP,
SIGMETRICS, SIGMICRO,
SIGMINI, SIGMOD, SIGNUM,
SIGOPS, SIGPLAN, SIGSAM,
SIGSIM, SIGSOC, SIGUCC, SIL,
SIMP, SIMSTRAT, SIS, SLADO,
SLIM, SMAC, SMF, SMS, SNA,
SNAP, SOLACE, SOP, SOS,
SPACES, SPAR, SPEED, SPIDAC,
SPIRIT, SPLASH, SPREAD, SPSS,
SQUIRE, SRS, SRTOS, SSCS,
SSD, SSDS, SSET, SSIS, STAN,
STAR, SATARS, STEPS, STIC,
STOP, STORES, SURV, SWALCAP,
SWORCC, SYMRAP, TAD, TAG,
TAGS, TALISMAN, TAP, TDS,
TEPIGEN, TERCO, TERN,
THINGS, THROE, TIDEDA, TIFI,
TIFR, TIGER, TIM, TIP, TMS,
TOLCCS, TOM, TOPCOPS, TOPS,
TOS, TOSAR, TRACS, TRANSYT,

TRC, TRMS, UCHIS, UKCA,
UNIMS, UNIPARSE, UNIS,
UNISYM, URL, UTLAS, UVS,
VAMP, VAST, VIARCO, VISPA,
VM, VMM, VOICES, VRX, VS,
VSAM, WAMP, WAP, WASP,
WEST, WISE, WP, YARDS,
YPCS

Dentistry
UEPMD

Desalination (see Water)

Design
CADC, CADD, CADE, CADSYS,
EDAC, ICCAD, NADFAS,
NCDAD

Disposables
EDA, EDANA

Documentation
AACR, ABC, ABTICS, ACRiLIS,
ACS/DCI, AEBIG, AGLINET,
AIOPI, ARPL, ASIDIC,
BADADUQ, BIS, BOSS, BSRIA,
CABS, CAIRS, CAN/OLE, CAN/
SDI, CAN/TAP, CANTAP,
CARIS, CCC, CIDST, CISTI,
CISTIP, CO-ASIS, COFIPS,
CONSER, COPICS, DEVSIS, DLA,
ECDIN, EDC, EMS, ENDEX,
EUDISED, FID/CCC, FID/CLA,
FID/CR, FID/DC, FID/DT,
FID/ET, FID/II, FID/LD, FID/
RI, FID/TMO, GIRL, ICTED,
IDC, IIIC, IRA, IRIS, ISBD (m),
ISBD (NBM), ISBD (S), ISDS/IC,
ISI, ISODOC, KWUC, LEC, LINOC,
MARBI, MARLIB, MERLIN,
MIDONAS, NDC, NORASIS,
NUTIS, OASIS, ORION, OSTI,
OTIU, PANSDOC, PASTIC,
PATS, PDIN, PDIS, PHILSOM,
RELIPOSIS, SAA, SAIT, SALINET,
SCHOLAR, SCORPIO, SELDOM,
SIG/, SIS, SOASIS, SQUIRE,

SSIS, STORES, TDB, TIS, TISC,
TOS, TOSAR, TRC, TRISNET,
URL, UTLAS

Drainage
DID

Drawing
SPEED

Dredging
ISDT

Drilling
CDRA

Dyeing
IMP

Earthquakes
CANCEE

Ecology
(see also Environment)
ITE, MAB, TIE

Economics
AIB, AUTE, CIEC, COMECON,
DIW, ECAFE, ECWA, EDF,
EMCF, EMU, ESA, ESCAP,
EUMOTIV, FDES, GES, IEA,
MIRAC, MOF, OEA, PAMS,
SEPD, SER, STATEC, SUERF

Education and Training
AAC, ABLIS, ACFHE, ADCIS,
AFPA, AHEAD, ALECSO,
ASCD, ASEE/CoED, ASET,
AST, ATEC, ATFAS, ATI, ATM,
AUCAS, AUTA, AUTE, BEC,
BGTA, BOTEX, CAL, CAMET,
CAPT, CARISED, CAVEA,
CCETSW, CEI, CELS, CET,
CLASSIC, CODAS, COPQ, DANTES,
EARDHE, ERIC/CLIR, ERIC/
CLIS, ERIC/EM, ERIC/IR, ERSTC,
ESAN, ESPRI, EUDISED, FRTC,
GLS, HELPIS, ICET, IEP, IMHE,

IMTEC, ITRU, LEC, LSA, LSM, MSTC, NAHT, NCAE, NCECA, NDPCAL, OMTC, OSE, PATS, PEPCO, PETANS, PITAS, RESCAM, RPPITB, SCET, SCOPE, SCOTBEC, SEAMEO, SEAMES, SECA, SENA, SETEP, SIS, SISTAC, SLS, SPE, STA, TAMA, TIFI, TOPS, TSA, TTRI, WCCI, WCOTP

Electrical Engineering
AIM, ASEB, BASEC, CEDA, CERL, CLCCS, CLD, CSEE, DEMKO, EEIA, EERA, EPDC, ERA, ESAEI, ESB, EUREL, EWB, EWZ, GEEC, HPSEB, ICWA, IEEJ, INECEL, LIM, LSM, LVD, MANTRAP, MOCB, NEPA, NORDEL, OSEB, OVE, REC, RETRA, RWC, SEE, SEMKO, SMHEA, TEWAC, TVC, UFIPTE, UHE, UPSEB, WBSEB

Electro-chemistry
ASV, CIEP, COE, ECF, HMDE, PIE, POGO, SAEST, TLE

Electro-magnetism
EDM, EES, ELINT, EMV, REPS, SEW, TEMPS

*Electronics (see also
Radar, Telecommunications)*
ACEARTS, ACIA, AECE, AEWB, AEWIS, AEWSPS, AFACO, AFLOSH, AIDATS, AMIS, AMOS, AMS, AOC, APLL, ASIC, ASRADI, ASTAP, ATEWS, AUDDIT, BALUN, BAMP, BCCD, BEAMOS, BMS, BOLDS, BPS, BRISC, BVA, CAJE, CASH, CATT, CAWS, CCIRID, CCM, CCRT, CD, CEL, CEMAC, CEMEC, CEPEC, CMM, CONCAP, CONSTRONIC, CONTRAC,

CPS, CSERB, DFGA, DICE, DIOS, DPEWS, DTPEWS, EARS, ABAM, EBES, EC&D, ECQAC, EECA, EEIA, EERA, ENEWS, EQUATE, ESM, ESSCIRC, ETIA, ETTDC, EWAC, EWACS, EWSM, ExRAY, FACCM, FACE, FAP, FDNR, FILTAN, FPLA, GIMIC, GWS, HEI, HEMLOC, HERMES, HI-PI, HiNiL, HPLL, HTOT, HTRB, HTS, HUDWAC, IECE, IMAC, IMAD, INSPECT, ISMLS, ISON, ITCM, J-SIIDS, LARAM, LIM, LLCCA, LNTWTA, LOCMOS, LPSTTL, LSI, MCEB, MCI, MHIC, MIBAR, MIFIL, MLPWB, MSI, MSPS, MST, MTA, MTL, MULTEWS, MWS, NACE, NADEEC, NEDA, NEDELA, NEGISTOR, NELDIC, OXIM, PACE, PAMF, PANEES, PCCD, PHIB, PIA, PIC, PLA, PLARS, PMOS, PPDI, PTDL, PVM, RASE, RENS, RFS/ECM, SACCM, SAEW, SAILS, SAWD, SAWO, SBG GEDD, SCCD, SCTL, SEE, SERL, SEW, SFGA, SHIELD, SIP, SIPOS, SIR, SLR, SLUG, SLVC, SMPS, SPAR, SPS, SSA, SSAS, SSI, SSS, STEP, STEWS, STI, STL, SUSIE, TACELIS, TACELRON, TACJAM, TACOM EWS, TAP, TAPA, TBL, TBW, TED, TEDS, TEOSS, TERPES, TEWDS, TEWS, TJS, TRSB, TSR, TSS, UDAM, ULA, UMD, UMS, UNIHEDD, UPM, V/HUD, VASCA, VFET, VIBS, VLSI, VMOS, VS, VSC, WAMP, WAP, WIT, ZBS

*Energy (see also Atomic
Energy, Solar Energy)*
ACEC, ACORD, AEI, CERI, DEIS, DEn, ECAS, ECUBE, EIC, EMS, EPO, ERDA, ERG, ETSU, EUCON, FEA, FEO, IEA, IECEC, ITEC, LERC, MISER, NECAP, NEIC, NIECC, OEC, OEP, OETP, OTEC,

PEG, RECAT, SEQ, SLT, SPC,
TERA, THEME, WAES

Engineering–General
ACE, ACEI, ACENZ, ACEQ,
ACESA, AIEI, BEC, CNIF,
CSRE, EASA, EF, EPI, FAE,
FASFID, IDC, IEAust, IEI,
IFME, IGTechE, JIE, NEL, NSE,
OEQ, PEL, SCPEA

Environment (see also Ecology,
Air Pollution, Pollution)
AEQA, AESO, CIPRA, CNI, DES,
DESCNET, EAP, EDCC, EIA, EIS,
ENDEX, EPOSS, EQI, ERIM,
ERL, ESRU, FES, GLERL, HESC,
ICEF, ICEL, ICESA, ICIE,
INCPEN, IPIECA, IRS, LIFE,
NASN, NCC, NEPDB, NEPSS,
NESO, OES, OGC, PAECT,
PAPTE, PNERL, SESO, UNEP,
WERC

Ergonomics
CAPABLE, CPT, EIAC, ERSTC

Explosives
AFAM, APC, APCBC, APCR,
APFSDS, EOGB, EOR, ESSEX,
EXIAC, FAESHED, FASCAM,
GVMDS, HEAFS, HVAP, ICM,
JCAP, JIEA, LGB, OMC, PGM,
SAFEORD, SIAM

Fasteners
INTERFAST

Films
PFB, SFC

Finance (see Economics)

Fire Protection
(see also Safety)
AFFF, FFVMA, FIRTO, IFSSEC,
MAINLINE, NFDS, NFPCA,
NFRS

Fishing and Fisheries
ABFL, AFVOA, BIM, CIFA

Flour
FAB

Food
(see also Catering)
ASCN, BML, EUSAFEC, FACC,
FEL, FSC, FSL, HANES, HRD,
ICAFI, IFMA, IGD, JCO, MCI,
MRI, NYSNI, RDI

Forensic Science
AAFS

Forestry
BML, CTFT, FSGTR-NC, INCEF,
MAF

Forging
FIA

Foundries & Foundry Work
(see also Iron & Steel)
ATFAS, EICF, SAIF, SFAI

Futures Research
(see Planning)

Galvanising
(see Metal Finishing)

Gas
AFECOGAZ, AGRE, APRAGAS,
BGC, ENERGAS, ERS, GC, IGAT,
IGCA, LRS, MRS, OGDC, SBGI,
WGC, WGPORA, WOGA

Geodesy
(see also Mapping)
AGILE, GALS, GLAD, GUGK,
NGS, NIIGAIK, WGS

Geology
AEG, CAG, GSI, IAL, IGC,
IGGCI, INHIGEO, INTERAN,
MGMI

Geophysics
CGU, ELMS, GMCC, IAGUSP,
IGGCI, LAGEO, MOSPO,
NGSDC, SEG

Glass
CFRG, CFRGC, DGAS

Gliding
BHGMF, NHGA, RAFGSA

Graphics
GODAS, ICON, LCGT/IGS

Health
(see Medical Science)

Heating
CIRA, HVRA, IHVE, MARC,
MRT

Helicopters
AAELSS, AAH, ARH, ASH,
BAH, DELS, DSTR, FAESHED,
HelCIS, HEMLAW, HEMLOC,
HENILAS, HERMES, HHCC,
HySAS, LORAS, PLARS,
RODAR, RPH, SPAL

Highway Engineering
(see Roads & Road Transport)

Hire Purchase
HPTA

Horology
(see Clocks and Watches)

Horticulture
(see also Agriculture)
BAHPA, HTA, NFT

Housing
(see Building)

Hovercraft
(see Air Cushion Vehicle)

Hydraulics
HEIAC, HFI, HSTRU, MDRSF

Hydrography & Hydrology
DHN, HDL, IHSS,

Hygiene
(see Medical Science)

Illumination
CFF, ESI, IRDM

Industrial Relations
ACAS, CAC, CAS, EAT, FMCS,
IR, IRIS, OLMR

Industry
DOI, EGOTI, EUMOTIV, FIDA,
GIDEP, IAC, IDAB, MIR, PSIDC

Information Science
(see Documentation, Libraries)

Infrared
ABIRD, AFLIR, ALAIRS, ALIRT,
ARH/IR, BLIP, CCIRD, FAIR,
FIRTA, HAISS, HENILAS, INSPECT,
IRAS, IRCCD, IRDU, LADIR,
LODIF, LWIR, MIRS, SIRE, SIRTF,
TIRS, TTNS, VIRA, VISSR

Innovation
ACTI, CDI, CERI, OII

Inspection
(see Testing Quality)

Instruments
SIMA, SIREP, WIB

Insulation
NCIC

Insurance
ABAS, AIMIC, AIRMIC, CILA,
CRILA, HILA, IIHS, ILA, IUMI,
LILA

Inventions
AMINA, IPB, OII

Inventory Control
AIM, CASH, COMICS, CRISP,
DISC, DOQ, ERLS, ETOC, IBALS,
IBE, INCA, INSITE, MRP,
ORBIT, PIT, POQ, SLIM, SPIRIT,
UNIS

Ionosphere
EISCAT

Iron & Steel
ASPA, CONSIDER, CSN, ECCS,
ENSEC, EUROTEST, FSG, HSCR,
HSS, MUSTARD, OBM, OHT,
Q-BOP, SIDINSA, SIP, SSG,
TAASA, YS

Irrigation
CRUESI, DID, IIIC

Laboratories
ABFL, CERL, CORAL, CPL, EEL,
EMBL, ERL, FEL, FNAL, FSL,
GLERL, GSL, HDL, ILRAD,
IMLS, INEL, JEOL, JPL, LAC,
LASL, LCS, LGR, LRCC, LSM,
NAL, NCSL, NEL, NPL, NPRL,
NWL, ORNL, PEL, PMEL, PNERL,
SERL, ULC, WEL, WPRL

Lasers
ALL, ALT, ATLIS, AVLOC, BLHS,
CAPS, CLEOS, COAT, EDL, GLLD,
GRASER, HELLFIRE, IM/FM,
INLAW, LAGEO, LAHAWS,
LAMMA, LARIAT, LATAR,
LBIR, LEE, LGB, LIA, LIFE,
LIS, LLRS, LPCG, LRMTR,
LSA, LSIS, LTM, LTM/R, LWD,
MULE, PILLS, SFRL, SMTD,
SPAL, TCL, TIR-FPL, VET

Lead
LIA

Libraries & Library Science
ABIISE, ABLISS, ACLO,
ACRiLIS, ACURIL, AMCOS,
ANSTEL, ARLIS/NA, ATLA,
BARC, BCSLA, BIALL, BLOCS,
CACL, CALL, CALP, CAPL,
CARML, CASLIS, CATSS,
CCLN, CELS, CHSL, CIDBEQ,
CLTA, CLUMIS, COLA, CONSAL,
CRS, CSLA, DBV, DLA, GBIL,
HAL, IAML, IAMLANZ, IASL,
ILA, ILLINET, INIBON, IOL,
IRLC, JLA, LARC, LMRU,
LOIS, MARCCO, MLA, NACILA,
NLS, NMLA, NSDC, NSL, OLA,
OULCS, RLG, RTD/CCS, SCAN,
SCAULWA, SCL, SCMAI,
SCOLCAP, SConMeL, SKCSR,
SLICE, SLLA, SLS, SMCL,
SOLINET, SOLIT, SPEC, SPRD,
STISEC, SWALCAP, SWLA,
SWULSCP, TESLA, TIE, TINFO,
UCB-ILR.

Lighting
(see Illumination)

Local Government
ACOMPLIS, ADCT, AMA, IMTA,
LALUC, LAMSAC, LBA,
LBMSU, SCALA

Logistics
ALC, ALMIDS, AMA, CALS, CCS,
CLAMP, DEPMIS, LEADER,
LOGC

Lubrication
(see also Tribology)
JSLE

Machinery
BCMEA, BPPMA, CEEMA,
CEEMAT, CUMM, DEULA,
HMBP, JMI, MEMAC, MMMA,
NIMTSM, PIMR, SEAM, TAMTU

Machining & Machine Tools
CAMOS, CECIMO, EDIT, GNC,
IMS, JMTBA, MEMTRB,
OPOMP

Maintainability
(see Quality & Reliability)

Management
(see also Industrial Relations,
Personnel Management,
Production)
ABE, AMACON, ARIS, ATM,
BASE, BSE, CALB, CASH,
CbO, CEI, CIOS, CLAMP,
CMA, DAF, DIMS, DYNAMIT,
EPROI, ESAN, EZPERT, FWH,
GST, HRD, I&O, IAM/TMD, IIS,
JAIMS, LCLSC, LCMS, LSM,
MABSC, MANMAN, MAP,
MAR, MAS, MIMS, MIRADS,
MMAS, MSTC, NAB, NYMAC,
OLCC, OSCAR, OST, PMBO,
PMD, PNA, POP, PROI, PSM,
PVQ, PVS, RAMIS, RDN, ROOI,
SAIM, SENA, SPC, TAG, TIFR,
TSD, UMI, UNIMS, WPR, YPO

Manpower
IMS, MPQ, MSC, UMS

Mapping
CASC, CLUMIS, CONRAD,
GEMS, GUGK, IMT, INSIGHT,
NIIGAIK, ROTSAL, RSO,
SACARTS, SIFET, SUC

Marine Engineering
(see also Naval Engineering,
Oceanography, Ships)
ASRY, AWES, BRITSHIPS,
CASCADE, CEBLS, CLCCS, CPCH,
CSH, DAISY, GOLD, ICCAS,
IFMI, JAS, LOPS, LR-SAFE, MA,
MARCS, MECOM, NASD, PEV,
SAIMENA, SAJ, SFOLDS,
SSDS, SSIT, STG, TPU

Marketing
(see Trade)

Market Research
IMRA

Materials—research and testing
AAMCA, AMC, AMIC, CORRIM,
DBTT, EMMSE, ICM, IFHTM,
IRG, MIDAS, OMCB, SPT

Materials Handling
AICH, HOB, IPRO, MHTU, RMI,
ROMAN, SAM, SEMA

Mathematics
(see also Statistics)
CAMAL, CAMET, CRM, IMSL,
MFCS, SIMS

Measurement
SAIMC

Mechanical Engineering
CHAM, MERADO

Mechanics
USNC/TAM

Medical Science
(see also Dentistry,
Pharmaceutical Chemistry)
AACP, AAD, AAEE, AAMD,
AAOS, AAPSC, AAV, ABHP,
ABIH, ABLR, ABPM, ACOSH,
ADA, AES, AFMMO, AFOG,
AHC, AHL, AIHA, AIUM, AMDA,
AMI, AMIEV, AMPA, AOHC,
AOMA, ASA, ASCO, ASMT,
ASO, ASSH, AUCAS, AVST,
BCG, BDA, BMPA, BNW, BPT,
BSC, BT, CAE, CAP, CARS,
CCRESPAC, CDP, CF, CGL,
CHAMPVA, CHSL, CIMC, CINP,
CIOMR, CISHEC, CMS, CODAP,
COS, COTRANS, CPHA, CSA,
CSM, CSSI, CTA, CURB, DARIAS,
DAWN, DBS, DIC, DMD, DRG,
201

DTP, DVT, EAR, EBV, ELEP,
ELISA, EMAS, EMC, ERA,
ESDR, ETR, FAS, FEP, FHP,
FLV, FMR, FOCMA, FPT,
FRWI, FTA, FTA-ABS, FTI,
GCA, GMT, GSR, GTT, HAL,
HANES, HBsAg, HBV, HCG,
HCM, HCSA, HEADS-UP, HELP,
HeSCA, HISSG, HMG, HMO,
HMSS, HRD, HSC, HSE, HSI,
HSRC, HSV, IAA, IAAP, IACPAP,
IASL, ICAA, ICBL, ICDRG, ICHT,
ICPFR, ICTS, IDD, IFCC, IgG,
IHA, IHD, IHS, ILEP, IM, IMA,
IMBLMS, IMLS, IMMAPI, IOM,
IPA, IPPV, IRDS, IRMMH, ISM,
ISPO, ITC, IUAT, JCMC,
KAMEDO, KMS, LARC, LGV,
LHR, LMI, LRC, LSEB, LVAS,
MAA, MAPW, MAST, MEDINFO,
MHB, MIIA, MIND, MISER,
MMFR, MMIS, MOC, MODS,
MPAD, MPAI, MRC, MRFIT,
MSD, MSSNY, MSUSM, MTST,
MVE, NACOSH, NCCLS, NEISS,
NEORMP, NFCPG, NHS, NIA,
NIAAA, NIDA, NIPG, NSU,
ODT, OGTT, OHSPAC, ORT,
OSAHRC, OSUK, PAHOCENDES,
PAP, PET, PHA, PHT, PNKA,
POLARS, PP, PPLC, PPSA, PVD,
PVP, QAM, QEP, RAAP, RAPID,
RCM, RCN, RCPI, RCSI, RDS,
REDY, RHCSA, RPE, RPHA,
RPR, SAB, SAIMR, SAODAP,
SAT, SCBF, SFA, SID, SIDS,
SMON, SN, SSC, STAI,
STARPAHC, STD, SUA, SVS,
SWS, TBE, TCC, TD, TDB, TIA,
TPHA, TPI, TPP, TPT, TRCHII,
UCHIS, ULPZ, UMML, USUHS,
VMH, VWD, VWF, WASP, WIMA,
WMA, WPA, ZIG

Metal Finishing
ATEG, BAA, EGGA, EURAS,
VOM

Metallurgy
AustIMM, CENIM, COCOR, CRM,
ESFP, FATT, FCGR, IHP, MA,
MECON, MGMI, MMIJ, ODS, RA,
ULI

Metals
BHMA, BNFMRA, JMI, MIDCOM,
MS, UNS

Meteorology
AASIR, ACOMR, AFOS, AMS,
AMTEX, ANMRC, CABLE, CARD,
CEWT, CLIMAP, COMEDS,
COSAMC, DALE, DMSP, EMTN,
EWI, GMCC, GRC, GUGMS,
IMO, MOWOS, MPC, NMIA,
OBOE, OWS, PA, PAD, PMR,
RSMAD, SALR, SCAMS,
SMOROMS, SPLASH, SPM,
SSOS, STOMP, VAI

Metrication
ANMC, MCB

Microform
AME, ANCIRS, COMPAC, FGMC,
FISAR, IMS, MFUSYS, MIDONAS,
MIMIC, MIRAC, MMS, MOST,
NMA, RADRU, SQUIRE

Microscopy
CCSEM, CEM, HVEM, OEM

Minerals
PMA, PMDC

Mining
APCOM, APMC, ATM, AusIMM,
CPRM, CUMM, DOMES, IMA,
ISMS, MESA, MGMI, MMAJ,
MMIJ, SMRE

Missile Technology
(see also Rockets)
ACTV, ADM, AIRS, ALCM,
ALIRT, ARH/IR, ASALM, AT/
GW, BGW, BMDATC, BMDSCOM,

BPDMS, BRAZO, FLIMBAL,
HACLS, HARM, HELLFIRE, HIT,
IRR/SSM, LABRV, LRAAM,
MAARM, MASU, MIA, MIDAS,
MIMS, MIRV, MOAT, MRAAM,
PARM, PGRV, PMR, RAM,
SCARE, SCM, SHAG, SIMS,
SLCM, SOM, SOMM, SPARM,
SSSM, TETAM, TTNS, VERLAC

Mycology
ISAHM

Naval Engineering
(see also Marine Engineering,
Oceanography, Ships)
ANA, DTNSRDC, SAIMENA

Navigation
AIN, ANMI, ATNAV, AUTRANAV,
AZTRAN, CERNAI, DHN, DRL,
ENRI, ESGM, GPS, ICS, IDNE,
IFN, IIN, ILT, IMS, IN, IOA, LINS,
LNB, MABS, NAVSTAR, NI,
NTS-1, PINS, RAPS, REINS,
RIN, SPIRE, TERN, VNAV

Newspapers
ANZWONA, CCNA, GTMS, IAPA,
NEWSCOMP, NEWSTEC, PANPA,
SNPA

Noise
(see Acoustics)

Nutrition
(see Food)

Observatories
NHO

Oceanography and Ocean
Engineering
ACODAC, ADS, AMS, ARMS,
BATHY, BODS, CAPS, CIM,
CMAS, CONDEEP, CONDRILL,
CONSUB, CTD, CUEA, DOMES,
DOT, DUMAND, EB,

EUROCEAN, FAMOUS, FLOAT,
FPEC, GESMA, IODE, IOE, IOSA,
IPOD, JOIDES, JONSDAP,
JONSIS, JONSWAP, KORDI,
MODE, MSV, NADOT, NAMDI,
NAVOCEANO, NDBO, NORS,
NSESG, NSOSG, OAC, OFFINTAC,
OFINTAC, OSAS, OSD, OSFLAG,
OTD, PHOCIS, PLUSS, POAC,
ROSCOP, SALM, SCIMP, SCODS,
SEASAT, SEMP, SMTRB, SPM,
SSV, STVP, TAMPA, TLP, TRACS,
USIC, WASP

Oil
(see also Petroleum)
ADMA, ADNOC, AFECOGAZ,
BNOC, BRINDEX, COS, DMO,
HPDO, HSD, HVGO, ICOO,
IMINOCO, INOC, IOCC, IOE,
IOM, IOSA, IPAC, LDDO, LDO,
LVGO, LVW, MWV, NADOT,
OCIMF, OGDC, OIWP, OPCC,
OSAS, OSCO, PGO, PNOC, POC,
RAOT, RBOT, ROSE, SCCOP,
SECLF, SOM, SSC, SUMED, TIP,
VCO, VRDS, WGPORA, WOGA

Oil Pollution
(see Pollution)

Operational Research
ALB, AORS, BABO, CABS,
CAMEL, CHAPS, DP, ECORS,
EMORG, GALS, IP, LASEORS,
LRM, MINOS, MOLP, MORS,
NEORMP, NWORG, NZSG,
OPRAD, ORGS, POLKA, RPW,
SLUMT, SOL, SORG, SWORDS,
TOPAZ, WISE, WORDS, YHORG

Optics
ALOFT, AOCM, ASE, BPM,
HOE, IOOC, JCII, JEOL, JOERA,
LSI, LWPF, NVD, ODA, PIVS,
PROM, RSI, SEWIO, STEP,
SWPF, TFIO

Organisation & Methods
IPWSOM, IWSOM, MSTC, OMS,
OMTC

Packaging
ACODS, AFCMA, BPBF, BTSA,
CETIE, COCS, CSSCG, EPOCS,
FEDES, INCPEN, INTACT,
IPACK, MIPS, POP, TRICON

Paper
APF, BP&BMA, BPBF, BPBIF, BWPA,
CEPAC, CMPC, CRP, EFPB, ENCC,
EUROGROPA, FBA, FIPAGO,
HOPES, IMP, IPPTA, IWPPA,
JWPAC, LWC, PIF, PIMA, PSCC,
PWA, SODEPADOM, SONIC,
TMP, WAPRI

Patents
CLAIMS, INPADOC, INPI, PCT

Personnel Management
BASIL, HRIS, HRS, PERSIS, PIRL

Pests
COPR, GCMRU, IPM, OPP

Petroleum
(see also Oil)
ACPS, ADCP, AMPTC, APR, CAIS,
CBMPE, COPE, CPC, CPM,
DMBC, EGPA, EGPC, FCC,
FCCU, GPA, GUPCO, HPCL,
InstPet, IPAC, IPIECA, IROPCO,
JAPEX, KNPC, LAPCO, MALN,
PETANS, PFB, PHILIRAN, PITAS,
PMA, PPD, QGPO, SIRIP,
SOFIRAN, SPE

Pewter
GZC

Pharmaceutical Chemistry
AIOPI, IDMA, IMMAPI, OPPI,
SCHOLAR, SSIS

Photogrammetry
ALBANY, ARME, CIPA, GEMS,
PHOCIS, SFP, SIFET

Photography
APT, BLIP, CAPS, ICPS, IPC,
JCII, PSPA, SEGAIP, SPE

Physics
ABHP, AES, APS, ARPS, AS,
CPL, EPS, EXAFS, HADIS, HEP,
HRS, HTS, InstP, ISS, MI, NPL,
NPRL, PAS, PEL, POPA, QM,
SS, SSC, XPS

Planning
AFF, AIPA, EAROPH, ESCSP,
IAPS, NASCP, PEI, SEPP, SLRP,
SZF, WFSF

Plastics
(see Rubber & Plastics)
NAGPM, NAPIM, NAPL, NAQP,
NCA, PPA, SPAI, YMP

Pollution (see also Air Pollution)
ASPEC, CGA, CLEAN, COW,
CPAR, DESCNET, IOPEC, NEPDB,
NEPSS, NESO, NPDES, OGC,
OPOL, PAECT, SESO, WPRL

Postal Services
APO, MINPOSTEL, MPT, MUA

Powder Metallurgy
HFPAC, PAC

Power Presses
BPPMA

Printing
APHA, BFMP, BPIF, CPI, ESP,
IFRA, ITCA, KNVD, NAGPM,
NAPIM, NAPL, NAQP, NCA,
PPA, SPAI, YMP

Production Management
ACC, ACO, CALB, CPC, CREDD, DAP, DTUPC, GOCO, MEDIA, NPI, PAC, PACE, SAGT, SRAC

Psychology
(see also Behavioural Sciences)
NIIP, PSE

Public Relations
IPRA

Publishing
AAUP, ABDP, ABP, ACP, ACUP, AEMP, AMOP, AMPA, CBPDC, CPA, CPPA, EDITERRA, ELSE, EPC, EUROSTRUCTPRESS, FAEP, IASP, IPA, JBPA, PEPCO, SAMANTHA, SGPA, STM, TRACS

Purchasing
AAPC, BME, IFPMM, InstPS, PMAC, RIB

Quality & Reliability
CARS, CASE, COQ, DQABE, ECQAC, FAIRS, IACQ, IAQR, IMQ, ISQA, JCII, JMI, MTBMA, NCSR, NEQCC, NPRDS, PSQL, QALD, QPR, QTM, QTR, QuAD, RAM-D, STAQUAREL, SYMRAP

Quantity Surveying
FACET

Quarrying
BQSF

Radar
ABIR, ACEARTS, AGIPA, AIDS, AIRCAT, ALCOR, AMRAD, ARCADE, ARCAS, ARPS, ARRES, ATARS, ATLAS, BANS, BARBI, BTH, CAST, CONRAD, CORAL, COSAR, CSLC, DFDP, DIR, DVARS, EAR, EARS, EATS, EISCAT, GEMS, HRRM, IMFRAD, LOBO, LPI, LRD, LRRS, MALOR, MARRES, METE, MLR, OTH-B, OTH-F, PDES, PDNES, PRDS, RA, RADS, RANC, RAPPORT, RAPS, RBOC, RDP, REINS, RODAR, RRE, RSRE, RVP, RWR, SARIE, SCARE, SCDS, SNOE, SOTAS, SSR-CAS, STEG, TDLR, TSAR, VARES, WASCAL

Radiation
ARMS, ARPS, ASRO, ASTRA, BHP, COMAR, CORM, DWL, HARES, HARIS, IARP, INDI, IRAP, KSS, MIDAS, MPAD, MPAI, RADMAP, RAP, RMRS

Radio
(see also Broadcasting, Television)
ARRA, IARU, JAMSAT, MARS, MPT, NIRT, NRRL, ORTF, RACES, RETRA, RTRA, SEE, UMRCC, WMARC

Railways & Railway Engineering
AICMR, AMTRAK, CABS, CEH, CELTE, CP, EPOCS, FEPASA, FOCS, JOT, LRC, LRT, LRV, NRPC, ORE, RATP, RDA, REF, RIDE, RITES, SOR, TEN, UNIFE, URRVS, USRA, VTU, YARDS

Recycling
NARI

Refrigeration
NARAC, RUAG, SNEFCA

Reliability
(see Quality & Reliability)

Remote Sensing
CCRS, CORSPERS, ERTS, LACIE, LANDSAT. RSAA, RSMAD, RSS

Rice
WARDA

Roads & Road Transport
AARB, AASHTO, AFMS, APSTC,
AWARE, CTMA, DVLC, EAS,
FAST, FMC, IGTDS, IMTA, IPR,
MAC, MOVIMS, PARCS, PVM,
RRU, SFS, SMAC, SST, THINGS,
TRANSYT, URF

Rockets
(see also Missile Technology)
AUTOCOM, FFAR, HVRAP, IRR,
LRES, MRL, RAIR, RPE, RVSN,
SRB

Ropes
COMICORD, EUROCORD,
FIDUROP

Rubbers & Plastics
ADICEP, ARTT, BAHPA,
BRUFMA, CRI, CUMA, DBBD,
DBTU, DCPA, DETU, DMETU,
DRG, DRPG, DSR, EHD, ESPRI,
EV, FEF, GEPOC, GRP, HELP,
IBK, IIP, IPS, IRI, IRSA, JRIA,
LIM, LRCC, MRRDB, NYRG,
PBT, PET, PI, PMA, POE, PPDC,
PRC, PRI, PS, RAC, REPLAC,
RIM, RPM, RPPITB, RRIM,
SGF, TETMTU, TPU, TR,
TRIMTU, TSU, UHMWPE, UPR,
VDCM, VHMWPE

Safety
(see also Fire Protection)
ACDS, ACOSH, ACRS, ARPS,
ASLAB, ASLB, BCISC, BPS, CCOU,
CHEMSAFE, CIIT, CISHEC,
DEMKO, EMAS, FAS, HMFI,
HSC, HSE, IARP, ILAMA,
INTASAFCON, IRAP, ISMaC,
ISRSA, KSA, MESA, NACOSH,
NEISS, NISCON, NISO, NLS,
OHSPAC, OSAHRC, RAP,
RNLI, SASI, SISGAC, SISTAC,
SMRE, TREMCARDS

Satellites
(see Aeronautics & Astronautics)

Seismology
SSSWP

Ships & Shipping
*(see also Marine Engineering,
Naval Engineering)*
ACS, ADT, AMVER, BSF, CAMP,
CENSA, CESA, CLICS, COCS,
CSUK, FACS, FONASBA, GCBS,
IAGLP, IAPHA, IFSMA,
INTASAFCON, IRS, ISLWG,
ISRI, LR-PASS, LRBC, MABS,
NI, OASIS, OWS, PALMS,
RANSA, RATAS, RMSC,
RNLI, RNSA, SCS, SMTRB,
SMTS, STA, STP, SWATH, TAD,
ULCC, USNSA, WEDAR,
WMARC, WSEV

Shops
ISAA, SMI

Simulation
ISAGA, WSO

Soil
PSTIAC, SAWMA, SMD, SMIAC

Solar Energy
CSEI, IESUA, SERI, SPIRT,
STC

Spectroscopy
(see Physics)

Standards
AFEI, APRAGAZ, ASCC, BASEC,
CENCER, CEP, COCOR,
CONCERT, DBS, DEMKO, DIN,
DMSPC, DNA, E, ES, EU, FSC,
ICCO, IFAN, IIP, IMQ, INN,
IRANOR, ISODOC, JAS, JCPDS,
KERMI, MA, NAAQS, NCSL,
NPRDS, NSB, OVE, PSST, REMCO,
REMPA, RMI, RTSA, SASO,
SEMKO, SWM, TECHNICHAR,
TECHNICOL, TISI, ULC, UNS

Statistics
ABS, ANCOVA, ARIMA, BSO,
BSP, CAPMS, CSO, ECTA, EMS,
EWMA, IMSL, KSH, MNLS,
NBD, SAS, SEWMA, SHAPE, SOS,
SPSS, SS, STAN, STATEC,
UMVUE, USAM

Steam
CNC/IAPS, IAPS

Steel (see Iron & Steel)

Submarines
ASSW, ASTI, CICAS, DTV

Sugar
MSIRI, SASA

Surveying
ACCESS, CARISED, CASLE,
FAS, GEM, IPS, MALSCE,
NIIGAIK, PBAS, SEMDA

Tanks—Fighting Vehicles
ETT, MAFVA, METT, STAGS,
TACOM, TALC, TASDC

Telecommunications
(see also Electronics)
ACC, ACRE, ADPCM, AFAM,
AIDUS, ANBFM, ANFI, APCM,
ARETO, ARMCOMSAT, ARRA,
ASAP, ASET, ATEMIS, ATU,
BBAC, BFICC, CARA, CBFM,
CEEFAX, CENCOMS, Comm/
ADP, COMSAT, COPE, COTC,
CPIC, CQMS, CTCA, CTCSS,
CTO, CTS, CVSD, DNIC, DUCE,
EMTN, FAIRS, FOM, GSC,
GUATEL, HRP, IAM/TMD,
ICATS, ICATS, ICSC, IECE,
INTELCAM, ISOCC, ISSLS,
LNR, MAC, MASAR, MHG,
MINPOSTEL, MISI, MPT,
MSRCE, MUX, NAIM, NETANAL,
NLETS, NPDN, NTSK, PACT,
PANAFTEL, PAT, PBC, PDM,
POLANG, PSSC, R&RR, RAC,
SAMSON, SCC, SCPC, SDMA/
SS, SELCALL, SLMS, SLUTT,
SPAU, SPE, SPEC, SPIRT,

SSRA, STATUS, SWAP, TATPAC,
TCA, TCC, TCOM, TCTS,
TDMG, TDSA, TDSCC,
TELEBRAS, TERCO, TEUREM,
TEXTEL, TIGER, TIP, TRC,
TTRI, UAX, USASATCOMA,
VANS

Telemetry
ATC, RTPS, STACS, TAC,
TIPS, TRACS, TT&C, TTAC

Telephony
(see Telecommunications)

Television
(see also Broadcasting)
ANCHOR, CAPS, CEEFAX, DICE,
GTE, ITE, LASCOT, NIRT,
ORACLE, ORTF, PERTVS,
RETRA, RTRA, RTTV, SITE,
TEPIGEN, TVG, TVID, TVSU

Terotechnology
ETSC, NTC

Testing
*(see also Materials—research &
testing)*
AATB, AEM, AFLOSH, AFTEC,
AINDT, ANFI, ARTT, ATS/JEA,
AUDDIT, BDWTT, BINDT, BSTM,
CENTA, COFREND, CSSL, CTL,
DSTR, DTOL, DUVD, EASTEC,
EQUATE, ETAADS, EUROTEST,
EWGAE, FIRTO, HFRT, HTOT,
HTRB, INCITE, INSPECT, IOT&E,
JCII, MCD, NDTAA, NDTS, NETE,
NTDSC, NTIAC, RBOT, SECLF,
SEMKO, SONDE, TDMG, TDSA,
TTU, UKSMT, USSST, XRD

Textiles
(see also Carpets)
AIUFFAS, BMMFF, BTC, CIRIT,
COMITEXTIL, EDA, EDANA,
FTMA, GSCCMF, ICMF, IRCT,
ITF, LSIS, MFA, NASWM, PCC,
POY, SAWTRI, TITUS, UPSTC

Thermochemistry
CALPHAD

Timber
AWWF, JATCA, PAPTE

Tin
ATIC, ITA

Tobacco
JTC

Trade
AECB, AIM, ASSOCHAM, BOTAC,
CACCI, CAPEXIL, CCC, CCL,
CCCPIT, CIETA, COCOM, COIE,
COMPROs, COREPER, CPA,
CPSA, CRE, DOT, ECI, EDC,
EGOTI, EMA, EUSAFEC, GATT,
GSP, GSTP, ICTB, IIFT, LCCI,
MMC, MPMI, MRTP, MTN, NTB,
OFT, OPG, OTAR, PMA, PNITC,
RTSA, SUSTA, UNCITRAL

Training
(see Education & Training)

Translations
ATA, BISITS, GPT, OFFI

Transport & Transportation
*(see also Aeronautics, Railways,
Roads, Ships)*
AMPTC, APTA, ATA, CTS, ECMT,
ICTED, IRT, MOT, MOTAT,
NCIT, NFTA, NSWPTC, PATRAC,
PBEIST, PTC, TNRIS, TOPAZ,
TRISNET

Tribology
(see also Lubrication)
TETJC

Tunnelling
ITA, PJA, SANCOT

Turbines
ASATT, ELRAT, ENSIP, HHT,
NGTE, TIGT, VAST, WATG

Tyres
ACT, ATI, CRI, DTUOC, TRIB

Valves–Electronic
BVA, VASCA

Ventilation
HVRA, IHVE, MARC

Veterinary Science
WAAVP

Warehousing
CABWA, ICAW, NAWK

Waste
HWMD, RH, WAO, WMAC

Watches
(see Clocks & Watches)

Water
CLEAN, COW, CRUESI, CWPU,
HFF, IDE, IEEF, IGDS, MED,
NASQAN, NPDES, NWWA, OSW,
OWRT, SAWMA, WNWDA, WPRL,
WRA, WRB, WRC, WRRI, WSA

Weights & Measures
SWM

Welding
DSA, ERIW, GMPA, LSC, NVEBW,
WATTee, WIMA, WMA

Wood
(see Timber)

Work Study
AWSG, IPWSOM, IWSOM, IWSF,
MAP, MOST, RA